THE
EXE VALLEY
RAILWAY

During a promotional tour of the West Country in 1961, No. 3440 *City of Truro*, with 'The Westward Television Train', made a stop at Tiverton on Tuesday 28th February in a bid to 'drum-up' custom for the new Independent Plymouth-based T.V. station.

Terry Harper Collection

ISBN 0 946184 15 1
© John Owen
& Kingfisher Railway Productions
December 1985

Typesetting by
Aquarius Typesetting Services
New Milton, Hampshire

Printed by
Netherwood Dalton & Co
Bradley Mills,
Huddersfield, Yorkshire

THE
EXE VALLEY
RAILWAY

John Owen

Published by

Kingfisher Railway Productions

188 Bitterne Road, Southampton SO2 4BE
Tel. (0703) 222032

A typical setting in the Exe Valley c. 1910. *Paul Karau Collection*

Acknowledgements

The inspiration for the book comes from a happy, if all too brief, personal association with the Line, and in this regard I am indebted to the enthusiasm and dedicated professionalism of former Exe Valley railwaymen, in particular Signalman Bill Mears, Driver Verd Redwood, and the late Reg Cole, station master at Thorverton.

Photographs provide a valuable, even vital, dimension, not only in illustrating points, details and locations mentioned in the text, but also in recording what is now part of history. For permission to reproduce their prints, I should like to thank British Rail, Lens of Sutton, O.P.C., L. & G.R.P., H.M.R.S., and Tiverton Museum. I extend especial thanks to a number of photographers who, through their interest in the line and technical expertise, have contributed pictures of considerable locational and operational worth; Hugh Ballantyne, Andrew Barnett, John Bell, Douglas Butterfield, Brian Davis, Stan Dickson, David Fereday Glenn, Peter Gray, Michael Hale, Ian Holt, Philip Kelley, Reg Kingdon, Ron Lumber, Richard Riley, Kevin Robertson, Max Stewart, Ronald Toop, Wilf Underhay and David Vaughan Davies.

With the historical research, I should like to acknowledge the assistance given by the staff of the Public Record Office, Kew; the West Country Studies Library, Exeter; and the Public Affairs Regional Office, Paddington; as well as J. P. Morris of the Signalling Record Society; A. P. Voce, Hon. Curator of Tiverton Museum; members of the Great Western Society, Didcot. For permission to survey Cadeleigh station my thanks go to Devon County Highways Department, whilst the survey itself was only possible through the invaluable assistance given by John Snow. My grateful appreciation goes to Hilary Rampton who cheerfully undertook the onerous but essential task of typing the manuscript.

Introduction

The Exe Valley line was more than a Railway; it was a way of life. For almost eighty years it ran like a vital artery along the length of the scenic Devonshire section of the valley from which it took its name, joining at the market town of Tiverton with the short but economically vibrant Tiverton Branch. It is not the intention of this book to wallow in nostalgia — although pleasant memories will, hopefully, be evoked — but, rather, to portray something of the day-to-day flavour of a hardworking line which, while unique in many ways, displayed many of the operational characteristics of Great Western branch lines everywhere; features which have largely disappeared on what is left of the modern branch railway.

Despite the glorious landscape setting of the line, it was not on the 'tourist route' to the coastal resorts of South Devon and Cornwall, and it is one of the aims of this book to put the Exe Valley 'on the map' — although to the many communities of Mid and East Devon who mourn its passing, it has always been there! Visitors to, or passing through, Tiverton are strongly recommended to call at the town's Museum in St. Andrew Street,

where there are many reminders of the Valley's devotion to the line; the whole display being dominated, appropriately, by 0-4-2 tank engine number 1442.

As the nature and volume of traffic changed over the years, this was reflected in alterations to track layouts and train services. To enable the reader to view these modifications chronologically, certain operationally significant dates have been selected; namely 1885, 1905, 1920, 1930, 1935, 1950 and 1960. Thus the timetables printed in the Appendix may be matched with the appropriate track-plan for each location.

To cater for the interests of the railway modeller, the diagrams of Cadeleigh and Bampton stations the 14XX loco and auto-trailer have been drawn to scale. The line offers a range of stations from the humble rural halt to the three crossing stations — each with a different style of freight working — and the substantial branch line junction layouts of Tiverton and Dulverton. The line is of sufficient length and economic diversity to allow a variety of locomotive and stock working and timetable operation, and affords considerable potential for landscape modelling.

Contents

Page No.

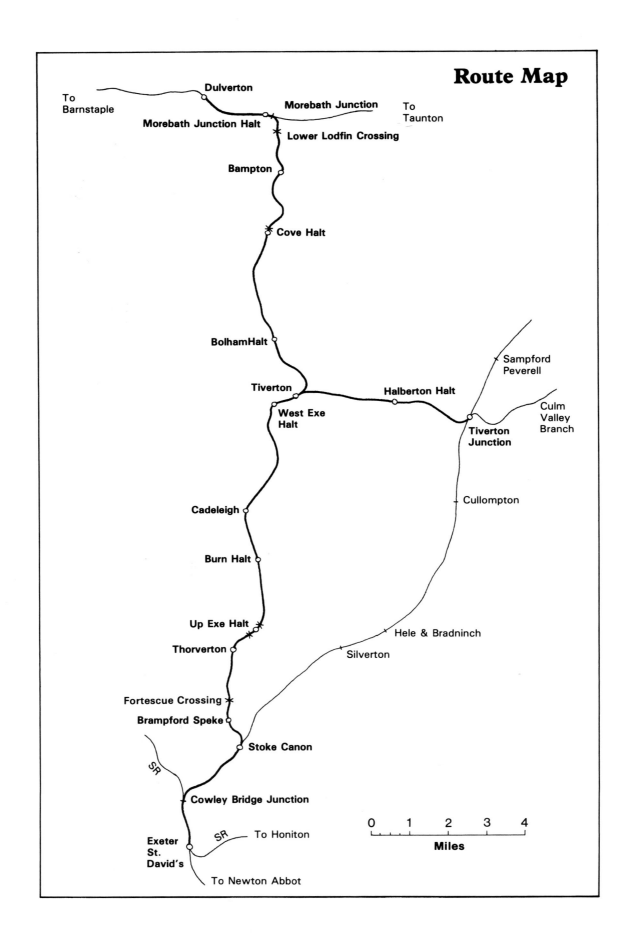

Route Map

To Barnstaple

Dulverton

Morebath Junction

To Taunton

Morebath Junction Halt

Lower Lodfin Crossing

Bampton

Cove Halt

BolhamHalt

Sampford Peverell

Tiverton

Halberton Halt

Culm Valley Branch

West Exe Halt

Tiverton Junction

Cullompton

Cadeleigh

Burn Halt

Up Exe Halt

Hele & Bradninch

Thorverton

Silverton

Fortescue Crossing

Brampford Speke

Stoke Canon

SR

Cowley Bridge Junction

SR   To Honiton

0 1 2 3 4
Miles

Exeter St. David's

To Newton Abbot

Chapter One
A Description of the Line

High on the open, windswept western uplands of Exmoor, at fifteen hundred feet above sea-level, rises the River Exe. For its first youthful 20 miles or so, the river flows eastwards and then southwards in the county of Somerset, gaining tributaries and thus growing in stature. Near the village of Exebridge the river crosses into Devonshire, and for the next 24 miles flows southwards towards Exeter. This southern section of the river has created a lowland corridor through the hilly terrain of Mid-Devon, a natural routeway which, betwen 1885 and 1963, was utilised by the Exe Valley Railway.

The first, and enduring, impression of the landscape bordering the Exe Valley is one of hills. Leave the valley and one is into a world of steep, narrow, winding lanes bounded by high, thick-set hedges punctuated at regular intervals by old and well-proportioned trees. Considerable variations exist, however, along the 24¾ miles of the line, due to both its geological and geographical evolution. The flavour of the line is perhaps best portrayed by describing a journey northwards from Exeter.

Passing through the ticket barrier on to Platform One of St. David's Station, Exeter, the passenger would be directed to the

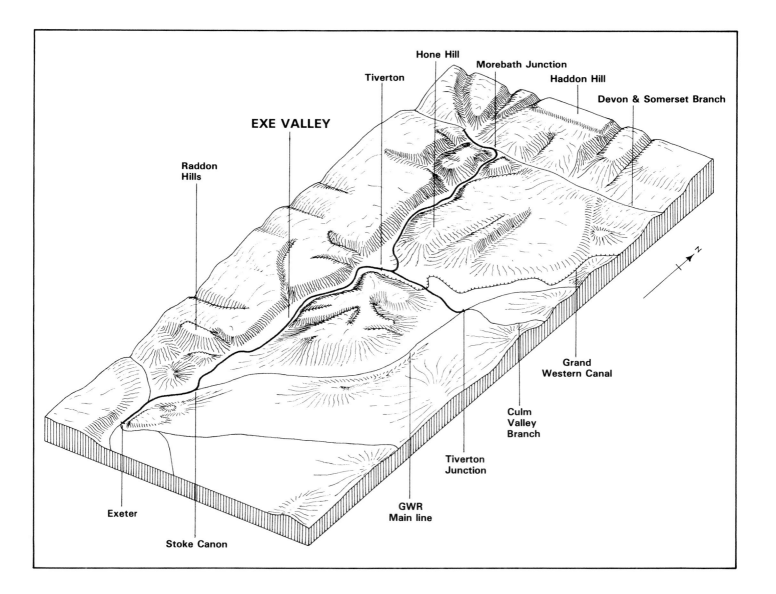

'14XX' class 0-4-2T No. 1442 with an Exe Valley train in the bay at St. David's station, Exeter. This locomotive is now the centre-piece of the 'Railway Gallery' in the Tiverton Museum.   *K. Alford; courtesy Tiverton Museum*

No. 1471 with its train, viewed from the level crossing at the north end of St. David's station on 3rd July 1963.   *R. C. Riley*

No. 1451 moving cautiously over pointwork at the beginning of its run to Dulverton on 16th July 1958.   *R. C. Riley*

right, past the Refreshment Rooms, Cloak Rooms and various offices to the bay platform (Platform Two) at the north end of the station. Exe Valley trains invariably left from 'the bay'. Waiting beyond the ever-present parcels vans would be the 'Valley' train, usually an 0-4-2 tank of the 14XX Class at the head of one or two auto trailers. Within a few yards of the platform end is a level crossing carrying a busy road to Exwick. The crossing and track layout is controlled by Exeter Middle signal box. The gates would not be closed against the road until the train was ready to leave, this being communicated to the signalman by a member of the station staff or by the guard (notification was achieved by pressing the 'Bay Ready to Start' bell plunger housed in a hinged

box on one of the platform canopy pillars). As a public right of way, the wicket gates at the crossing were not locked, thus allowing pedestrians to cross at any time. For this reason, a patrolman was on duty to ensure that non-one was run down. With the bay 'Start' signal lowered and the 'All Clear' given from the guard, a shrill blast on the loco's whistle would warn the patrolman that the train was about to move off.

Once over the crossing, the train joined the 'down' main line for a few yards until the trailing crossover took it over to the 'up' main. Rattling over the points leading to Riverside Yard, the train ran north along the floodplain of the River Exe. Signal checks were often a feature of this stretch. Very occasionally,

Pannier tank No. 3659 on a northbound Exe Valley train forging along the 'up' main line between Exeter Riverside Yard and Cowley Bridge Junction.
W. L. Underhay

on the northward journey, the distant signal for Cowley Bridge Junction would be 'on', as a Southern train would be signalled in from North Devon. On the south-bound journey, it was common to be 'checked' by Exeter East box and then stopped at Middle box's four-way bracket signal which controlled the 'throat' of the station. Once the train had stopped, the signalman would pull off the bay 'calling-on' signal and allow a cautious approach to the platform.

Just over a mile (1 mile 19 chains) from St. David's, the clatter of points marked the end of the long 'up' and 'down' loops and saw the Southern Region line to North Devon curve away westwards over the Exe. This is Cowley Bridge Junction, where the signalman would always be kept literally on his toes in an endeavour to keep trains moving (over 200 trains a day, for example, passed through the Junction on weekdays during the summer of 1962).

Curving to the north-east, and riding smoothly, the train was now running across the meadows to the north of Stoke Woods on a rising average gradient of 1:165. This section of track was popular with Exe Valley enginemen because they could run at speed, especially on the run down to Exeter. The maximum speed permitted on the branch was 35 m.p.h., with several more severe restrictions. Drivers reckoned a 14XX 0-4-2 tank could travel at 80 m.p.h., but admitted that the shaking and lurching motion engendered would make it impossible to stay on the footplate! Crews on this section quite often managed to get up to 60 m.p.h., but the wheel-noise and swaying motion of the auto-

coach markedly increased and detracted from the usual smooth ride. In the 2 miles between Cowley Bridge and Stoke Canon the train crossed the Exe twice, first on a low girder bridge (Stafford Bridge) and secondly on a trussed steel-frame structure. Immediately before the second bridge was the 'up' outer home signal of Stoke Canon Junction, a tall square-post signal dating from Great Western days. A whistle from the engine would alert the signalman to be ready with the Electric Train Staff for the single-line section about to be entered (track circuiting would in any case enable the signalman to follow the train's progress). 'Down' branch trains were frequently held in Stoke Canon station because they had to cross the 'up' main line in order to gain the 'down'. If delays were not caused by an 'up' train being signalled, a 'down' one was — or had yet to clear back from Cowley Bridge. This frequent signal stop would make Valley trains late, and consequently encourage drivers to 'open them up' once they had the all clear.

Stoke Canon was a station of red-brick, utilitarian design, dating from the complete rebuilding of the Junction layout in 1932. Slowing to 20 m.p.h. or less, the Exe Valley train would leave the main line and glide in over the facing points to the branch platform line. Passing behind the red-brick 1930s signal box, the train ran into the shorter west side of the island platform. Unless branch trains needed to pass here, they would run straight through after June 1960, when the station closed to passengers (a reduction in speed remained, however, to ensure safe negotiation of the points and handling of the Train Staff).

Cowley Bridge Junction in 1960. The view is northwards, with the former LSWR line curving to the left and the GW main line to the right.

Nelson Collection; courtesy OPC

Stoke Canon; 1960. The Exe Valley line curves to the left whilst the main line continues northwards to Stoke Crossing and Rewe, and thence follows the valley of the River Culm.

Nelson Collection; courtesy OPC

Once clear of the station the train entered the Exe Valley branch proper. The line curved sharply to regain the River Exe, while the main line continued north east to pick up the valley of the River Culm. The Railway's boundary posts are set very far apart at this divergence, this being a legacy from the earlier junction layout when there was a broad gauge siding running parallel with the standard gauge branch. The branch crossed the water-meadows between Stoke and Brampford Speke on a low embankment, punctuated by four regularly spaced masonry flood arches. Being the confluence between the Culm and Exe rivers, this whole area was liable to flooding. The Railway owned land at a distance of many yards from the track, and there are still one or

Brampford Speke 9th December 1961. No. 1471 propelling its train over the low embankment across the water meadows en route for Exeter. *Peter W. Gray*

A northbound train alongside the river near Nether Exe.   *Tiverton Museum*

two cast-iron boundary posts incongruously projecting out of the meadows. Running close up to the left bank of the river, the line curved north into Brampford Speke. Although a halt from 1923, all the original station buildings remained; the station master's house and station building both being lived in. The architectural style of the buildings is to be found, with only the slightest variations, throughout the southern half of the line.

Leaving Brampford Speke Halt the train immediately passed a platelayer's hut, the first of many along the branch (Valley men often referred to them as 'Packers' Huts). These wooden cabins, commonly made out of old sleepers, with their brick chimney and shuttered window, afforded a base for men when they were working on the line nearby. They contained a simple 4-barred wooden seat and adjoined a small square piece of level grass on to which the ganger's trolley would be placed while the work was in progress. These huts were about a mile apart, with larger workshops-cum-stores at the stations. Soon the train rumbled over the first of several bridges over the River Exe. The lattice-work steel girder decking, supported by masonry abutments, was carried over the river on two massive stone piers and was the standard design for the others on the branch.

Looking out through the carriage window, the traveller would see a low, but varied, landscape. The outcrop of red rock in the river bank at Brampford Speke pointed up the fact that the valley at this point is cut in a series of rocks known as the New Red Sandstone (a system of rocks well known to holidaymakers at Exmouth, Dawlish and Teignmouth). These soft, friable rocks underlie a subdued landscape of broadly convex hills, through which the Exe has cut a wide, flat-floored valley. The soft sandstones have weathered into a rich, warm, red soil. When ploughed, the resultant dun-coloured fields, interspersed with cropland and green pasture-land, build up a 'patchwork' scenery, the thickset hedges of the field boundaries highlighting the rectilinear nature of the landscape. Trees are generally restricted to the steeper slopes, river banks and hedgerows. The grazing of cattle on the valley floor was a feature which introduced move-

ment as well as further colour to the scene through which the train was now travelling.

With the river now away to the right, the line made for Fortescue Crossing. The gates here were opened and closed manually by the crossing keeper, the wife of one of the signalmen on the branch. The crossing existed in order to carry a farm track from the road and farmhouse on the west of the line to a few fields, bounded by the river, on the east; a situation elsewhere that was satisfied by an 'occupation crossing' where the gates were operated by the user. At Nether Exe, north of the crossing, the line took on a rustic charm. A tree-lined bank paralleled the line on the left, while immediately to the right was the river — itself overhung with trees — with level watermeadows beyond. The smoke from the engine mixed with the tree canopies as railway and river ran side by side for the next half mile.

Emerging from the trees, the train would coast down on a 1:100 gradient, approaching Thorverton on a long, straight embankment with the sunken Hulk Lane on the left and the watermeadows and old mill leat on the right. Crossing the massive stone skew bridge over Hulk Lane, the train rattled in over 2 sets of facing points and came to a halt in the 'up' platform. Thorverton (6 miles 11 chains from Exeter) was the first crossing station on the line and, as the village had no form of bus service until the line closed, was one of the best used of the rural stations. The attractive blue-grey stone buildings — station buildings, goods shed, weighbridge hut and station master's house — gave the station a unity of design and architectural style. With the 'Staff' from Stoke Canon given up to the signalman and the Electric Train Token taken on board, the train would be ready to leave. With the 'right away' from the guard, it moved off over the goods yard points and across the road which led to the village centre. The long siding to Thorverton Mill curved sharply away to the right, immediately beyond the substantial stone overbridge.

Soon after passing Thorverton's 'up' advanced starting signal — sited part way up a bank and away from the track so as to be

The approach to Thorverton from the south.
Tiverton Museum

Thorverton 17th August 1957. Auto fitted-tank No. 1469 arriving with a train for Exeter.   *Peter W. Gray*

visible from the station — the train rumbled across another river bridge almost identical with the one at Brampford Speke. Just downstream from the bridge would be seen Thorverton Wier; a wide, impressive feature built to give the mill a head of water via a leat or mill race. As the train continued along a low curving embankment, the distant signal for the level crossings at Up Exe came into view. There was one crossing on either side of the station. During the course of a day a few vehicles would pass over the crossings — indeed, compared with Fortescue they would be busy — and so once the train had passed, the gates were opened for road traffic. Drifting over Up Exe South Crossing, the train coasted into Up Exe Halt. This halt, like Brampford Speke, was a 'demoted station'. The station building was, and continues to be, occupied as a house, but the mossy nature of much of the platform pointed out the relatively small amount of use the halt latterly received. From 1954 a number of trains went straight through without stopping, 'whistling up' on their approach to warn the crossings.

smaller and the proportion of grassland over arable increased. The diminutive Burn Halt was little used, despite a nameboard grandiously proclaiming 'Burn Halt for Butterleigh'. As at Up Exe, a few trains were scheduled to stop in the last ten years of the halt's existence, those that did providing a basic 'peak time' facility for schoolchildren and shoppers.

Passenger trains were allowed 8 minutes to cover the 4 miles between Thorverton and Cadeleigh. Trains would 'tap' along this section of shallow cuttings and low embankments at the maximum speed permitted, the ride in the auto-coach being comfortable with just a slight lateral roll. The wheel noise of the auto-coach was distinctive when running at this sort of speed; a sort of dull, resonating 'roar' which was rhythmically enhanced by the rail joints.

On the footplate of an 0-4-2 tank, however, it could be a very different matter. The wheel arrangement encouraged a tendency for the rear to 'wag' if the train was lightly loaded or was running 'bunker first'. A footplate ride once on the pick-up goods from

Pannier tank No. 9629 in open country to the south of Burn Halt on an 'up' train on 8th July 1959. *Peter W. Gray*

Once over the North Crossing, the train was curving to the north, to run parallel with the Exeter-Minehead road. The passenger would soon become aware of a change in the view from the window. The valley floor appreciably narrowed. Although still half a mile wide its bluff lines are seen to be sharper and the valley sides to rise more steeply and to a much greater height. This marked the passage from the soft sandstones on to the older, darker, harder Culm Measures which make up much of the landscape of Mid-Devon. The tops of the hills are more plateau-like, but the numerous streams which drain into the Exe have dissected the land into a fret-work of steep hills and deep valleys which give it its characteristically broken appearance. As the train continued north, on the long straight to Burn Halt, the fields became

Thorverton to Cadeleigh was quite an experience; with only one covered box van and a brake van to 'weight' the locomotive, it was necessary to keep hold of a cab hand-rail to keep oneself steady!

Running in over the two sets of facing points to the 'up' platform at Cadeleigh, the train was now 10¼ miles from Exeter St. David's. The village of Cadeleigh, 1½ miles to the west-northwest of the station and over 300 feet higher, is a real hill-top settlement, reached by a steep winding road. The station was actually adjacent to the village of Bickleigh, a picturesque place much visited by tourists today. When the line opened in 1885, the station was actually called 'Cadeleigh & Bickleigh', but to avoid any confusion with the Bickleigh on the Plym Valley line north of Plymouth, the name was shortened to 'Cadeleigh' in 1906.

No. 9629 draws into Cadeleigh's 'up' platform on 30th May 1958.   *M. Hale*

Immediately to the north of the station the line crossed the Exe on another of the now familiar girder bridges. The land all around here was once the property of the Carew family (from the early 16th century). This family lived in Bickleigh Castle, and although they did not oppose the construction of the railway, they agreed to its passage through their land on the condition that they had the fishing rights from the river bridge. Trout would often stay in the vicinity of the bridge piers and so this was a superior location to the river bank! Although the Estate was sold up in 1922, the fishing rights were transferred to the new owner. Many a time when the ganger was walking over the bridge and saw trout beneath it, he would ring up the landowner from the station who would duly arrive with hook and line to land his catch (the ganger received due remuneration!).

Travelling north-northwest, the train soon found itself once again running parallel with the river. For the next mile and three-quarters the valley conspicuously narrows and steepens. On the hillside beyond the river the slopes are all-but continuously wooded. The trees, mixed deciduous, provide an attractive back-cloth to the pastures of the valley floor, while on the west-side of the valley the slopes are more varied, mainly grass but with some ploughland and wood. As the line turned north towards West Exe, road, rail and river ran very close together, all three being framed by trees and grassy banks. Passing below the main road, the approach to Tiverton was made on a sweeping embankment which turned the line almost through a right angle. The southwestern suburbs of the town were served by West Exe Halt, which was extremely well-patronised. It was convenient for the workers at Heathcoat's Mill and also served a sizeable housing development. All trains, except the first one up in the morning, stopped at the halt. It was the only one of the purpose-built halts

designed to accommodate a two-coach rather than a single-coach train; an indication of its degree of passenger use.

The old town of Tiverton developed on the high 'wedge' of land between the Rivers Exe and Lowman, which have their confluence at West Exe. The railway skirted this high ground, first crossing the Exe on a substantial, attractive four-arched stone viaduct, then cut beneath St. Andrew Street, bridged the Lowman and entered Tiverton station through a deep cutting.

Tiverton always possessed the air of a main line station; one half expected to see a train of several coaches arrive hauled by a 'Hall', 'Manor' or 'Grange', or at the very least a 43XX Mogul. The long platforms, each with a bay; the covered footbridge; extensive station accommodation complete with canopies; and wall-mounted advertisement boards, gave the station an ambience in keeping with the status of the town! This was further enhanced by an extensive goods yard and substantial signal box.

The station generated a tremendous amount of traffic, both passenger and freight, and was also a junction, being the western

Northbound from Cadeleigh.   *B. L. Davis*

No. 1451 entering Tiverton with a train from Exeter in June 1958.   *R. E. Toop*

Opposite page top: Approaching West Exe Halt from the south.   *W. L. Underhay*

Opposite page bottom: '14XX' class with trailer and parcels van crossing the River Exe at West Exe with an Exeter – Dulverton train. Not only have the trains gone, but so too has this riverside view; austere flood-prevention work has transformed the scene.
Peter W. Gray

Busy scene at Tiverton, with the '14XX' class auto-tanks monopolising the traffic. The northbound locomotive (No. 1421), characteristically, is taking on water while that in the 'down' platform (No. 1442) will propel its train on to Exeter once the 'right away' is given. The connecting service to Tiverton Junction — the 'Tivvy Bumper' — waits in the 'down' bay. 28th September 1963.
H. Ballantyne

No. 3659 running in over the junction at Tiverton with a Dulverton–Exeter train on 29th September 1962. The line to Tiverton Junction is in the right-hand foreground.
M. J. Fox;
courtesy Tiverton Museum

terminus of the former broad gauge Tiverton Branch which linked the town with the West of England main line at Tiverton Junction. Some Exe Valley 'up' passenger trains connected with the one-coach auto-train to Tiverton Junction, known locally as the 'Tivvy Bumper'. The times of this service were dictated by main line services at the Junction and, to a lesser extent, the Culm Valley trains between the Junction and Hemyock. The Tivvy Bumper usually worked in and out of the 'down'-side bay platform, but if a tight connection was to be made with an 'up' Valley train, the empty stock would be marshalled across from 'down' side to 'up', and then backed into the 'up'-side bay. The 'up'

valley train would pull well forward in the platform to allow passengers to transfer directly from one train to the other (and at the same time enable the engine to take on water). The train to the Junction would then leave first.

Thinking of the Exe Valley as a branch needs modification as far as Tiverton is concerned. Being a Junction, the signalling referred to 'main line' and 'branch'. The line to Tiverton Junction, although having been built back in 1848 and always handling more trains than the Exe Valley, was only 4¾ miles long compared with the 24¾ miles of the Exe Valley, and so it was classified as the 'branch', and the Exe Valley as the 'main line'.

No. 1471 propelling the 15.20 Bampton to Exeter train towards a local 'summit' north of Tiverton on 14th September 1963. *Peter W. Gray*

A northbound train scurries along the edge of the Exe Valley between Bolham and Cove.
D. Fereday Glenn

Scenically, the area around Tiverton closely resembles that south of Up Exe, for between West Exe and Bolham the line once again crosses the softer red sandstones, which have pushed westwards in a finger-like protrusion from the Culm Valley. Leaving Tiverton the train climbed vigorously to a local summit below Cowleymoor, where it crossed the 'toe' of the low ridge separating the Exe and Lowman valleys. A series of cuttings and embankments, followed by a half-mile stretch of tight curves — on which a 20 m.p.h. speed limit subsisted — brought the line back to its northward orientation. At the tiny Bolham Halt, two miles from Tiverton, the train was about to cross back on to the Culm Measures. The northern section of the line possessed a different character from the southern; architecturally, historically and geographically. The landscape is not any higher here but it is less dissected, and so begins to resemble a more conspicuous if undulating upland. The most dramatic change, however, is in the Exe Valley itself: the valley narrows markedly, and both sides be-

come steeper and more wooded. Between Cove and Bampton, the valley sides are very steep indeed on the outer bends of the river, and landslipping is a problem on the road between Bolham and Bampton. Unlike the road, which rises and falls along the east side of the valley, the railway kept to the edge of the floodplain, thus maintaining a constant line and reasonable grade. The stretch of line between Lythecourt and Fairby was one of the fastest on the branch for 'up' trains; the gradient was falling at 1:100; the line was straight; and there were no crossings, stations or halts for some way. On one occasion a driver had been reported for 'speeding' on this section, and so on a subsequent turn was timed and found to be doing 60 m.p.h. He took it more carefully for a while afterwards, but speeds often crept over the 35 m.p.h. maximum!

Between Fairby and Cove, road, rail and river ran close together in a wooded valley; the woods now containing a fair proportion of conifer trees. Cove Halt, situated alongside the

No. 1450 pauses at Cove Halt with a southbound auto-train. As the locomotive is propelling its train, the lamp is incorrectly positioned — a feature by no means uncommon on the Exe Valley. 3rd October 1963. *D. Fereday Glenn*

river, was the first of the halts to be built on the Exe Valley, opening in 1923. Apart from this distinction, and no doubt because of it, it had a different appearance from the other halts. Its platform was the usual one-coach length, but was adorned with a corrugated-iron pagoda-style waiting shelter; the only one on the line. Pulling out of the halt, the train passed over the level crossing carrying the road which gave access to the huge and visually intrusive Holmingham Quarry. The floor-mounted Cove signal box, technically a 'ground frame', locked the gates, but the gates — as at all the crossings — had to be opened and closed by hand. A short siding, capable of holding only 5 wagons, came immediately beyond the crossing. Goods trains would call here 'by request', but the siding received little use, and in 1954 the freight facility was withdrawn. Beyond the siding the line crossed the Exe on a two-span girder bridge; passed the towering quarried cliff of rusty-looking slabs of rock; and rounded a ridge to cross the Exe again. This last crossing allowed the line to gain the valley of the River Batherm to Bampton, as the main valley of the Exe turned away through a right angle to by-pass the town. In fact the line only crossed the Exe once more, near Exebridge half a mile from its terminus at Dulverton station (this last half mile following the southern margin of the valley of the River Barle). The train now had to start climbing hard, on a rising gradient of 1:63, through the narrow valley that lead to Bampton. The massively-bedded limestones of this area were once extensively quarried for roadstone, a network of tramways taking the stone to the sidings at Bampton. The whole hillside south of the town is marked with disused and largely overgrown quarries, all of which once yielded valuable revenue for the Railway, as did the October pony fair, for which the town is famous. The station was situated in a cutting on the western edge of the built-up area while the southern approach and goods yard were on embankments to help ease the gradient through the platforms. The station buildings and layout were different in detail from those at Cadeleigh and

No. 1471 entering Bampton with an 'up' train on 2nd July 1963. *R. C. Riley*

Thorverton, the section north of Tiverton having been built by a different contractor.

With the 'right away' from Bampton, the train passed beneath the bridge connecting Luke Street with High Street, and into a deep cutting which in places exhibited bare rock outcrops. The 'down' home signal was perched high up on top of this cutting. As the River Batherm flows into Bampton from the northeast, the railway used its tributary, the Shuttern Brook, to maintain its northern progress in order to join the ex-Devon and Somerset line at Morebath Junction. With the further reduction in stream-size, the valley accordingly narrowed. The line was climbing at 1:66 through a predominantly green-field hedge-bound landscape. At 68 chains (over ¾ mile) north of Bampton was a Stop Board, at which all 'down' freight trains had to halt to pin down brakes. This was about half way between Bampton and Morebath Junction, and was designed to prevent trains running away down the steep gradient through the momentum of the trucks exceeding

is towards this that the train was climbing. Lower Lodfin level crossing occupied the pass, for it is a useful road gap as well. The wooden signal cabin — as at Cove only classed as a ground frame — and the adjoining crossing keeper's house kept a lonely vigil in a landscape of many fields but few people. Whistling as the crossing got closer the train, still climbing, then began to curve to join the line from Taunton to Barnstaple. Even with Morebath Junction's branch home signal showing 'off' the train had to slow to 15 m.p.h. to run in over the points and exchange single-line tokens. The Devon and Somerset now became the 'mainline' and the Exe Valley 'the branch', while the train also changed description from an 'up' into a 'down' train!

Most of the time Valley trains would run in to the Junction without any signal checks, as any booked connections were made at Dulverton rather than the single-platform diminutive Morebath Junction Halt. On one occasion a late-running D & S train was given precedence over a Valley train by the signalman — a

No. 1421 passing Lower Lodfin Farm on 15th June 1963 on its climb from Bampton to Morebath Junction with the 15.25 from Exeter.   *Peter W. Gray*

the breaking ability of the locomotive and guards van combined. Restrictions were placed on the number of wagons permitted to freight trains; so that although a limit of 50 wagons existed from Bampton to Exeter, 28 was the limit from Dulverton to Bampton. In practice, trains were never this long, but it highlights the principle. Even before the stop board site was reached, the orientation of the line had become obvious. Ahead of the train, running from west to east, across the direction of travel, would be seen a pronounced ridge rising over 300 feet from the level of the railway (Surridge Knap on the west and Hukeley Knap on the east). The Shuttern Brook has cut a narrow gap through this ridge, and it

'Barnstaple man' — and the latter was held at signals. The friendly rivalry that existed between the two lines caused phones to ring in 'mock anger' and the Morebath man was informed in no uncertain terms of the Valley men's displeasure at this delay!

Morebath Junction Halt was the usual basic affair, and was built a long time after the station of Morebath, which was nowhere near the village of the same name (indeed, it was two circuitous miles by road). The halt was a mere quarter of a mile away across fields, and gave villagers access to the shops and markets at Bampton and Tiverton.

The remaining 1¾ miles to Dulverton, running now in a

No. 1450 propelling the 13.05 from Dulverton over the points at Morebath Junction, taking it from the former Devon & Somerset line to the Exe Valley branch. 7th September 1963.   *R. A. Lumber*

Morebath Junction Halt, looking east; 1956. This unprepossessing halt marked the highest point on the line (500 feet above sea-level).   *Mowat Collection*

No. 1421 running into the 'back platform loop' at Dulverton with the 17.48 from Exeter on 23rd July 1963.   *R. A. Lumber*

Dulverton. Change for Exe Valley Line

Most Exe Valley trains made a connection with Devon & Somerset services at Dulverton. In this case the branch train waits in the 'back road' while '43XX' class No. 6390 runs in with the 08.20 Barnstaple (Victoria) to Taunton train. 28th March 1959.

J. E. Bell

No. 1421 again on the 17.15 for Exeter waits for No. 6372 to arrive with the 16.10 Barnstaple Junction to Taunton train. 15th June 1963.   *Peter W. Gray*

westerly direction, were over the metals of the Barnstaple line. The gradient profile of this line as a whole resembled a switchback, with numerous grades of 1:58 and 1:60. For Exe Valley trains the highest point on their journey was reached just to the west of Morebath Junction Halt; namely, almost 500 feet above sea level (St. David's station, at the beginning of the journey, stood at 40 feet). The Valley train found itself passing through a series of cuttings on a falling gradient of 1:58, heading for its last crossing of the Exe on the single-span girder bridge just upstream from Exebridge. The maximum permitted speed on this stretch of 50 m.p.h. was appreciated by drivers, although on approaching Dulverton this would have to be brought right down as the limit imposed on trains entering and leaving the Exe Valley Plat-

form loop line was a mere 15 m.p.h. Two or three trains had a wait of only 15 minutes or so before embarking on the return run and, as the crew liked to have a cup of tea, there was sometimes a chance to gain a few more minutes by utilising the higher speed limit, falling gradient and generous time schedule from Morebath Junction.

Running in slowly off the single line and then over the two further sets of facing points, the train would come to a halt in the branch platform, and the end of its journey. The last half-mile of the run had been in Somerset, and had brought the train right up to the southern flanks of Exmoor; the birth-place of the river that had kept the line company for almost the whole journey.

Pannier tank No. 9685 and single trailer here make a connection with a train from Taunton to Barnstaple in April 1962.
R. E. Toop

No. 1471 and coach in the customary location at Tiverton on 28th March 1959: the 'down'-side bay platform. The combination of a '14XX' class tank engine and single auto-trailer formed the train known affectionately as the 'Tivvy Bumper', shuttling between Tiverton and the main line at Tiverton Junction.

J. E. Bell

The Tiverton Branch

Dating back to 1848, the Tiverton — Tiverton Junction line was originally a branch of the Bristol and Exeter Railway. With the opening of the Exe Valley line in 1885, it became a branch of that line as well. Although technically the Tiverton Branch was not part of the Exe Valley, it was in daily practice very much part of the system with locos, crews, passengers and freight interchanging between two lines, and even a few services being timetabled as through workings. The 14XX Class tank engine and single auto-trailer which worked the line in later years (the Tivvy Bumper) provided 12 to 13 trains each way every weekday, usually connecting with trains on the Exe Valley line, or main line, or both.

The Tivvy Bumper would make a cautious start from Tiverton to enable the driver to collect the single line token from the signalman. The train then moved over a considerable amount of pointwork, the final set of points taking the Exe Valley line, curving sharply away beneath Blundells Road to the north. The speed restriction over the junction was initially severe: 5 m.p.h. was the maximum allowed until 1912 when the points leading to the single line section beyond the junction were opened out. Even so, the speed limit was only raised to 10 m.p.h. Once over the last of the points, with the train heading east through allotment gardens, the driver would open up the regulator to get a run at the 1:91 rising gradient which began almost immediately. To the south of the train the lower hillside was covered with housing dating from the inter-war years (and now spreading even further eastwards). The Grand Western Canal, nearly 100 feet higher

than the railway, followed a parallel though markedly more sinuous route, with the land rising more steeply above. Once beyond the Tidcombe road over-bridge, the high ground recedes and the train ambled through a low, undulating green landscape with only minor earthworks necessary to maintain the constant upward grade. The line followed the 'wedge' of red sandstones referred to earlier; a broad swathe of landscape traversed by very small streams which gave only a general direction to, rather than narrowly confined, the course of the railway. The Alsa Brook,

'14XX' class No. 1420 hurries away from Tiverton on the 16.00 working to the Junction on 30th July 1960. The site of the original Bristol & Exeter terminus station may be seen behind the train. The tall Great Western signal, with its 5-foot arm, was installed in 1912 and survived until 1964. *D. Fereday Glenn*

Two of Tiverton's more interesting signals, viewed from the Blundells Road overbridge. In the foreground is the 'Up Main Advanced Starting Signal' with the 'Shunt' arm below (lever numbers 5 and 6 respectively). The other signal is the 'Down Main Outer Home' with a co-acting arm below (No. 40). On the Tiverton Branch, the 'Tivvy Bumper' makes a purposeful start on its 4¾ mile journey to the Junction.

Peter Slater

No. 1450 propelling its trailer towards Tiverton Junction in the undulating country between Tiverton and Halberton. This mode of operation was extremely rare on 'up' trains, the locomotive invariably hauling its coach out to the Junction and propelling it back. 18th August 1964. *I. G. Holt*

Below: The Grand Western Canal aqueduct west of Halberton Halt. No. 1463 with the 13.15 ex Tiverton on 4th November 1961. *Peter W. Gray*

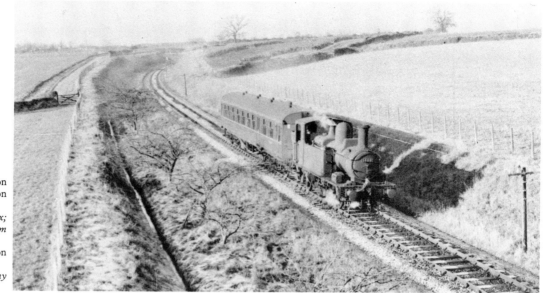

No. 1466 running into Halberton Halt with a train for the Junction on 21st December 1963.

M. J. Fox;
courtesy Tiverton Museum

Below: No. 1442 leaving Halberton Halt for Tiverton Junction.

W. L. Underhay

running immediately to the north of the line, together with the River Lowman, drain the western part of this 'wedge', while the Spratford Stream and its tributaries drain the east. The watershed between these systems, such as it is, is marked by the aqueduct carrying the Grand Western Canal over the line, just to the west of Halberton Halt. This landscape did not present the railway builders with any great problems, and consequently the Tiverton Branch was given the locomotive route classification of 'Red' under the Great Western's system of colour coding. Indeed, all locomotives except the 60XX 4-6-0 'King' Class were permitted to work over the branch, while the Exe Valley, as a 'Yellow' route, was only able to take a somewhat restricted range of smaller and lighter locomotives. The classification went from 'Double Red' at the top end of the scale through 'Red', 'Blue', 'Dotted Blue', and 'Yellow' to 'Uncoloured' on the humblest branch line. The speed

limit on the line was 45 m.p.h., although 'Red' engines were only permitted 20 m.p.h.

On reaching the aqueduct, the driver would shut off to coast the short distance into Halberton Halt. The aqueduct was a solid looking affair made from stone quarried in the Beacon Hill/Canonsleigh area a short distance to the northeast. The cast-iron trough carrying the canal is 40 feet above track level, being carried across the track bed by two masonry arches. The aqueduct was built in 1847, at which time a double-track broad gauge line was envisaged. In post World War Two days, the canal trough leaked very slightly, so that in frosty weather a long icicle hung down inside the northern arch right over the track. In the bitter winter of 1962-63 it grew to enormous size, so much so that the crew of the first train of the day — a goods train from Tiverton Junction — had to remember to keep well inside the cab as they passed

No. 1471 in the Tiverton Branch platform at Tiverton Junction with the 11.20 to Tiverton on 28th March 1959. *J. E. Bell*

through the arch and duly truncated the icicle! Apart from the redundant second arch of the aqueduct, the provision for a projected second track found other uses than the one intended. Halberton Halt, which opened in 1927, was built on the site for the proposed second track, and right beneath the wide-arched road bridge, which led from the village. The clearance for this bridge, and all bridges, was based on a requirement for two 7ft. 0in. lines with side and centre clearance. Thus a wide strip of land extended the 4 miles 54 chains from Tiverton to Tiverton Junction, and produced perhaps the strangest feature of all.

Running for well over a mile on either side of Halberton Halt, and occupying the site of the second line, was a single row of apple trees, giving an orchard over two miles long but only one tree wide.

During the second decade of the present century, apple merchant Mr. Joseph Diggle travelled from Lancashire to Devon each year to purchase apples (buyers would put in a bid for a full orchard as seen at the setting of the fruit, rather than paying a price per unit weight for the fruit when picked). He subsequently married a Halberton girl and settled in the village. Noticing the strip of 'spare' land running alongside the railway, he approached the GWR for permission to rent that part of it, near the village, for the planting of Bramley apple trees — a linear orchard which he tended for many years.

After a brief pause at Halberton Halt, the Tivvy Bumper continued its eastward progression for the remaining 2 miles or so to Tiverton Junction.

Now technically in the drainage basin of the River Culm, the topography goes through a series of minor inflections causing the line to rise and fall slightly (though keeping an average gradient of 1:86). Where more significant breaks of slope occurred the line crossed first a low embankment, then through a shallow cutting and so on until the final short climb to the Junction. Running in past the engine shed and sidings, decelerating and rattling over the cluster of points which 'gathered up' these sidings, the train came to a halt at the island platform built specifically for its use.

Chapter Two
The Historical Background

Railway promoters always hoped to make money from their enterprises. If capital was to be attracted, some hope of a return on investment had to be offered. The Bristol & Exeter Railway Company, whose aim was to link those two important commercial centres, had, in an endeavour to maximise eventual profits, to consider not only the most favourable geographical route for the line but also the traffic potential in a corridor on either side of the 'optimum' route. Commonsense would indicate the need to take the railway to Tiverton, an important market town in the mid Exe Valley. The Census of 1831 showed that Tiverton was the third largest town in Devon with a population of 9,766 (Plymouth was the largest with 78,633, followed by Exeter with 32,450). The commercial importance of Tiverton had already been realised by the builders of the Grand Western Canal. The canal company had an ambitious scheme to build a waterway from Taunton, with its access to the Bristol Channel, to the Exe estuary port of Topsham, and thence English Channel. A branch was planned from the main canal at Burlescombe, which would 'tap' the traffic at Tiverton. Work started on the branch first, due to major engineering problems further north. In 1814, the short 'landlocked' canal opened, giving the Canonsleigh and Beacon Hill limestone and sandstone quarries a cheap outlet to Tiverton.

The surveyors of the Bristol & Exeter Railway, like the Canal Company before them, decided to use the Lower Culm Valley route to Exeter rather than go to Tiverton and along the Lower Exe Valley. A number of factors favoured this decision. In the first place, the Culm Valley route was over 4 miles shorter. Gradients were not severe on either route, the Culm Valley averaged 1:264 and the Exe Valley 1:241. The significant difference here, however, was that a line built in the former would be on an almost continuous gently falling gradient to the south, while the Exe Valley route would be faced with rising and falling gradients in almost equal number unless heavy engineering work was undertaken. More importantly, the wider floodplain of the Culm allowed easier curves and, consequently, higher speeds: the maximum permitted speed of 90 m.p.h. was only curtailed on the reverse curves south of Cullompton (and that was 65 m.p.h.). In the absence of an expensive engineering commitment, a maximum of 35 m.p.h. came to be imposed on the faster sections of the Exe Valley branch.

If the main line was destined to avoid Tiverton, then a branch to connect it to the system was essential. Indeed, the Tiverton Branch was included in the proposals forwarded to Parliament by the Bristol and Exeter, and this made it one of the very first branch-lines planned in Britain. The Act was to enable the Company to raise funds to build their line, much of the money being needed to pay compensation to landowners through whose land the Railway would pass. The Act was passed on 19th May 1836. Work began immediately on laying out the main line, but not the branch. The 4¾ mile branch was intended to join the main line at what became Tiverton Junction, but as no branch existed as yet, the station was known as Tiverton Road. The line from Taunton to Exeter opened on 1st May 1844, and was, like the other Great Western lines of the day, on the seven foot gauge (actually 7ft. 0¼in.).

Their main task complete, the Bristol and Exeter now sought to build their line to Tiverton, but found that the powers granted in 1836 had lapsed. They once again approached Parliament, but this time ran into opposition. The Grand Western Canal Company had in the meantime woken up to the threat the railway posed to their monopoly of trade, notably in coal and stone. Road transport was painfully slow and was low-bulk and labour intensive. The bright future envisaged by the canal company had never materialised and the plans for a railway would end any hope of recouping some of the heavy losses made during the canal's construction. It was only in 1838 that the canal was finally opened all the way from Tiverton to Taunton; the expense having been so great that the planned extension to the south was abandoned. Given their dire financial situation, it is hardly surprising that the canal company objected to the Bristol & Exeter's intentions. The economic arguments against the railway carried little weight, but a more serious obstacle was the need for the railway to pass beneath the canal just southwest of the village of Halberton. An aqueduct would have to be built to effect this. As construction of the aqueduct would mean disruption to the operation of barge traffic, the Grand Western made a last-ditch stand to block the railway, but even this objection was overruled.

The Bristol and Exeter was therefore, after many months' delay, given Parliamentary approval. Construction of the line began almost straight away. The anticipated volume of traffic led the engineers to plan for a double-track line on the 7 foot gauge. Although only a single track was initially laid, all engineering works and structures — including the twin-arched stone aqueduct at Halberton — were designed for two tracks. In the event, a single line was able to cope with the traffic and the second track was not laid. So concerned was the Bristol & Exeter to open the line, that the engineering work and track laying was finished before the terminus station at Tiverton, so that when the line opened on 12th June 1848 passengers had to join or leave the trains at track level. Tiverton Road was then renamed Tiverton Junction.

The first train to run over the Tiverton Branch was hauled by 'Bristol & Exeter' No. 58, seen here with footplate crew and other branch personnel on Opening Day, 12th June 1848. *Tiverton Museum*

The hostility between canal and rail was bound to remain, given their conflicting outlook and recent history. In an effort to attract traffic, both companies cut freight rates, ultimately to their mutual disadvantage.

With its passenger revenue and general merchandise traffic, together with a more regional catchment area, the Railway was able to absorb the heavy losses in coal traffic caused by this trade war. The canal company borrowed money in order to remain operational, but was incurring collosal debts. For five years this insane war continued, until in 1852 the canal company offered to sell out to the Bristol & Exeter. The B&E refused an outright purchase, but agreed to lease it for £2,000 a year. The Grand Western had no option but to agree and as soon as the arrangements had been finalised, in 1854, the B&E promptly raised the

inclined plane at Wellisford. The Somerset section of the canal was abandoned in 1865, whilst the section from the Holcombe Rogus/Westleigh quarries to Tiverton was kept open. Later, in 1924, even this trade stopped following serious leaks in the clay lining and bank, and caused the railway company to put in its own mineral line from Burlescombe station to the quarries. By a strange quirk of fate, however, it was the railway that came to rely on the canal, or at least on its water. As long as trains plied the short distance between Tiverton and Tiverton Junction, they would take on water at the latter (this also being the location of the engine shed). However, with the opening of the line from Exeter to Dulverton in 1885, Exe Valley trains needed to take on water at Tiverton. A large water tower was built on the bank just to the east of the station, and was gravity fed from the canal basin

Repairs being carried out to the bed of the Grand Western Canal which had failed near Halberton; April 1921. Further leaks in the same area in 1924 created a dry section around which the GWR had to pipe water until the necessary repairs were completed. Leaks continued, however, and in the 1930s the Railway stanked-off a half-mile length near the village.   *British Railways/OPC*

rates on water-borne freight. This drove traffic off the canal and on to the railway, and with a virtual monopoly now secured, railway freight rates were put up as well.

In 1863 the Bristol & Exeter offered to buy the canal for a sum of £30,000. Not surprisingly, the offer was accepted. If the canal company could not, or did not, want to see the future, others could. The Tiverton firm of Goodlands (coal and builders merchants) set up in the town in 1830, and located at the canal basin. With the coming of the railway, the firm soon moved to their present site, adjoining the former Bristol & Exeter terminus.

The section of canal from Taunton to the summit on the Somerset-Devon border had always been expensive to maintain, in particular the boat lifts at Trefusis and Nynehead and the

some 80 feet up the hillside. The canal was fed by the Lowdwells springs north of Holcombe Rogus, and by a number of small streams draining in from the high ground near Sampford Peverell and Tiverton. Occasional checks had to be made to ensure that the intake grille, on the north side of the canal basin, was clear of any debris. The importance of this supply was illustrated in the serious leakage at Halberton in 1924 which all but drained the section. Stop locks were inserted on either side of the break and water was piped round the dry section to maintain the supply to the railway. In 1948 responsibility for maintaining the canal passed from the British Railways Board to the British Transport Commission. The closure of the Exe Valley line in October 1963 removed the need to maintain the canal as Tiverton Branch trains could take on water at the Junction, and it quickly fell into a poor state of repair. There was a very real possiblity that the canal bed would be filled in, but local action groups and eventually the county council took over its restoration.

With the opening of the Tiverton Branch in 1848 railway building in Devon came to be concentrated elsewhere. The villages of the Exe Valley continued their time-honoured self-sufficient existence, with only an occasional need to travel farther than the nearest market. Pre-rail transport was slow and doubtless uncomfortable. In the village of Thorverton, 6½ miles north of Exeter, two local carriers Messrs. Cummings and Downing, ran horse-drawn covered wagons with seats in. Twice a week they went to Tiverton, and twice a week to Exeter in the years before the railway opened. Many villages had their own carrier for moving goods or were served by one from elsewhere. Somebody was generally on hand with a horse and trap for hire for those people who wished to travel further afield.

A growing awareness of the benefits of the railway saw a tremendous boom in railway construction in Devon in the last 30 years of the 19th century. To be without a railway created a sense of isolation or even deprivation. The evident success of the Tiverton Branch encouraged the establishment of an Exe Valley Railway Company in the 1860s, with the aim of building a direct link between Exeter and Tiverton via the Exe Valley (not until 1876 was it possible to reach Tiverton via the main line without having to change trains at the Junction, but it remained a slow journey). After considerable initial interest, the plans foundered. On the 1st November 1873 the Devon and Somerset Railway Company opened their line between Barnstaple and Taunton, providing a rail-head for the Upper Exe Valley villages at Dulverton (Dulverton station was actually a misnomer as it was situated in the village of Brushford, some two miles down the River Barle from Dulverton itself). This made the idea of an Exe Valley Railway all the more attractive: a direct line could be established from the remote villages of southern Exmoor to Exeter, while Tiverton would be made more readily accessible to its existing hinterland. In fact, the line actually started out as two separate companies.

An Exe Valley Railway Company — a completely separate body from that of ten years before — was set up, and petitioned Parliament for powers to raise funds and purchase land between Stoke Canon and Tiverton (running powers were also sought over the Bristol & Exeter main line between Stoke Canon and Exeter). The Company gained authorisation under their Act of 30th June 1874. Some time before this, a different organisation, the Tiverton & North Devon Railway Company, was set up. A meeting to elect members was held in Tiverton on 22nd September 1865, the meeting being chaired by J. H. Heathcoat-Amory. The aim was to build a line from Tiverton, through Bampton, to Dulverton. The Company was incorporated by Act of Parliament on 19th July 1875, and its Prospectus was issued at the end of January the following year. The amount of capital required was £65,000, a figure which proved to be a considerable under-estimate. The scene should have been set for a significant amount of railway building in Mid-Devon, but then the problem of money raised its head again — there wasn't enough.

While the two companies scratched around for funds, another issue entered to add yet further delay; namely, the question of gauge standardisation. As early as 1846 an 'Act for Regulating the Gauge of Railways' required all new lines to be of the 'narrow (i.e. standard) gauge' of 4ft. 8½in. The Great Western and associated west of England lines had exemption, as they already operated the 7ft. gauge favoured by Brunel. The 'change of gauge' necessitated when travelling from 'narrow' to 'broad' rails was becoming an increasing irritant as the volume of rail travel grew. The 7ft. gauge soon became the exception rather than the

rule, on the network as a whole, and so a 'third rail' began to be added to allow both broad and narrow gauge trains to run. By the mid-1860s this 'mixed gauge' had reached Exeter, and then from 1869 the Great Western decided to abandon the broad gauge, bit by bit. The last line to be dealt with was that from London to Penzance: the 168 miles from Exeter to Penzance being converted in just 31 hours on May 21st and 22nd, 1892. With mixed gauge from Stoke Canon to Exeter, broad gauge from Taunton to Barnstaple and broad gauge on the Tiverton Branch, the two companies with schemes in the Exe Valley would have to decide which gauge to use or await the inevitable demise of the broad gauge.

The financial problems of the Exe Valley Railway Company were a real handicap, but the potential of their plan appealed to the Bristol & Exeter. After negotiations, the Exe Valley Railway Company transferred its powers to the Bristol & Exeter, this being confirmed by Act of Parliament on 19th July 1875 (at the same time as the Tiverton and North Devon was incorporated). No sooner was this done than the Bristol & Exeter's attention was diverted to more far-reaching matters — an amalgamation with the Great Western Railway. Discussions were lengthy. On the 1st January 1876 the Bristol & Exeter was leased to the Great Western, and from 1st August of the same year was amalgamated with it, so losing its separate identity. After a short period of consolidation, the Great Western Railway took over the Exe Valley project, and in 1877 preliminary work started. The contractor appointed for the line was W. Moss of Stafford, while the engineers were F. Fox and C. E. Mountenay.

The building of the Exe Valley line, as with any railway, was a long and skilled task and the arrival of the navvies caused considerable excitement in the villages along the route. Three steel girder bridges had to be built over the Exe (at Brampford Speke, Thorverton, and Cadeleigh) and a four-arch stone viaduct at Tiverton. Numerous over and under bridges, culverts, cuttings, embankments and retaining walls all had to be built using only 'pick-and-wheelbarrow' technology, while the stations, station-masters' houses, level-crossing keepers' houses, weighbridges, cattle-docks and goods sheds were built out of local stone and to a unity of design. Not only did the railway bring unaccustomed activity, it also brought in people from far and wide with much of the work being sub-contracted to local firms. The Contractor, Mr. Moss, brought his whole family from Stafford to live in the village of Thorverton while the line was under construction. The activity here even inspired a poem with one of the verses stating:

'It is only for Mr. Moss to move a little faster
and Thorverton will have a station master'.

One of the carpenters working on the station at Thorverton pencilled a few autobiographical details on the back of the booking office counter before it was secured beneath the ticket window.

'This counter was fixed by William Alfred Pering,
ninth child of Nicholas and Ann Pering.
Born at Blackawton, County of Devon,
Thursday, January 14, 1847, ten minutes after 2 a.m.'
Dated, March 27, 1884

While the Exe Valley Railway was underway in the south, the Tiverton and North Devon Railway was experiencing mixed fortunes in the north. This project got off to a slower start than its neighbour. Surveyors had begun work on the route to be followed by the line from its junction with the Devon & Somerset Railway near the village of Morebath, but money for land purchase remained a problem and caused further delays. The contractor

H. C. Sanders, Engineer, Tiverton & North Devon Railway.
Tiverton Museum

appointed by the Company was N. B. Fogg of Liverpool, and the engineer was H. C. Sanders. With the route finally surveyed, the first sod was cut by Sir John Heathcoat-Amory, M.P. for Tiverton, on 3rd May, 1880, and the initial earthworks were begun. A year later, in May 1881, the Devon & Somerset 'narrowed' its line from Taunton to Barnstaple, and so when it was time to start laying track, the decision was taken to begin at Morebath Junction and work south to Tiverton, a distance of 8 miles and 54 chains (80 chains in a mile; 1 chain thus being 22 yards). The line got to within 2 miles 17 chains of Tiverton, and then financial difficulties stopped it.

At this juncture the Great Western Railway stepped in. With the southern section well under way, the Great Western Railway could see the advantage of combining the two operations and running trains right through from Exeter to Dulverton. There was little practical point in the T.& N.D.R. trying to struggle on, but they were a fiercely independent organisation, and even though the Great Western completed and operated the line, the Company kept its name and a nominal form of independence for the next ten years. The Company had spent £85,980 on building the line, while the income received proved to be far short of that expected: £1,395 in 1885; £1,843 in 1889; and £2,150 in 1893. In return for operating the line, the G.W.R. received 50% of the gross takings, an arrangement which lasted until February 1894 when the T.& N.D.R. Co. was wound up.

With the involvement of the Great Western, work resumed and moved on apace, the opening being planned for Wednesday 2nd July 1884 — ahead of the Exe Valley Railway. However, even the Great Western Railway could not escape the delays that

The Line Under Construction Photos by Sanders; 1882-84.

Tiverton's new station under construction. The original B & E terminus and goods yard are in the background.
Tiverton Museum

32

had accompanied the project from the start. The official sent by the Board of Trade to inspect the line was Colonel Yolland, his visitation taking place on Thursday 26th June 1884. Although he reported that the, 'Line is in very good order throughout', there were two items which required remedial action, and so he refused permission for the line to open on the planned date. The main problem was at Morebath Junction. Crossing loops of 300 yards in length had been provided on both the Tiverton & North Devon line and the Devon & Somerset in advance of their joining, followed by a 65 yard continuation of the double track to the west of the junction, towards Dulverton. To operate such an extensive layout with the signalling technology then available and the Board of Trade's minimum distance requirement for the working of points by mechanical means, required two signal boxes: the main junction box, controlling all signals and the western facing points

opening celebrations were put into cold storage. Within a month, however, all the necessary modifications had been attended to and inspected, and the line opened with due ceremony on Friday 1st August 1884.

In addition to his Report, Col. Yolland had been involved in other correspondence concerning the Tiverton & North Devon line, in respect of both legal and operational matters. On July 3rd 1884 he had written to the Board of Trade informing the Secretary that the powers granted to the Railway Company under their Act had lapsed, and stating that until this problem had been sorted out, the line could not open because it possessed no legal rights. At the same time, a Mr. Looseman of Tiverton contacted Col. Yolland regarding a 'cut' he had made under the line during its construction. He had taken legal advice in an effort to clarify any liability he might incur should his engineering endeavour

Retaining wall under construction.
Tiverton Museum

and the junction; and a subsidiary box, 110 yards east of the former, to work the loop points on both the T.& N.D. and D & S Lines. Both boxes were to be worked by one man. The Inspector was unhappy about this arrangement, stating:

'I have pointed out that it would be quite impossible for one signalman to do the work properly in two signal boxes situated at a distance of 110 yards apart, and I have suggested that the length of the loops should be shortened so that the whole of the work may be done by one man in the junction signal box. I am told that no very large amount of traffic can be expected on this new line for many years to come and the steepness of the Incline, 1 in 66, will limit the number of Wagons that will be taken up these lines'.

He was also concerned about the sharpest curve on the line, south of Bolham. The need to join up with the Tiverton Branch at the B. & E. station necessitated a diversion away from the Exe Valley, this being referred to as the 'Bolham Deviation' in the deposited plans. The most severe curve here had, or should have had, a radius of 12 chains, but Yolland noted that, 'some little adjustment is wanted at this spot as the curve laid in has a radius of less than 10 chains for a short distance'. Gangs were set to work immediately at Bolham and Morebath Junction, and the

cause an accident. As he received contradictory and inconclusive advice, he suggested to the Inspector that the opening be postponed until the legal situation was resolved. Yolland, however, was not persuaded and informed Mr. Looseman that 'if he performed any act that ultimately caused any serious accident to happen, he would probably be placed in a very uncomfortable position.' This view was conveyed by letter to the Board of Trade on 5th July. Two days later the Inspector was writing again; this time about the provision of turntables. He noted that the old 35ft. turntable at Tiverton had been removed, and asked if a new one was to be provided. The Great Western replied that a turntable was unnecessary. The Colonel disagreed, and in a letter of 24th July stated that the G.W.R. was acting illegally and should put in tables at Tiverton and Dulverton forthwith. Any delay in the opening of the line would be the fault of the Railway. The Board of Trade and Great Western reached a compromise solution: the former would drop the demand for a turntable at Tiverton, while the latter undertook to install one at Dulverton, in the meantime running tank engines over the line to obviate the need for turning. In the event, the Dulverton table had a diameter of only 23ft. 9in., while train services were worked by tank engines throughout the line's life. Col. Yolland, however, re-

Bampton station building. *Tiverton Museum*

mained unhappy, writing on 18th October 1884: 'The Great Western Railway Company do not seem inclined to comply with my requirements and it is for the Board of Trade to determine whether they are to be allowed to do as they choose.' This was one battle the Colonel lost!

The standards to which the line had been built are detailed in the Board of Trade Report. The Report thus gives an insight into the planning and construction of a branch line, as for example with regard to the Permanent Way:

'The width of the line at formation level is 13 feet in cuttings, 17 feet on embankments and 20 feet in cuttings under 5 feet deep. The width between lines when double is 6 feet. The gauge is 4 feet 8½

inches. The permanent way consists of double headed steel rails that weigh 80 lbs per yard in lengths of 32 feet, fixed in cast iron chairs that weigh 33¼ lbs, by means of wooden keys placed inside the rails. The chairs are fastened on transverse sleepers by means of two long bolts to each chair. The sleepers are 9 feet long, by 10in. x 5in., placed 3 feet apart from centre to centre, except at the joints where the distance is 2 feet apart. The joints of the rails are fished with two plates and 4 bolts to each joint, the plates together weighing about 24½ lbs. The ballast is of broken stone and gravel and is stated to be 10 inches in depth below the undersides of the sleepers. The line is fenced with wire standards 6 feet apart and the top wire is 3ft. 9in. above ground and there are 7 wires. Cast iron straining pillars with winding barrels and ratchet wheel. Four double or eight single pillars per mile'.

Once the Great Western Railway had taken over the two schemes in the Exe Valley, it turned its attention to the Tiverton Branch and the station facilities in the town. With the imminent increase in both quantity and variety of traffic at Tiverton, the 'narrowing' of the line out to the Junction made operational sense as it would allow trains to move between the three parts of the system. The 4¾-mile branch was converted to the 4ft. 8½in. standard gauge on Sunday 29th June 1884. Associated with the scheme inherited from the Exe Valley Railway Company was the plan for a new station at Tiverton. For the time being, however, the Tiverton Junction and Dulverton trains continued to use the old two-platform Bristol & Exeter terminus with its attractive wooden train shed. Services were only transferred to the new station when the southern section opened for business. At this time the original station became part of the goods depot and, although the buildings were soon demolished, the track layout remained almost unchanged until the rails were lifted in 1968.

The spotlight now shifted south of Tiverton. With the final touches to the stations completed, the villages of the lower Exe Valley prepared for the big day. The line was inspected by a Board of Trade official, this time Major-General Hutchinson, in

Bampton goods shed. *Tiverton Museum*

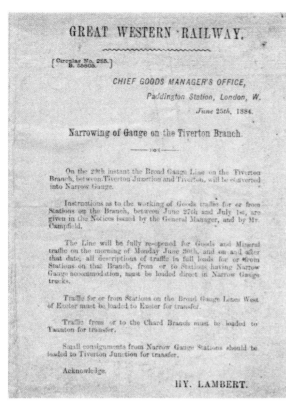

the third week of April 1885. He reported that the, 'Line is generally in good order', but there seemed a real possibility of history repeating itself when he outlined six items requiring attention before he would permit the line to be opened (this being planned for 1st May). Although these items were only of a minor nature (attention to fencing, working of facing point locks, telegraph insulators and the like), the Inspector required notification from the Superintendent of the Line by Tuesday 28th April that the work had been satisfactorily completed or he would have to 'report that by reason of the incompleteness of the works the aforementioned line cannot be opened for passenger traffic without danger to the public using the same'.

One interesting and potentially serious feature noticed by the Inspector related to the section of line at Fortescue, both the level crossing and southern approach. He reported that:

'Considerable improvements have been effected in curves and gradients from those shown in the deposited plans and sections; but in carrying these out, an unauthorised lateral deviation has been made for about 12 chains from 0.78ch to 1m 10ch without any certificate for such deviation having been obtained from the Board of Trade. No objection has, it is stated, been made by the Landowner of this deviation, but nevertheless the railway for this 12 chains is . . . an unauthorised undertaking possessing no legal rights'.

Fortunately, the Inspector chose not to follow this up, while his criticisms were rapidly attended to, and given the 'all clear'. So after 20 years of planning, frustration and delay, and over seven years of construction, the Exe Valley line opened from Exeter to Tiverton, and thus throughout to Dulverton, on Friday 1st May 1885.

'517' class 0-4-2 tank, No. 529, and station staff pose at Tiverton on the opening of the new station in 1885. The locomotive has just run-round its train following arrival from Tiverton Junction.

Poster announcing the opening of the T&NDR. In the event, it had to be postponed for a month. *Tiverton Museum*

Chapter Three
Stations, Halts and Crossings

An Edwardian period view of Bampton. *L&GRP; courtesy David & Charles*

The stations were constructed during the early 1880s. The builders were fortunate in having a choice of suitable stone available locally, in the quarries at Bampton, Beacon Hill and Canonsleigh. The stone, of Carboniferous age, was tough and coherent while at the same time capable of being cut and dressed. Of the four main materials present, the one most favoured was the tough, massively-bedded sandstone series, ranging in colour from blue-grey with patches of brown to a reddish-grey. The roofing slates and decorated ridge tiles were grey, while the door and window surrounds and corner stones were of honey-coloured oolitic limestone. This pattern applied to the goods sheds and weighbridge houses as well as the main platform building. The waiting alcoves were made of wood panels. Doors and internal woodwork were painted a chocolate-brown, while all external woodwork — including fencing — was painted a 'Great Western Cream', actually a light 'stone' colour.

Standardisation of building materials created a unity of design and thus a sort of 'Line Identity', or at least it did on the southern section. The Exe Valley Railway let out the station contracts to W. B. Berry of nearby Crediton, so that an identical form was found at Brampford Speke, Thorverton, Up Exe and Cadeleigh. Being a special case Tiverton was purpose-built, although the same materials were used. The only station which remains unaltered today is Cadeleigh, and this may be taken as the archetypal station on the southern portion of the line. Only the slightest differences in internal details would be found between the four stations, although the colour balance of the stone varied somewhat, reflecting the nature of the individual rock bed or quarry face. The Tiverton and North Devon Railway, with their Contractor, Nathaniel Fogg, only needed to build one station: at Bampton. A number of differences existed between this station

and those further south. The waiting alcove for instance, with its forward-sloping roof, was built in front of, and not integrated with, the longitudinal part of the building (this part being the Booking Hall and Booking Office instead of the stores in the other stations). The Gents was actually inside one transverse wing of the building, while the Ladies Waiting Room and lavatory occupied the whole of the other. There were also external differences, notably, the plain finish of the facade. In the southern stations the stone part of the building had bay windows, while the weather boarding was patterned.

In late 1923 Brampford Speke and Up Exe lost their status as full stations and were reduced to halts. Between 1923 and 1929 a number of purpose-built halts opened as part of a campaign to attract passengers from the villages, hamlets and farms which were close to the line but not near an existing station. The new halts were fairly basic affairs, and possesed standard overall dimensions even though they showed a surprising variation in detail. Their length was 109 feet, comprising a 72-foot long platform and two 18ft. 6in. ramps (the ramp used to join or leave the platform was longer — and thus more gently graded — in some cases, from 20ft. to 26ft.). Waiting accommodation was confined to a centrally-located shelter (12ft. long by 7ft. wide), which contained a wooden bench along the side and back walls. A timetable/notice board was either displayed at the entrance to the halt or inside the shelter. Two lamp posts surmounted by tapered glass cases housed oil lamps supplied by the station to which they were 'affiliated', although from the late 1930s, a simple hurricane lamp hung over the shelter doorway usually sufficed. Fencing, universally, consisted of regularly spaced concrete posts with 5 or 6 strand wire in between.

Cadeleigh Station: Layout of Main Buildings

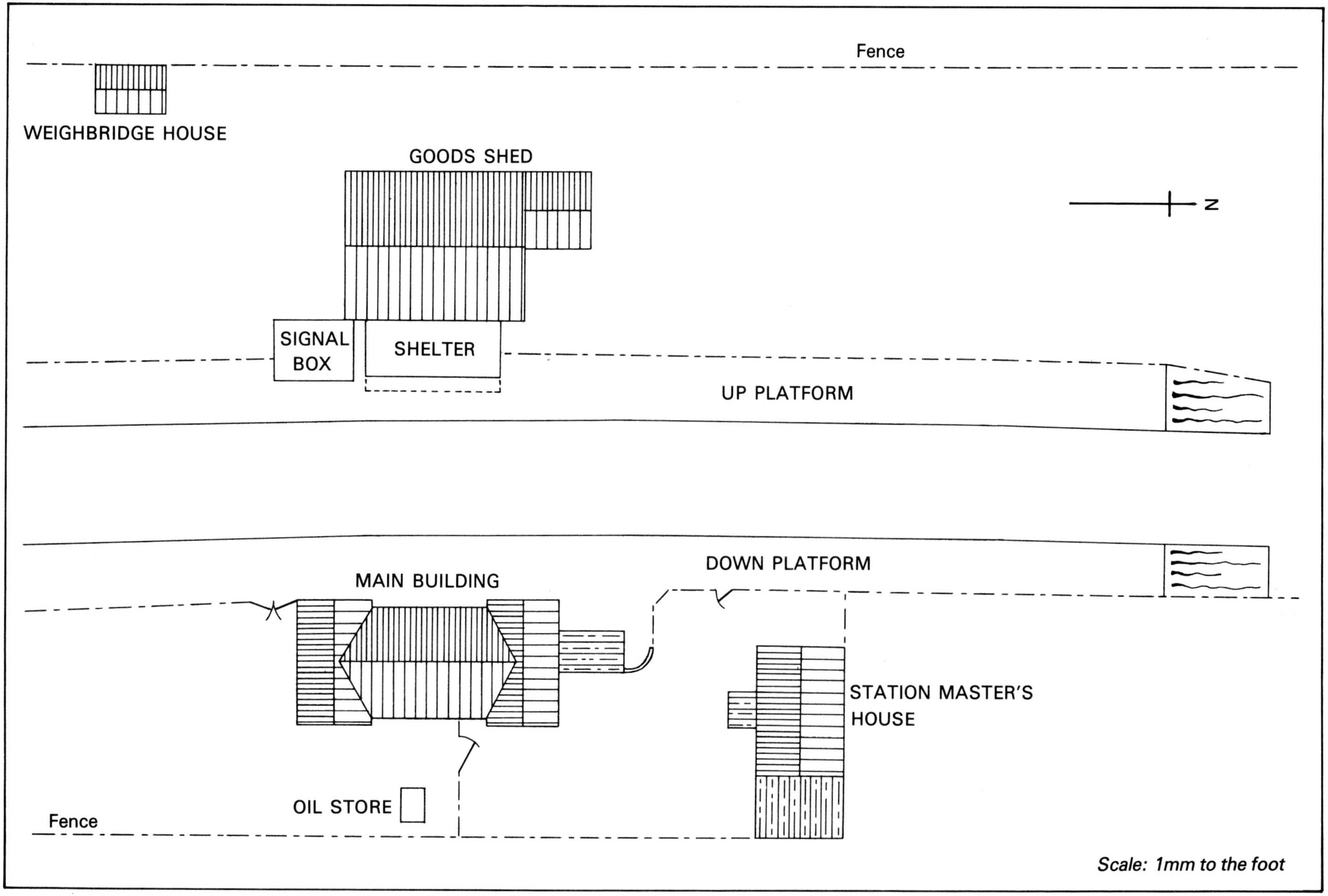

WEIGHBRIDGE HOUSE

Fence

N

GOODS SHED

SIGNAL BOX

SHELTER

UP PLATFORM

DOWN PLATFORM

STATION MASTER'S HOUSE

MAIN BUILDING

OIL STORE

Fence

Scale: 1mm to the foot

Cadeleigh: main station building

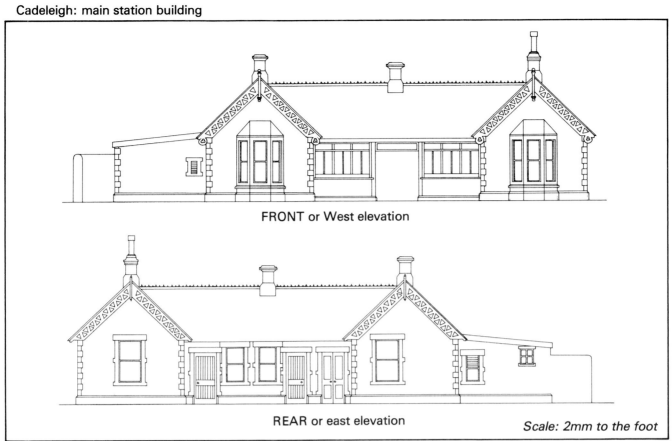

FRONT or West elevation

REAR or east elevation

Scale: 2mm to the foot

Cadeleigh main station building; 'down' platform.   *P. J. Kelley*

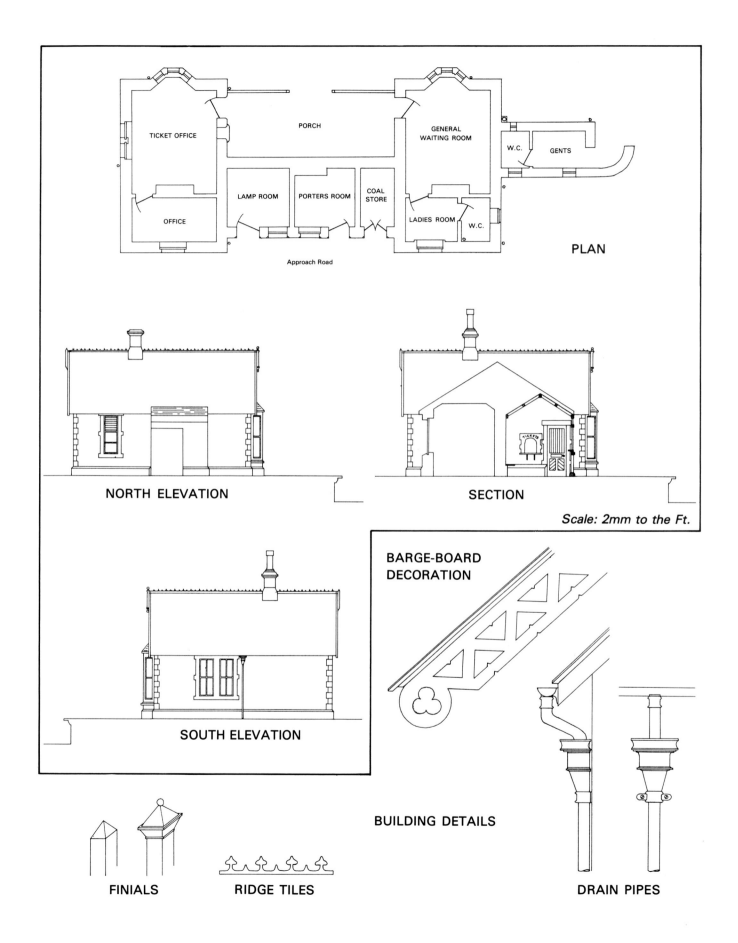

PLAN

TICKET OFFICE

PORCH

GENERAL
WAITING ROOM

W.C.

GENTS

OFFICE

LAMP ROOM

PORTERS ROOM

COAL
STORE

LADIES ROOM

W.C.

Approach Road

NORTH ELEVATION

SECTION

Scale: 2mm to the Ft.

SOUTH ELEVATION

BARGE-BOARD
DECORATION

BUILDING DETAILS

FINIALS

RIDGE TILES

DRAIN PIPES

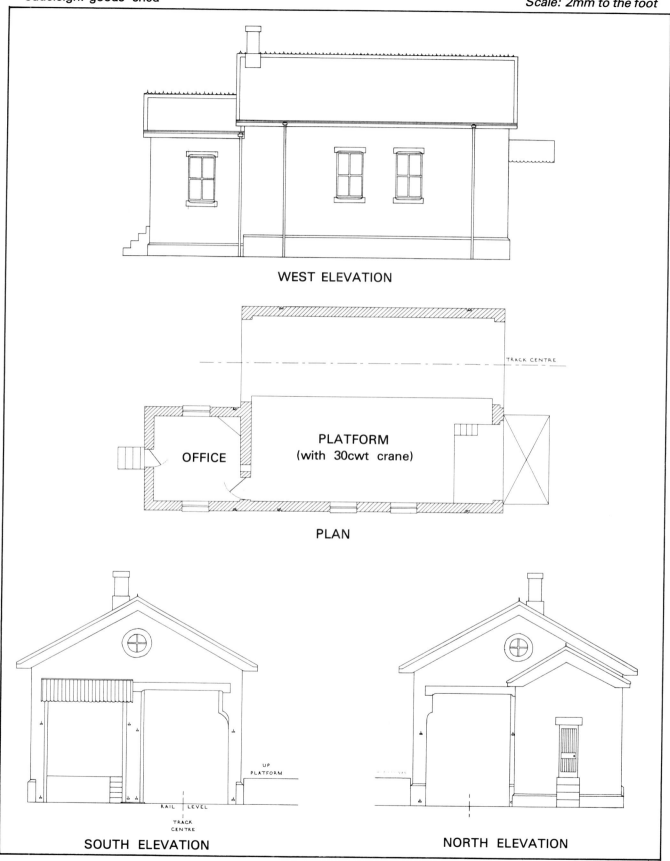

WEST ELEVATION

TRACK CENTRE

OFFICE

PLATFORM
(with 30cwt crane)

PLAN

SOUTH ELEVATION

NORTH ELEVATION

Cadeleigh goods yard details: yard crane; goods shed and office; weighbridge house.

B. L. Davis

Cadeleigh, details of up-side buildings: signal box, waiting shelter (or alcove) and goods shed. *P. J. Kelley*

Cadeleigh: weighbridge house

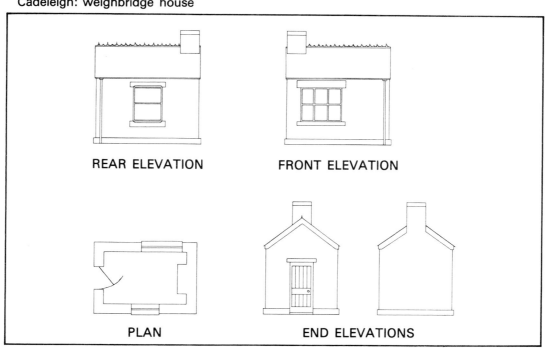

REAR ELEVATION   FRONT ELEVATION

PLAN   END ELEVATIONS

Administration

The Exe Valley stations formed Circuit number 999 of the Exeter Division. While overall supervision of the branch thus came from Exeter, the day-to-day responsibility for the stations, halts, level crossings and signal boxes rested with the individual station masters. With the opening of the purpose-built halts, an operational pattern was established which remained for the rest of the line's existence; namely: Stoke Canon looked after Brampford Speke Halt and Fortescue Crossing; Thorverton supervised Up Exe Halt and its two crossings; Cadeleigh looked after Burn Halt; Tiverton looked after West Exe and Bolham Halts; Bampton administered Cove Halt and crossing, Lower Lodfin Crossing and Morebath Junction Halt; while Tiverton Junction looked after Halberton Halt. The appropriate station master was responsible for writing out and posting up the timetable, a task which was necessary when the schedules changed — generally twice a year — or if the notice became damaged or illegible. The signalman from the 'mother' station had to go to the halt occasionally to sweep out the waiting shelter, while the platform and approaches were the responsibility of the ganger. Walking the line, the ganger would pass any one halt at frequent intervals and so could easily check that the platform was in a sound state of repair. He also had to organise the cutting of grass on approach roads or footpaths and the clearing of snow from the platform and environs when occasion demanded.

These tasks were occasional; attending to the lamps, however, was a daily chore for signalmen and guards combined. For some fifty years station lighting was provided by oil lamps, the lamps being housed inside a square-sectioned, tapered glass case on top of a square wooden post. When the oil lamps were replaced by hurricane lamps, the old posts were modified: the glass cases were removed and a shallow circular metal tray was fixed to the top of the original post. The diameter of the tray matched that of a hurricane lamp base, while three 'claws' were arranged at 120 degree intervals around the circumference. Their purpose was to grip the basal section of the lamp to hold it steady, while an adjustable screw fixed in the front claw gave increased stability in windy weather. In a number of cases, however, the old wooden lamp posts were replaced by metal poles, hooked over at the top, on to which hurricane lamps were hung by a loop attachment at the top of the lamp. Up until September 1954 all trains stopped at the halts and so platform lighting was required for much of the year. This lighting normally consisted of a solitary hurricane lamp hung above the entrance of the waiting hut. Taking Burn Halt as an illustration, the signalman at Cadeleigh would attend to the lamps in the mid-afternoon on a winter's day. The paraffin was kept in a padlocked corrugated iron hut behind the station building. From the large 40 gallon oil drums, the required amount was 'tapped off' into a smaller can which was then carried the short distance to the Lamp Room. The lamps were kept in a large galvanised metal cabinet beneath the window, on the lid of which the lamps would be filled and trimmed. As dusk descended the lamps would be lit and primed. One would be hooked up over the entrance to the waiting alcove on the main station building; one on the post by the double gates leading in from the station approach road; one by the 'board-walk' between the platforms at the south end of the station; one on the 'up' platform near the signal box steps and one above the entrance to the 'up' waiting alcove. The lamp for Burn Halt would be left on the platform for the guard of the next 'down' train to take on board and convey to the halt, where he would hook it up over the doorway of the waiting shelter. As the last train of the day was an 'up' train, its guard would extinguish the lamp, put it in the carriage vestibule, and return it to Cadeleigh. Occasionally if there was a relief guard or man new to the line, he would forget the lamp, and arrangements

had to be made in the morning to get it back. At Thorverton there was no oil store; the drums being kept on a 'base' made of two pieces of wood situated at the back of the station building. The lamps were kept in a corrugated hut nearby, where they were filled, but they were lit and primed in the signal box. The booking office had its own oil lamp in situ, but if the signalman needed to go into the office after dark he would usually carry a tilly lamp (pressurised paraffin vapour lamp) from the signal box rather than light up the office lamp specially.

Illuminating the halts was relatively straightforward, but trying to stop at some of them was not so easy. Brampford Speke and Up Exe Halts having been built as full stations were perfectly alright, for while they could comfortably accommodate four coaches, Valley trains were rarely more than two coaches long. The problem of 'overshooting' arose with the purpose-built halts: Burn, Bolham, Cove and Morebath Junction. West Exe Halt, being so well used, had been lengthened to take two coaches, while the 109-foot long Halberton Halt on the Tiverton Branch only normally received trains of one coach. The single coach platforms required some skill on the part of the driver, the exact position at which he would stop his locomotive depending on the sort of rolling stock he was in charge of. The most delicate manoeuvre, and the one which was required most often, was to stop a train of two auto-coaches (trailers). These coaches only had one door for the passengers to alight or en-train, and by judicious positioning it was possible to get both doors at the platform (door centres were 68ft. 6in. apart and the platform 72ft. long). Regular drivers had their own particular 'markers' on the trackside which they would match up with something on the locomotive — markers such as a broken sleeper edge; an identifiable fence post; a particular telegraph pole; a piece of concrete block; or an 'arranged' mound of ballast. Similar markers had to be organised when the driver was in his vestibule on the leading auto-coach when the train was being propelled. When trains were composed of ordinary stock — as they often were in the late 1950s due to a shortage of auto-coaches — the coach on which the guard was travelling was the one which would be drawn up at the platform. A third variation was to have one ordinary carriage, adapted for auto working, and one auto-coach. In this arrangement the auto-coach had to be farthest from the engine, and as it conveyed the guard, it would be the vehicle which was drawn up at the platform. The Valley guards knew their passengers and would ensure that those for the short-platformed halts travelled in the correct coach (similarly, most regular passengers knew about these operational subtleties!).

One of the daily rituals at the stations on the branch was concerned with the paying in of fares and other monies. The previous day's takings had to be handed into the guard of the first train to Exeter in the morning. Very strict procedures were followed here, notably that the money pouches could only be accepted from a uniformed member of staff. The preparation of the pouch was the last main job of the station master before he went off duty. The takings would be counted and recorded, and then placed in the pouch — a padlocked leather container — before it was locked in the safe. The name of each station was written in gold lettering on the front of the pouch. Should any tickets be sold in the evening, this money was added to the following day's accounts, and locked away separately. The guard on the first 'down' train carried a large 'Circuit Box' on the floor of the carriage vestibule; this was a portable tough wooden chest with a half-hinged lid which allowed the pouches to be dropped in but not taken out again. On arrival at St. David's station the guard would carry the Circuit Box to the Divisional Office on Platform One. Here the box could be unlocked, the pouches released and the money counted and checked against the station masters' return slips. Boxes would arrive from all over the Exeter Division, and only when a grand total had been concluded would the divisional money and return be sent off to the central office at Reading. The empty pouches were taken back up the Exe Valley in the early afternoon and handed over by the guard, so allowing the process to happen all over again.

At the halts the guards sold the tickets. They had a wooden frame with sprung metal clips to hold the tickets, which were issued by value rather than by destination, very similar to the old ticket racks used by bus conductors. These ticket sales were entered in a book carried by the guard, which resembled the excess fares book carried by the guards today. The sale was recorded and the monies paid straight into Exeter, where the accountants attributed the receipts to the appropriate station. Thus the takings from Cove Halt were accredited to Bampton, and so on.

One vital function of the station master, as far as the staff were concerned, was the handing out of pay packets every Thursday. The wages were made up at Bristol and sent down to Exeter in the early hours. The Wages Office at Exeter broke up the wages into the appropriate 'Circuits' and put all the Exe Valley pay packets into a sturdy tin box which was then locked. The box was transferred to the late morning passenger train up the valley, the guard having a key so as to dispense the 'largess' at each station. At each station the station master would sign for the money, and then hand out the wage packets to his staff. At Thorverton for example the signalmen would get their money at the changeover between shifts, around one o'clock. To get the money to the keepers at the two Up Exe crossings, the station master would catch the train in the early afternoon to Up Exe Halt, pay the keepers, have a chat with them, and then come back on the next 'down' train. The only time Mr. Reg Cole, the last station master, wore his hat was when handing money in to, or receiving wages from a train! The station master was also responsible for making out wagon labels for loads to be dispatched; arranging for their collection; recording all financial transactions; dealing with parcels; and requisitioning all the materials necessary for the running of the station.

The institution of the station master was central to the rural branch line, and often he was a respected figure in the community. Reg Cole at Thorverton exemplified this tradition. His railway career spanned almost 50 years in which he acquired knowledge of all aspects of railway operation. A long-standing and enthusiastic member of the railway St. John Ambulance organisation, he quickly established a reputation at Thorverton as a thoroughly professional railwayman. Of smart appearance — always with buttonhole — soft speech and ingenuous manner, he was respected by passengers and staff alike. A keen gardener, he would often be seen in the evenings in the garden of 'Station House', which ran behind the 'down' platform. The station masters at Thorverton, Cadeleigh and Bampton had small staffs to look after — just signalmen and crossing keepers — but Tiverton was a different matter. Around 30 people were employed at Tiverton, ranging from signalmen through to porters, parcels clerks, goods agent and shunters to permanent way personnel. Whether numbers were large or small, the administrative machinery was such that the Exe Valley always ran smoothly.

Level Crossings

There were five controlled level crossings on the Exe Valley line. Working from south to north, with distances from Exeter St. David's, they were: Fortescue (4m. 58ch.); Up Exe Crossing, later Up Exe South (6m. 63ch.); Up Exe Station, later Up Exe North (6m. 77½ch.); Cove (19m. 20ch.); and Lower Lodfin (22m. 23½ch.). The keepers lived in 'tied' houses adjoining the crossings. None of these crossings were on important roads, but

when the line opened all were worked as signal boxes, though not as 'block posts'; that is to say, they had no way of accepting or refusing trains entry to their section but could stop them at signals if the crossing was occupied. The crossing signal boxes were ground-mounted wooden structures. They contained a stove with brick flue at the back and sliding windows on the side facing the track. The lever frame was in front of these windows. The keeper had to know when trains were 'on line', and so above the levers was a shelf on which there were visual display instruments, these being activated by, and exactly responding to, the block instruments in the signal boxes to either side. A bell was necessary to give audible warning to the keeper, and as it was not reasonable to expect the keepers to sit in their cabins all day, the bell was fixed on the outside gable end above the door so that it would be heard inside the house nearby as well as in the cabin. The imminence of a train would be indicated by a single beat on the bell, the 'attention' code; this would be answered by the signalman of whom the request was made. The beat 3-1 would then be tapped out (3 if it was the goods), and also answered. The first signalman would draw out his train staff or token and turn the pointer on his block instrument to show 'Up Token Out' or 'Down Token Out', whichever was the case. This would be repeated on the instrument at the level crossing, and so tell the keeper which way the train was coming. The gates would be closed across the road by hand. The keeper would then return to the cabin and pull the lever which bolted the gates. The interlocking mechanism of the lever frame was such that no signal could be pulled until the gate was properly locked. In the early years of the branch the crossings were protected by home as well as distant signals (except for Lower Lodfin which had distants only). With the gate bolt lever pulled, the home would be pulled, which would in turn release the distant lever. Only at Up Exe North, by the station, were there 'wicket gates'; a way of allowing pedestrians to cross the line even when the road gate was closed. With the passage of the train out of the section and the bell code to clear the line (2-1 on the 'block'), the repeater instrument moved to show 'token in'.

The volume of road traffic using the crossings was not very great, particularly at Fortescue, where the road was in fact a farm track that led to a dead-end. At Up Exe the road simply looped round between the two crossings, serving a mill and a few farms between the railway and the river. Only at Cove and Lower Lodfin were there through roads, only minor ones but with a fair amount of traffic (especially Cove). In the summer of 1907 the Great Western reduced the three 'southern' crossings to ground frame status; the terminology mattered because it affected wage levels! All 'stop' signals were removed, so that the gates were protected by distants only.

Red targets (large red discs) were fixed to the centres of the gates; these acted as 'stop' signals when the gate was across the track. A lamp was centred on the top bar of the gate, showing a red light to the direction across which the gates were closed. The bells, block repeaters, signal repeaters and distant lamp indicators were of course retained. Cove and Lower Lodfin received similar treatment in 1923. At Cove the now defunct levers were simply removed from the frame, and here and at Lower Lodfin, nothing else was touched (indeed, even today the cabins remain as 'conservatory' style additions to the former keepers' houses). At Up Exe and Fortescue matters were more drastic. A small wooden shed-like structure was built to house the necessary instruments and the three levers. At both the Up Exe crossings the new ground frame was built on the opposite side of the track to the signal box. Once the levers were tested, the signal boxes were then demolished. The Fortescue frame was built immediately next to the existing signal box. At these three 'southern' crossings, the bell was moved inside the keeper's house: it was located in the hallway high up on the wall near the front door.

Although all the crossing frames performed the same function, there were minor variations which gave them individual identity. All the crossings, except Lower Lodfin, had two working distants, one for each direction. Lower Lodfin was provided with a 9-lever frame, but only used numbers 1 and 9, the others being 'spares'. Number 1 worked the 'down' distant and number 9 the gate bolt. The 'up' distant was fixed and was only 41 yards from the crossing, whereas the 'down' distant was 869 yards. With northbound trains pulling up the 1:66 gradient (1:58 in one place) and with a clear view of the crossing for a good quarter of a mile, the fixed distant was deemed adequate. The same signal also doubled-up as the branch distant for Morebath Junction, being 1,070 yards from that box. The 'down' distant was also unique in being a twin arm signal (the stop signal above it being the branch starting signal from Morebath Junction). The distant would only come 'off' when the starting signal above it showed 'clear'.

At Cove there was a 13-lever frame; number 1 worked the 'down' distant, number 6 the siding points, number 7 the facing point lock, number 10 the 'up' distant and number 13 the gate bolt. The crossing keeper actually could only use numbers 1, 10 and 13, the point levers being locked in the frame. Their release could only be effected by unlocking that part of the frame with the key token used between Tiverton and Bampton (that then locked the distants in the 'on' position).

The Up Exe crossings were sufficiently close together to share the same distants. Here, the signal would only show 'all clear' when both crossing keepers had pulled off their levers. Such signals are said to be 'slotted'. This action is achieved by three balance weights and slot bar near the base of the signal (the centre weight ultimately connects to the signal arm, and can only move when the other two have been pulled). While both levers must be pulled to lower the signal, the first lever put back to 'on' causes the arm to return to 'on'.

At Fortescue it was customary for the gates to be kept open for rail traffic, with both distants pulled 'off'. The crossing keeper, whose house was on the wrong side of the line would have to be hailed if use of the crossing was required. This crossing remained until 1963, at which time it was attended by the wife of one of the signalmen at Thorverton. It was not uncommon for the signalman to walk or cycle the 1½ miles to work to book on at 06.00, and catch the first 'down' train of the afternoon back; the train stopping momentarily, and conveniently, on the crossing! The rapport of the staff was a notable feature of the valley — as on so many rural branch lines.

It had been the practice for decades to employ the wives of railwaymen — usually signalmen — to work the crossings. The job had mixed blessings. The biggest 'plus' was the house that went with the job, but although the work was not strenuous it required keepers to be 'on call' for from 14 to 16 hours a day six days a week, and in the case of the three 'southern' crossings, a split shift on summer Sundays. When there were sizeable gaps between trains, domestic and gardening chores could be attended to. Meat, fruit, bread and other foodstuffs could be obtained from mobile shops; a rural community came to depend on these visitations. Even so, occasional shopping expeditions had to be undertaken, and the keeper would be out of earshot of 'the bell'. During the late morning 'lull' between trains, one sunny day in the summer of 1962, the signalman on the early turn at Cadeleigh decided to go fishing (Bickleigh being a favourite haunt of anglers). The only possible train that might run at this time would be the 'goods', but that ran almost exclusively for the grain traffic at Thorverton mill, and then only 'as requested' from there to Cadeleigh (and in any case, it usually left Exeter at 09.05). The Cadeleigh man rang Thorverton box and informed the signalman there of his plans. This presented the young Thorverton man with a chance to play a joke, but he forgot about the crossing keepers. The 'goods' had already come and gone again that morning, but the Cadeleigh man was informed in all sincerity that the 'goods' was shunting mill traffic at that very moment and had a stores truck (box van) to take to Cadeleigh. This manoeuvre would lose the Cadeleigh man a clear hour's fishing, and he doubted the existence of the freight. A couple of minutes later, the Thorverton signalman duly tapped out 1 beat on the bell plunger of the token instrument; this was answered, and was followed by a further 3 beats (the code for a freight train). So far so good, but then the phone rang in Thorverton box. One of the crossing keepers at Up Exe was just putting her coat on to go out when the bell rang in the hallway; if the 'goods' was running this meant the keepers would lose an hour as well. At this point the bluff collapsed and the instigator was very pointedly told that his joke was not appreciated!

Every so often the crossing keepers would be given a day off. On these occasions, as on their annual holiday (or 'leave' in railway jargon), relief signalmen had to work the crossing. This was a most unpopular duty in the three 'southern' crossings because of the cramped accommodation in the ground frame hut and the general lack of interesting activity. On a fine day, the signalman could take the chair and sit outside, but in winter or on a rainy day the misery can be imagined! There was no fire and no room to swing a cat. The bell in the house could either not be heard at all or only faintly, and so reliance had to be placed on the repeater block instrument and knowledge of the train times. When the keeper was only off for the day and had gone into Exeter on a morning train, the guard on the return trip would sometimes arrange for the train to stop at the crossing. If the weather was bad or the keeper was loaded up with shopping, the walk from Brampford Speke to Fortescue or even from Up Exe Halt to Up Exe South was unpleasant. As the keeper had to alight at track level, this was one of the rare occasions on which the extending steps on the auto-coach would be used.

A regular duty of the keepers was to top up the lamps on the gates. The paraffin for the lamps was kept in 10-gallon drums, and these would periodically need replenishing. The crossings were superintended by a particular station, and the drums would have to be refilled there. Stoke Canon covered Fortescue Crossing; Thorverton the two Up Exe Crossings; and Bampton the crossings at Cove and Lower Lodfin. The keeper would inform the station a few days in advance so that the station master could arrange for the pick-up goods to stop at the crossing and exchange drums (these were carried in the stores truck or sometimes in the guard's van). The stations received their oil in 40 gallon drums which were kept in corrugated iron sheds near the station building or signal box. The crossing distant signals were attended to by signalmen and not by the crossing keepers. The only overtime allowed to signalmen at Thorverton, Cadeleigh and Bampton was for tending the distant signal lamps. (Stop signals and discs were relatively close to the signal box and could be done during the shift). Half-an-hour's overtime could be added on to the end of the 'early turn' for this purpose, but at Thorverton and Bampton, who had crossings to look after as well as their own fixed distants, this was hardly adequate. The work would normally be done during slack periods between trains. The 'down' distant signal for the Up Exe Crossings was a tall structure, and would sway slightly in a strong wind. Being over 30 feet tall it was usefully provided with a lamp-hoist; a pulley arrangement to raise and lower the lamp. A ladder also existed as the amber and green spectacles had to be cleaned and the arm made accessible in case it needed attention. The lamp-hoist had rusted up, however, and so Thorverton signalmen hoped for clement weather! The signalman at Stoke Canon Junction was too busy to leave his box to do the distants at Fortescue, and so these were attended to by the lampman who was based at the Junction and spent most of his time on the main line.

Chapter Four

Motive Power

By the time the Exe Valley line opened throughout in 1885, the staple locomotive for passenger work on such branches was the Armstrong '517' Class of 0-4-2 tank. These locomotives had been around since 1868 on the standard gauge parts of the Great Western, and had proved their worth on lines with sharp curves and ever changing gradients. The '517s' dominated Exe Valley passenger traffic from the outset, a typical train comprising one of these engines and three or four coaches of the 4 or 6-wheeled variety. Freight trains in the early days were generally hauled by 0-6-0 saddle tanks. These attractive engines with their large brass domes, half-cabs and outside frames (complete with 'buffalo-horn' type spring mountings) gave sterling service, with number 737 of the '1076' Class being a 'regular' on

and this corresponded with the recently appointed Chief Mechanical Engineer C. B. Collett's aims to either draft new locomotive designs or make improvements to existing models. The '517' Class thus came to be gradually superseded by the '48XX' Class of 0-4-2 tanks. In many ways they resembled their forebears, but in trials were found to be an all-round improvement: they not only consumed less coal and were cheaper to run, but needed less maintenance 'on shed' and also reduced the wear and tear on the track. Exeter received four of these engines in September 1932, a further one in October (numbers 4805-4809) and then five more between 1933 and 1936. One was sent to the sub-shed at Tiverton Junction to work the Tiverton Branch, while the others worked the Exe Valley and Teign Valley routes. All

'517' class 0-4-2 tank, No. 1468.   *British Railways/OPC*

the line. The 'pick-up' nature of the goods service yielded loadings which were well within the capacity of the locomotives.

This pattern of working continued for almost 40 years, providing a reliable service to the villages of the Exe Valley. The early years of the twentieth century saw the appearance of steam rail motors and auto-trains on other parts of the Great Western, but this hardly impinged on the established operational pattern of the branch. In 1908 a steam rail motor (integrated engine and coach) was allocated to Exeter, and although it made very occasional trips out to Dulverton and back, its main sphere of operation was the Teign Valley branch and on main line stopping trains to Newton Abbot. However, the auto-train method of working was proving its worth: cutting down on 'turn round' times, allowing greater operational efficiency and more capacious accommodation. It was only in the autumn of 1923 that the '517s' could be seen hauling or propelling auto-trailers along the branch on any sort of regular basis. By this time the '517s' themselves were beginning to age,

the engines were auto-fitted and so, providing the auto-trailers were available, ran the more demanding schedules that the now expanded timetable required. Shortly before Nationalisation, in 1946, the number sequence classification of locomotives was changed, so that the '48XX' Class became the '14XX' Class. The allocation of individual engines to Exeter changed, but numbers 1405 and 1469 spent their whole working lives there. In the last few years of the Exe Valley's life numbers 1405, 1429, 1434, 1442, 1450, 1452, 1462, 1469, 1470 and 1471 were regular visitors to the line. Two 14XXs were always allocated to Tiverton Junction, one to work the Tiverton Branch and one the Culm Valley line to Hemyock (replacing two old but reliable 2-4-0 tank engines of the 13XX Class, and formally of the South Devon Railway).

On the last day of passenger services on the Hemyock Branch (Saturday September 7th 1963) number 1421 was the booked locomotive. The engine had been cleaned up for the occasion but

'1400' class 0-4-2 tank, No. 1451, in the 'up' bay at Tiverton on 24th July 1962. *D. Fereday Glenn*

ran without a smokebox number-plate. This locomotive may be seen in a number of photographs throughout this book. Several rumours circulated as to who was responsible for the disappearance of the number plate, with souvenir-hunters being the most strongly favoured.

The missing plate was neither found nor replaced, but her crew preferred it, because they said she now resembled a Great Western engine! (which had the number painted on the buffer beam and not on the smoke box). Fortunately, three of the 0-4-2s which worked the Exe Valley at the end of its life have been preserved in Devon, although ironically they were not the real stalwarts of the line, having been moved to Exmouth Junction for the last few years only. One is number 1442 now preserved as a static display in the excellent Tiverton Museum, and the others, Nos. 1420 and 1450, are alive and well on the Dart Valley Railway.

The 14XX Class were the mainstay of the branch for 30 years, and so deserve closer examination. A list of technical specifications are of interest, but the bald facts cannot convey the spirit and efficacy of these hard-working engines. One of the most distinctive features of the Class is the large dome. This was simply a collecting point for steam; the regulator would control the outflow of steam from the dome to the inside cylinders. The regulator handle, arranged for right-hand drive, was in the cab and fitted up for auto-working, which allowed the driver to control the train from a regulator handle in the driving compartment of the coach; the movements of which were exactly replicated in the cab.

The tall, rather elegant chimney is also an immediate eye-catching feature, something of a rarity on many classes of post-war Western Region locomotives. On many locomotives a large, angular box-like structure may be seen on the boiler casing between the chimney and the dome. This housed the top-feed

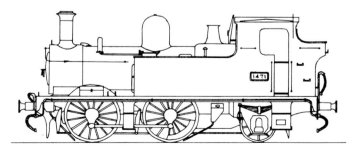

4800/1400 CLASS

1. Introduced:	August 1932	7. Wheel diameters:	
2. Designer:	C. B. Collett	(a) coupled wheels:	5′ 2″
3. Number series:	1400-1474	(b) trailing wheels:	3′ 8″
4. Overall length:	29′ 11″	8. Water capacity:	800 gallons
5. Overall width:	8′ 7″	9. Coal capacity:	2 tons 13cwt
6. Weight:	41 tons 6cwt	10. Cylinders (2):	16″ x 24″
		11. Boiler pressure:	165 p.s.i.
		12. Tractive effort:	13,900lbs
		13. Power classification:	1P
		14. Route availability:	all routes

apparatus. G. J. Churchward, who was Locomotive Superintendent of the Great Western from June 1902 until December 1921, first introduced the top feed principle, but it was not fitted to Exe Valley engines until after the War. The apparatus was designed to distribute 'feed' water evenly over the length of the boiler so as to avoid the occurrence of 'cold spots'. The 'feed' water from the tanks was piped to the top-feed apparatus by way of injectors located in the cab. There were two injector controls namely a left hand and a right hand, which were situated at the back of the cab. The two pipes leading to the top-feed apparatus ran from the cab along the top of both tanks. On leaving the pipes, the water would percolate into the boiler barrel over a series of perforated trays to ensure a more equal distribution.

Tool boxes with hinged lids were mounted in front of the wheel arch of the leading driving wheel, and contained a whole range of useful bits and pieces like a wrench, spanner, lengths of cable and a short-handled wire brush. The bayonet type of angle brackets for carrying spare lamps were situated on the left running plate only.

The canopy or hood-like structure behind the vacuum pipe on the front buffer beam housed the electrical cable connections which 'plugged in' to similar equipment on the auto-trailer and so provided a system of bell communication between driver, fireman and guard. A similar device was fitted to the rear buffer beam, though without the hood. Protruding beneath the right hand side of the rear buffer beam, near the steam heating pipe, was the square-sectioned housing which received the auto-coach's sleeve coupling and thus enabled the locomotive to remain at the rear of the train while being driven from the leading coach. The 14XX Class possessed two whistles; a 'shrill' one for normal use and a much deeper sounding one used as a warning along the track and to alert the guard.

The introduction of auto-working gave the '517' class and later 48XX/14XX class a virtual monopoly of passenger motive power from 1924 to 1957. In the mid-1930s a steam rail motor was rostered for just one turn on the branch, leaving Exeter just after 16.30 for Tiverton, later working out to the Junction and then returning as a through working from Tiverton Junction to Exeter via the Exe Valley. By the late 1950s there was a shortage of auto-

trailers; many were old and had been withdrawn, and even though the closure of the Teign Valley line in June 1958 contributed a few extra vehicles, the level of service on the Exe Valley required 'ordinary' coaching stock to be used on a number of trains. These had to be loco-hauled in both 'up' and 'down' directions and consequently could be worked by any of the engines permitted on the branch.

The appearance of the ubiquitous Collett Pannier Tanks from 1929 added a new dimension to the Exe Valley's motive power. Many of the 0-6-0 tank engines were intended as replacements to the reliable, though ageing, saddle tanks. They began to arrive at Exeter Shed, in one's and two's, over the next few years, but with passenger work sewn-up by the 0-4-2s, they were more or less restricted to freight work. Only at the end of the 1950s were a very few Exe Valley passenger rosters allocated regularly to panniers, the most frequent visitors being of the 36XX, 77XX and 87XX members of the class. Their stock had to be of the conven-

Non auto-fitted pannier tank No. 9685 leaving Dulverton with an Exe Valley train in April 1962. *R. E. Toop*

THE PANNIER TANKS

These 0-6-0 tank engines belonged to an enormous class of locomotives, only some of which were fitted for auto-working. Most were members of the '57XX' class, although only 100 actually began with the number 57. Other number sequences started: '36XX', '46XX', '67XX', '77XX', '87XX', '96XX' and '97XX'.

Auto-fitted pannier tank No. 6400 leaving Cadeleigh with the 15.25 from Exeter. Only the '54XX' and '64XX' classes of pannier tanks were fitted for auto-working. 16th March 1963.

Peter W. Gray

'45XX' class 2-6-2 tank, No. 5555, entering Bampton with the 10.25 from Exeter. This small prairie class appeared under two series of numbers, viz. 4505 to 4599, and 5500 to 5574. Number 5555 was auto-fitted, while the non-corridor coach behind it had been equipped with the necessary transmission rod allowing it to run as part of an auto-assemblage. 2nd October 1963.
R. A. Lumber

THE PRAIRIES

'61XX' class 2-6-2 tank, No. 5183, passing Up Exe Halt on 2nd August 1959. This was one of the 'large' prairies.
D. Fereday Glenn

tional loco-hauled variety as they were not fitted for push-pull working. At the same time, Exeter Shed received just one auto-fitted pannier — of the 54XX type — number 5412. Early in 1963 No. 6400 arrived at Exeter (the 64XXs were also auto-fitted) and worked regularly on the branch, but had arrived very near the end of the line's life.

The 45XX small prairie 2-6-2 tanks made very rare appearances on the Exe Valley line until the last few years. Being unable to operate on the push-pull system they were to be seen as pilot engines on emergency diversions over the branch, or, occasionally, on freight. Fifteen of these locomotives were modified in 1953 for auto-working in the valleys of South Wales. Subsequent

dieselisation here brought a few of these engines to Exeter, although their stay was only short, anything from a few months to two years. Numbers 4589, 5524, 5555 and 5560 spent brief periods at Exeter Shed from September 1958. By this time, freight traffic was dwindling and the passenger work was well covered by the 0-4-2 and 0-6-0 tanks. These and other non-auto prairies did, however, appear on both passenger and freight trains but only really 'looked the part' on the summer Sunday trains, especially the through morning working to Newton Abbot when the train would be made up of four or five coaches filled with day-trippers to the coast.

Diesels were never given regular working on either the Exe

A very rare appearance of a diesel multiple unit on the Exe Valley: the 12.50 from Exeter on 22nd June 1963. *M. J. Fox; courtesy Tiverton Museum*

One of the North British diesel hydraulic Type 2 locomotives (No. D6318) on a 'down' train at Bampton on 28th September 1963. This was the penultimate Saturday of the line's life; this class were being given 'knowledge of the road' prior to their 'last day' appearance. *H. Ballantyne*

Valley or Tiverton branches before 1963. In the summer of that year a very rare sighting might have been had of a diesel multiple unit working the lunch-time 'up' Valley train on a Saturday, while the 'last day' services, much to everyone's disappointment, were hauled by the Class 22 of diesel hydraulic. These same diesels began to work in to Tiverton on freight trains from the main line from 1964, while the Sunday working from Tiverton to Exmouth and Sidmouth in the summer of that year was the preserve of a diesel multiple unit.

Tiverton Branch

The first train over the Tiverton Branch, on 12th June 1848, was hauled by Bristol & Exeter broad gauge 2-2-2 tank engine No. 58. The 'shuttle' nature of the service involved the locomotive running round at each end of the line, and so the Bristol & Exeter decided to try a new and innovative mode of working. On 1st May 1849 they put into service the steam railcar *Fairfield* (Bristol & Exeter locomotive — No. 29). This had been built by the firm of W. B. Adams in Bow, London, and had undergone trials on the West London Railway. As with the standard gauge railcars of later years, it consisted of an engine and coach combined, although unlike its descendants, the engine was not integrated within the coach body. The engine consisted of a vertical boiler with central chimney mounted on an open match-truck type of frame. The coach had seating for 16 first class and 32 second class passengers. There is little information regarding the operation of *Fairfield*, but it cannot have monopolised services because of the statutory requirement to run 'Government' trains, with provision for third class passengers.

In 1851 the Bristol & Exeter took delivery of five 2-2-2 tank engines; Nos. 30 to 34. One of these was allocated to the shed at

Tiverton Junction to work the branch in place of the railcar. (*Fairfield* now moved to the northern part of the Company's system, working mostly on the lines to Clevedon and Weston-super-Mare, although the engine had now become separated from the carriage. It was sold to a Bridgwater firm in June 1856 and was further modified.) The 2-2-2 locomotives worked the branch for the next 25 years. Their driving wheel of 5ft. 6in. diameter was situated between the 3ft. 6in. diameter leading and trailing bogie wheels, while their 'back' and 'well' tanks were able to hold 480 gallons of water.

The amalgamation between the Bristol & Exeter and Great Western Railway in 1876 provided a greater variety of motive power for both companies. Indeed, soon after the amalgamation, a wider variety of tank engines began to appear on the branch, especially with the inauguration of through workings to and from Exeter. It was only in 1884, with the conversion of the branch to standard gauge, that the class of locomotive appeared on the scene which was to monopolise passenger workings for almost 50 years. This was the '517' Class of 0-4-2 tank engines, so well suited to branch line work.

Until 1927 they operated conventional loco-hauled trains, and only in that year did they switch to auto-working. In the autumn of 1932 these ageing engines were superseded by the 48XX Class (later renumbered 14XX) of 0-4-2 tank, and these likewise monopolised passenger and light freight work. The heavier daily morning freight was entrusted to a more powerful engine, being a through working either from Taunton or Exeter. Panniers and prairies were used on this freight roster, and before World War Two, a 22XX (0-6-0) or even a 'Hall' Class were very occasionally seen on this turn.

Driver Clarke in the cab of 0-6-0PT No. 3794 at Bampton. As a 'regular' on the Valley, Fred Clarke was well known to station personnel and passengers alike. *Tiverton Museum*

ENGINE LOADS FOR PASSENGER TRAINS

SECTION		0-4-2T 14XX	0-6-0T 'A' Group	Diesel (D63xx) 22XX 32XX / 0-6-2T 'B' Group	B.R. Std. Cl. 3 (82xxx) 45XX 55XX / 36xx 37xx 46xx 57xx 77xx 87xx 96xx 97xx / 34xx 84xx 94xx	B.R. Std. Cl. 4 (75xxx & 76xxx) 78XX / 53xx 63xx 73xx 41xx 51xx 61xx 81xx / 56xx 66xx
From	To	Tons	Tons	Tons	Tons	Tons
EXETER	BAMPTON	150	190	–	240	–
BAMPTON	DULVERTON	130	170	–	220	–
DULVERTON	BAMPTON	130	170	–	220	–
BAMPTON	TIVERTON	150	220	–	240	–
TIVERTON	EXETER	180	240	–	260	–
TIVERTON JC.	TIVERTON	170	220	250	280	310
TIVERTON	TIVERTON JC.	170	220	250	280	310

MAXIMUM LOADS FOR AUTO ENGINES

The tonnage loads shown in the 'Standard Loads Table' above did not apply when Auto Train services were being worked by engines of the 14XX, 45XX, 54XX and 64XX classes, the authorised loads for which were as follows:

GRADIENT	RAIL MOTORS	
	0-4-2T	0-6-0T; 2-6-2T
	Tons	Tons
1 : 40	72	90
1 : 50	96	120
1 : 60	120	150
1 : 80	144	180
1 : 100	168	210

Fireman Lyne in the immaculate ex-works No. 1471 at Cadeleigh. On this occasion he was firing for Mr. Clarke. *Tiverton Museum*

Tiverton Junction shed and coaling stage on 2nd April 1961. The single-road shed could hold two tank engines: one for the Tiverton Branch and one for the Culm Valley line.

P. J. Kelley

Above: No. 1450 at Exmouth Junction MPD (the 'Southern' shed at Exeter) awaiting removal to the privately owned Dart Valley Railway in South Devon. 18th September 1965.

R. A. Lumber

Right: A peaceful Sunday morning at Tiverton Junction finds its two 0-4-2 tanks 'on shed'. No. 1470 would have to be awoken from its slumbers in the early afternoon in order to work 'engine and brake van' over the Culm Valley line to pick up milk tankers at the dairy at Hemyock.

D. Fereday Glenn

Exeter St. David's Motive Power Depot.   *Nelson Collection; courtesy OPC*

A somewhat incapacitated 0-4-2 tank, No. 1434, 'on shed' with illustrious companions No. 5020 *Trematon Castle* and No. 7018 *Drysllwyn Castle*.

Nelson Collection; courtesy OPC

Chapter Five

Auto-trains

The special type of carriage used in the push-pull style of working was known as an Auto-Trailer (the terms Trailer or Auto-Coach were also commonly used). The auto-trailer was very often used in conjunction with the 14XX Class of tank engine on the Exe Valley; indeed, it was the ideal combination. The coaches were hauled by the locomotive in the normal way on the 'up' run from Exeter, although an electric cable connection allowed the guard to communicate with the driver by using a bell-push near either vestibule door. The guard could thus see his passengers on and off the train, close the door from the inside and give a single press on the push button which would

crank passed the vertical motion into a horizontal transmission rod which ran beneath the coach and connected to another rod on the second coach and then to the engine. The connection was made by a square-sectioned telescopic shaft on the rear (or 'blind') end of the coach. This was clipped back to the coach itself when not in use. To connect it, it was unpinned, lowered and swivelled on its universal joint, extended and locked in to the square housing on the front of the other coach or the rear buffer beam of the engine.

The auto system catered for coaches on either side of the locomotive, so that in these instances the driver was never in the cab at

The classic combination, ie. '14XX' class with two trailers (in the 'up' main platform at Tiverton; most northbound trains took on water here).

Tiverton Museum

ring a bell mounted in the engine's cab. Many drivers answered this with a single blast on the whistle before moving off.

The great advantage of the auto-train was the absence of the need to 'run the engine round' before making the return trip. A special compartment in the trailer allowed the train to be driven from there. From the regulator handle pivoted to a triangular plate above the centre window of the compartment, an actuating rod passed vertically down between the left-hand and centre window and through the floor. The lower third of this rod was protected by a cylindrical 'guard' or housing. At its base a bell

all. This double-ended method of operation was used on stopping trains between Plymouth and Saltash for example, but not on the Exe Valley. None-the-less, a rod passed from each of the sleeve couplings underneath the locomotive and up through two holes in the cab floor to the right of the firebox door. These rods, one from the front of the locomotive and one from the back, ran vertically to a point level with, and just behind, the regulator handle. When not in use, the rods were clipped back out of the way. On a 'down' Valley auto-train the rod from the back (bunker end) of the locomotive was released and the pin pushed through the keyed

hole in the top centre of the regulator handle and then clipped in place. The driver now had control of the regulator from the trailer.

The trains were always prepared for auto-working even on outward journeys, because even if the control rods were all engaged they had no effect if they were not attached to the regulator handle. The bells were left wired up between the driver's compartment and locomotive cab. There was no bell in the guard's vestibule; he could communicate with the driver at whichever end of the train he was, but the only way the driver could get in touch with the guard was by using the engine's whistle. There was therefore a need to connect the driver in the coach with the whistle on the engine. This was achieved by having a chain running through a cylindrical housing the length of the auto-trailer just below the roof and slightly off-centre. The free-hanging lengths were not equal. The longer chain hung down at the driver's compartment end, while the shorter hung down at the opposite end by the luggage compartment. The two ends would

Above: The classic combination once again, this time on a southbound train. No. 1442 is propelling its trailers into the 'down' platform at Thorverton.
late F. Alford; courtesy Tiverton Museum

Left: Auto-tank No. 1451, with non-auto stock, leaving Tiverton on an Exeter–Dulverton service in June 1958.
R. E. Toop

Variation on a theme. By placing an adapted ex-brake non-corridor coach between an auto-fitted locomotive and an auto-trailer, the push-pull mode of operation would still apply. The train here is approaching Cowley Bridge Junction on a northbound service. *R. C. Riley*

join up across the gap between coaches and would be secured with an S-type of clasp connection. The short chain hanging from the luggage end of the trailer, next to the engine, would marry-up with the long chain from the locomotive's whistle which passed through the back of the cab and over the coal bunker. The train was now ready to operate on a push-pull basis.

When the locomotive was propelling its train the driver had control of most of its functions, but would also need to rely on the fireman. When stopping at a station the driver was able to put the brake on, but not to release it. When the guard gave the single 'Start' ring on the bell, the driver would give 2 rings which would repeat on the bell in the cab and which meant 'Blow off Brake'. The fireman would turn the ejector handle to the right which would recreate the vacuum and so take the brakes off. A single blast on the whistle would indicate to the driver that this had been done, and the train would set off. If the station was on the level,

it was possible to stand with the brake off, in which case, on the guard's 'All Clear', the driver would give a single toot on the whistle to alert the fireman who would acknowledge in like manner, and the driver would start the train. When the coach was being pulled in the normal way, with the driver's compartment empty, the large ratchet brake was left in the 'off' position and its handle was secured by a chain to prevent it 'coming on' due to the movement of the carriage. It was necessary of course that the compartment was locked when not in use.

When running 'auto' it was considered desirable to have another form of audible warning to alert, for example, men working on the line, passengers at halts and keepers at the level crossings. On a two-coach train running into a headwind the full impact of the engine's whistle might not be heard (although it was fairly piercing!). For this reason a gong was fixed to the front of the coach — seen left of centre when viewing the coach from the

No. 1462 leaving Bolham Halt with the strengthened 09.45 Dulverton to Exeter train on 18th August 1962. *Peter W. Gray*

outside. It was activated by a foot-operated treadle on the floor of the driver's compartment, just to the right of the brake mounting.

Many of the later trailers were fitted with Automatic Train Control (A.T.C.) equipment which audibly informed the driver of the disposition of approaching signals. A ramp set in between the rails made contact with a shoe underneath the coach, which produced either an 'All Clear' bell or 'Warning' sound depending on the signal (the ramp and the signal were electrically connected). Its use was restricted to the section between Exeter and Stoke Canon, such refinements being unnecessary on a branch with a 35 m.p.h. maximum speed limit.

Some drivers preferred to stand up when driving from the trailer, although there was a tip-up seat near the right-hand door to allow them to sit down and still reach the regulator handle.

One other noteworthy feature of the auto-trailer was the sanding apparatus, for when running 'auto' the leading wheels of the coach would run into trouble first on greasy rails. Just inside the two doors of the driver's compartment was a brass plate let into the floor. Set into this was a hinged 'pull-ring' which was used to

groups — would have to run round at Dulverton and haul their coaches on the return run as well.

Auto-fitted 45XX 'small' prairie class locomotives, the heaviest engines normally allowed on the line, made occasional forays along the branch with auto-train workings. Other prairies that found their way on to the Exe Valley passenger rosters would have to run round.

An auto-fitted engine was not always combined with auto-fitted coaches, while not all auto-fitted coaches were trailers! The so-called 'recognised' Exe Valley workings from Exeter were for 14XX and trailers, but depending on the availability of the 0-4-2s, a non-auto fitted pannier or small prairie was sometimes given the turn. The procedure to be followed at the end of the journey involved certain demarcation patterns which depended on the type of train. The full auto-train was a straightforward matter; the fireman had to change the lamp on the coach. The lamp on the engine was moved from the chimney bracket to the centre buffer beam bracket and changed to red. This was the driver's responsibility. A square red-coloured shade with a wire

A highly improper working, on 7th September 1963, with the locomotive propelling three trailers into Thorverton on the well-patronised mid-morning Saturday shoppers train to Exeter. The correct sequence should have been either: loco-trailer-trailer-trailer; or: trailer-trailer-loco-trailer; or: trailer-loco-trailer-trailer.

R. A. Lumber

raise the plate. Beneath the hole in the floor now revealed was the sand tray. From the tray, a pipe led down to the leading edge of the front bogie wheel on either side, the sand being prevented from moving down from the tray by a moveable flap at the top of the pipe. The two flaps, left and right, were connected by a rod to a black-painted lever in the driver's compartment, situated to the right of the gong pedal. When this lever was pulled, the flaps moved laterally and allowed sand to drain down to the wheels. The sand trays needed to be kept under the coach in order to keep the sand dry and thus able to flow when required. The sandboxes on the 14XXs were more accessible, and in the case of the rear driving wheel much more obvious, being filled from track level. The sandbox for the leading driving wheel was filled through discreet gaps at the back of the buffer beam.

The practice of auto-working was not confined to the 14XX Class. The 54XX and 64XX number series of pannier tanks were specifically built for light passenger work and were auto fitted. Only Nos. 5412 and 6400 worked the line on any regular basis, and this very near the end of its life. The other panniers at work on the branch — notably of the 36XX, 77XX and 87XX

handle was kept in a slot at the back of the lamp; this was lifted out and inserted into the slot behind the lens at the front of the lamp. The reverse procedure applied to the lamp on the coach, i.e. red to white. If a non-auto fitted locomotive was in charge of the train — whether the coaches were auto or ordinary stock — then it was the fireman's job to uncouple and recouple the engine on the run round. If on the other hand the locomotive was auto-fitted but the coaches were not, then a porter at Tiverton or Dulverton had to do the work. If a run round was involved, the driver had to attend to the lamp on the engine while the guard saw to the tail lamp on the coach.

All sorts of coaches found their way on to the branch over the years, even corridor coaches from 'foreign' regions, but where trailers were not available the preferred alternative was the all-second class suburban coach. From the early 1950s some of these had been fitted with the longitudinal transmission rod beneath, allowing them to run in an auto formation. There was no means of driving the train from these coaches, and so they had always to be between the engine and an auto-trailer. A few of these found their way on to the Exe Valley at a time when there was a short-

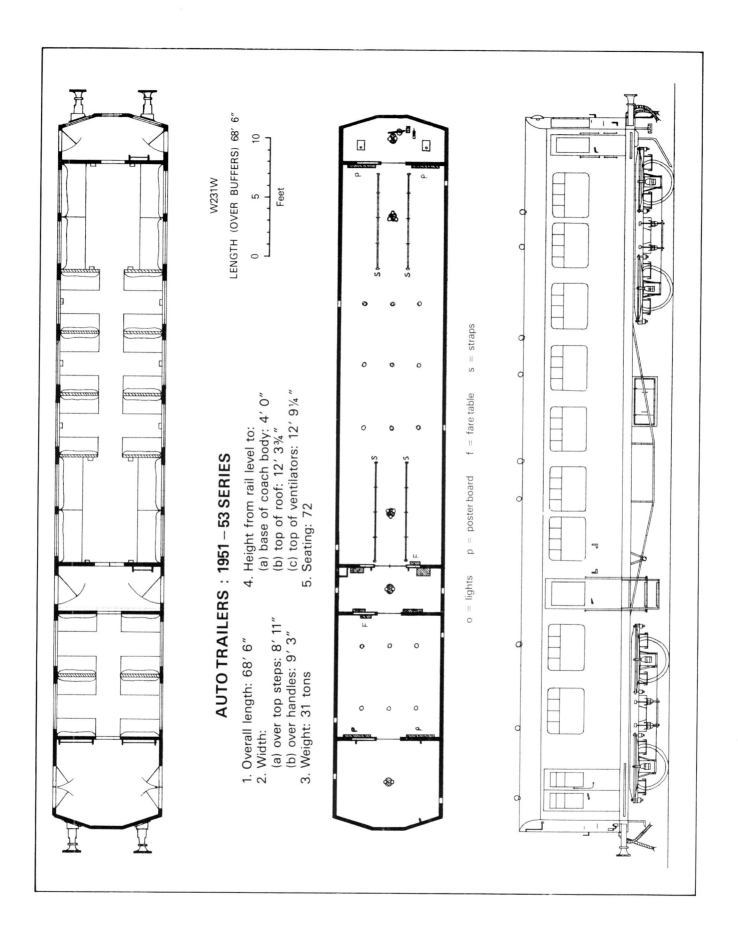

AUTO TRAILERS : 1951 – 53 SERIES

1. Overall length: 68' 6"
2. Width:
   (a) over top steps: 8' 11"
   (b) over handles: 9' 3"
3. Weight: 31 tons
4. Height from rail level to:
   (a) base of coach body: 4' 0"
   (b) top of roof: 12' 3¾"
   (c) top of ventilators: 12' 9¼"
5. Seating: 72

W231W

LENGTH (OVER BUFFERS) 68' 6"

0   5   10

Feet

o = lights   p = poster board   f = fare table   s = straps

age of trailers. Rules governing the operation of auto trains did not permit the propelling of more than two trailers. Although each trailer could hold 72 seated passengers with perhaps a further dozen holding on to the ceiling straps and 6 more crammed on to the emergency tip-up seats in the luggage compartment, some trains were becoming crowded. The Saturday mid-morning train into Exeter was particularly busy, right up until 1963, and an extra coach would be fitted on to the earlier 'up' working to cater for these passengers on the return. The locomotive would have to run round at Dulverton, auto-trailers or not, and treat it as an ordinary train. On at least one occasion, however, the driver propelled all three coaches back to Exeter; certainly not an approved working.

The auto trailer itself is worthy of closer inspection for on its inception it was a new style of coach which became the forerunner of the diesel multiple unit. Most of the photographs show the pressed-steel trailers which worked the branch from the early 1950s.

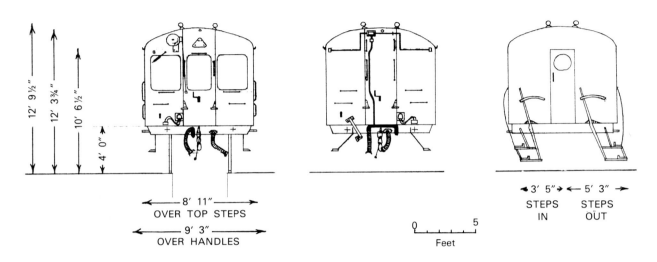

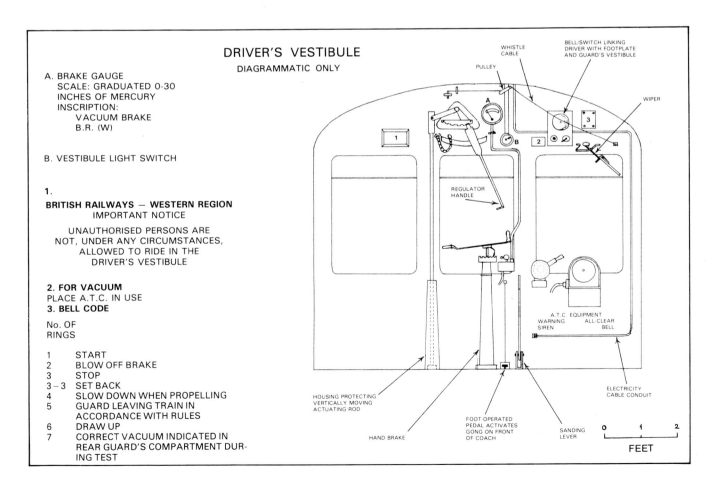

DRIVER'S VESTIBULE
DIAGRAMMATIC ONLY

A. BRAKE GAUGE
    SCALE: GRADUATED 0-30
    INCHES OF MERCURY
    INSCRIPTION:
        VACUUM BRAKE
        B.R. (W)

B. VESTIBULE LIGHT SWITCH

1.

BRITISH RAILWAYS — WESTERN REGION
    IMPORTANT NOTICE

    UNAUTHORISED PERSONS ARE
    NOT, UNDER ANY CIRCUMSTANCES,
    ALLOWED TO RIDE IN THE
    DRIVER'S VESTIBULE

2. FOR VACUUM
PLACE A.T.C. IN USE
3. BELL CODE

No. OF
RINGS

1	START
2	BLOW OFF BRAKE
3	STOP
3 – 3	SET BACK
4	SLOW DOWN WHEN PROPELLING
5	GUARD LEAVING TRAIN IN ACCORDANCE WITH RULES
6	DRAW UP
7	CORRECT VACUUM INDICATED IN REAR GUARD'S COMPARTMENT DURING TEST

The Western Region's intention had been to name the fifteen trailers built in 1951 after British birds. No. 220, the first of the series, was named *Thrush*, and 221 *Wren*, the policy then being discontinued (*Thrush* appears in a number of photographs).

The earlier trailers only differed in details rather than basics: some had a central guard's vestibule; some a greater allocation of transverse rather than longitudinal seats; and some had hinged seat-backs which would allow the passenger to always 'face the front'. Right from the outset of their use on the Exe Valley the trailers were one class only, and this, combined with their open saloon-style seating, made them very different from the other trains of the 1920s. The vestibule doors provided the only passenger access to and from the trailer, the vestibule itself separating the smoking and non-smoking saloons which were closed off by sliding doors. The sweeping out and cleaning of the coaches was the responsibility of staff at Exeter.

With the exception of the driver's compartment, the trailer was in the charge of the guard. The trailers were nothing if not functional, and the vestibule was the 'nerve centre' of the coach. On the wall facing the smoking saloon, to the left of the sliding doors and rising from the floor, was a metal rack for stacking destination boards. There were two metal angle clips on the outside of the coach into which the destination boards could be slotted, but they were never used on the Exe Valley and the rack always stood empty. Above the rack was a locked wooden wall-mounted box with slotted top. This was for used tickets and was divided by partitions into three sections, each fed by a slot. The slots were not labelled, and guards would devise their own classification, such as left slot for used single tickets; centre slot for returns; right slot for 'off-line' tickets (i.e. originating beyond the Exe Valley). Most used tickets were collected by the guards at the unstaffed halts. The ticket would be cancelled by using a ticket punch, and then dropped into the appropriate slot. The box was unlocked and cleared at Exeter. On the opposite side of the doors was a large black tin box containing First Aid materials, and below that was an inverted cone-shaped flag-holder. Below that again was the guard's tip-up style seat. On either side of the saloon doors was a coat hook.

On the other side of the vestibule, facing the non-smoking saloon, was another array of equipment. On the floor, and just inside the doors, were the levers which operated the moveable steps. By pulling the lever inwards (i.e. towards the saloon doors) the steps outside and beneath the vestibule door would extend outwards and allow passengers to leave or join the train from ground level. Above the lever to the left of the saloon door — this was only a single sliding door — was the light-switch housing. The guard used his discretion as to the necessity of providing lighting. There were no tunnels on the line — just one or two rather long bridges — and so lights were not required in normal daylight. A bell-push, together with a bell-code notice board, were situated high up just inside the vestibule doors, allowing the guard to communicate with both driving compartment

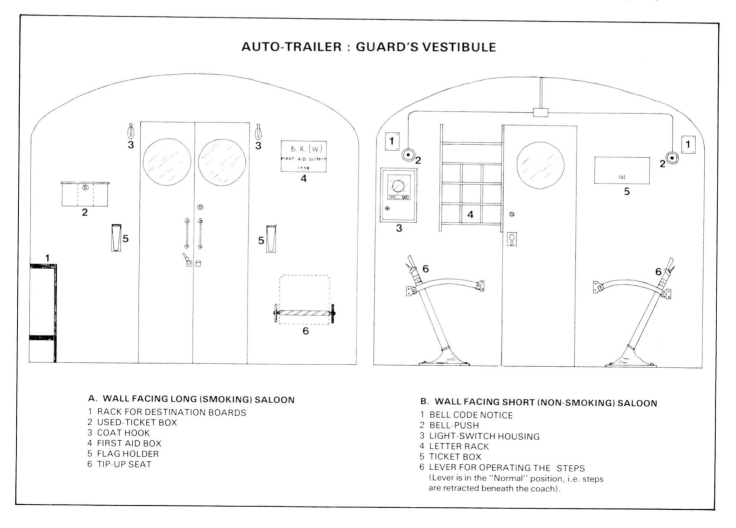

AUTO-TRAILER : GUARD'S VESTIBULE

A. WALL FACING LONG (SMOKING) SALOON
1 RACK FOR DESTINATION BOARDS
2 USED-TICKET BOX
3 COAT HOOK
4 FIRST AID BOX
5 FLAG HOLDER
6 TIP-UP SEAT

B. WALL FACING SHORT (NON-SMOKING) SALOON
1 BELL CODE NOTICE
2 BELL-PUSH
3 LIGHT-SWITCH HOUSING
4 LETTER RACK
5 TICKET BOX
6 LEVER FOR OPERATING THE STEPS
 (Lever is in the "Normal" position, i.e. steps
 are retracted beneath the coach).

and engine cab. To the left of the saloon door was a pigeon-hole style letter rack which was used as a form of internal post for inter-station notices, letters, forms and documents. The guard would have his own system. On the opposite side of the saloon door was another wooden ticket box. This box, which was not slotted like the other one, was where the hand-held ticket rack and fare-table was kept. The tickets were stacked in the rack in price categories, and held in position by a spring-clip. Exeter issued the tickets for all the Exe Valley stations and halts, while Tiverton Junction issued them for Halberton Halt. The tickets, stiff paper rather than card, were printed on both sides, one labelled 'up' and one 'down'. The names of the stations and halts of both the Exe Valley and Tiverton Branch were printed along the borders of both the long edges of the tickets. The guard would punch the ticket opposite the name of the station of destination and put the money in a leather money bag rather like that used by bus con-

ductors. Passengers wishing to travel from a halt to a destination 'off line', would have to re-book at the ticket office at Exeter, Tiverton, Tiverton Junction or Dulverton. A record of the ticket sales made by the guard had to be recorded on the appropriate form and this, together with the money, was paid in to the booking office at Exeter (or Tiverton Junction in the case of Halberton Halt).

Men were assigned to the branch on a regular basis, so that the train crews got to know one another well. As many of the passengers were regulars too, the guard got to know them and the pattern of traffic. Some passengers would always, out of preference, sit in the non-smoking saloon; others would always aim facing the direction of travel; while others would aim to avoid the longitudinal seats at all costs. Staff and passenger identity, and thus that of the branch, was strong, which made — and still makes — the closure of the line such a sad loss.

Auto-train, Dulverton, 22nd September 1950. The rather conspicuous 'chocolate & cream' trailer with its white roof was toned down during the last war, being repainted in plain brown with grey roof. Following Nationalisation, this colour scheme was gradually replaced by carmine and cream — often more crudely known as 'blood and custard'. Two such trailers are seen here on the Exe Valley train. The maroon livery of most of the trailers seen in this book was introduced from 1956.
                                                                                                      D. Butterfield

Chapter Six
The Passenger Services

If a railway is to be successful in gaining passenger revenue, it must reflect and fulfil the travel requirements of the people it serves. In an essentially agricultural area, in the days before widespread commuting, the need to travel was minimal; communities were close-knit and insular, and self-sufficient in many of their day-to-day needs. Passenger services on the Exe Valley line might seem very thin in the early days, but their temporal context should be remembered.

From the opening in May 1885 right up until the end of 1914 the pattern of services remained remarkably constant. The typical Exe Valley train consisted of an 0-4-2 tank engine with three or four coaches. The 'chocolate and cream' coaches were of the short, four-wheeled or the six-wheeled type and, collectively, offered first, second and third class accommodation. The first and last coaches were of the 'brake' variety, possessing a protruding side-light window to allow the guard to look along the train. All trains were conventionally loco-hauled in 'up' and 'down' directions, so that the only change the passengers would notice over the years was the disappearance of the second class category in the coaching stock. Six trains traversed the branch in each direction on Mondays to Saturdays, the timings varying only slightly from year to year. As World War One got into its tragic stride, services were cut back as part of a programme of economy. Brampford Speke was closed as an economy measure from 1915 through to the end of 1917; a strange decision, as it was a well-used station, much more so than Up Exe which stayed open. Only four passenger trains were now running each way, with an extra one on Friday evenings. Friday evenings were busy on the branch, with people returning from market day in Exeter and with schoolchildren who had 'boarded' during the week and were returning home for the weekend. With the end of the War this sparse service continued; indeed, by the end of 1919 even the Fridays only train had been withdrawn. Very gradually the Great Western

began to realise the need to provide a more responsive service, and in the late spring of 1922 provided a Market Day special on Tuesday afternoons between Tiverton and Bampton, and a return evening working from Exeter on Thursdays and Saturdays.

The introduction of auto-trains in the autumn of 1923 did bring a slight improvement in services, with six trains running each way between Exeter and Dulverton (with an extra one on Thursdays and Saturdays) and a further one between Exeter, Tiverton and Tiverton Junction. Even at this stage there was no commuting in the modern sense, a feature reflected in the fact that it was impossible to be in Exeter before 10 o'clock in the morning until 1928. Times and habits, however, were beginning to change. The need and the desire to travel at various times through the day began to increase. With the appearance on the roads around Tiverton of the solid-tyre Devon General buses from the mid-1920s, the Great Western Railway would ignore this trend only at their peril.

So began the biggest expansion in the passenger sector of the Exe Valley since the line's opening. A programme of halt-building was undertaken between 1923 and 1929 in a drive to capture traffic hitherto ignored and now likely to be wooed by the bus company. The summer service of 1926 saw the inauguration of Sunday trains between Exeter and Tiverton; only two each way — one in the early afternoon and one in the evening — but it was a start. In July 1928 came the improvement in service which was to remain until the end. Twelve trains now left Exeter each weekday, eight to Dulverton and four to Tiverton and Tiverton Junction; three trains ran between Exeter and Tiverton on Sundays, with a morning departure from Tiverton to enable day-trippers to visit the coastal resorts of South Devon. The best way to appreciate the change is to study the sample timetables in the Appendix.

Northbound train at Bampton, circa 1910. An 0-6-0 saddle tank is hauling a substantial train of 4 and 6-wheeled coaches. These engines were usually to be found on freight rosters.

R. J. Kingdon collection

Above: The Exe Valley bay at Exeter in 1921. As all branch trains were conventionally hauled in both directions, the platform was provided with a run-round loop.

L&GRP; courtesy David & Charles

Left: Two Exe Valley trains in the bay at Exeter, forming consecutive departures on 1st June 1963.

Peter W. Gray

Small prairie No. 5546 in Platform 3 at St. David's with the 13.15 from Tiverton on 28th March 1959.

J. E. Bell

Another measure of the changing travel regime on the Exe Valley is to look at the pattern of ticket sales from 1925. More and more people were travelling daily, and so purchased season tickets rather than visit the booking office every day. Thus in 1925 Tiverton sold 177 season tickets. Successive years' sales inevitably fluctuated, but the overall trend was upwards: 207 sold in 1929; 386 in 1932; 889 in 1935; and 1,288 in 1938. Numbers fell during World War Two, but quickly picked up again afterwards, reaching 1,130 in 1953, and hovered around the 1,100 mark right up until 1962, the last full year of the line's operation. A number of people who used West Exe Halt every day bought season tickets at the Tiverton booking office to save buying a ticket from the guard on the train. A similar picture emerges at the other stations, with Thorverton jumping from 65 season ticket sales in 1925 to a peak of 672 in 1954. Bampton rose rather more slowly from 70 in 1925 to its peak of 695 in 1953, but sustained a better post-peak record than Thorverton which was feeling competition from the car-owning commuter on the short distance to Exeter. In terms of the total daily passenger usage of the Exe Valley, the boost in services from the late 1920s was certainly reflected in the numbers carried, with the peak being reached in the early 1950s before private road transport became a serious contender.

The train services in the period 1928 to 1940 showed little variation in numbers, times and destinations on weekdays, although the summer Sunday service was increased from three to five trains from 1937. The daily pattern comprised twelve departures from Exeter with eleven return workings (the last 'up' train working to Tiverton Junction and then returning via the main line). The service was cut back to eight 'up' trains from the beginning of 1940, and the Sunday trains were withdrawn. As at the end of World War One, it once again took time for the services to be restored at the end of hostilities. In May 1946 a new timetable was implemented which somewhat modified the established pre-war pattern of working. This was the instigation of a train leaving Exeter at 06.00, running as 'Empty Carriage Stock' to Tiverton, and then as an advertised train to Dulverton. This was followed at 06.30 by an advertised service stopping at all stations. The purpose of the 06.00 was two-fold; firstly to get stock to Dulverton to work back the first, and very busy, down 'commuter' service to Exeter; and secondly to put out newspapers up the branch. The newspapers were bundled up, tied and labelled at St. David's station and placed on the floor of the guard's vestibule in one of the auto-trailers. Stops were made at Stoke Canon, Thorverton, Cadeleigh, Tiverton and Bampton to put out the papers. Dulverton received its papers off the first train from Taunton. As the train had to stop at some stations between Exeter and Tiverton anyway, it was changed to an advertised train from 1948. However, as the newspaper distribution system changed locally, so did the stops, advertised and otherwise, of the 06.00. At first, Stoke Canon was dropped from the schedule and was then put back in again as an unadvertised stop. Bolham Halt was added to the list of official stops because arrangements had been made to put off papers there. Burn Halt was added to the list of unadvertised stops, though for no apparent reason. With the closure of Stoke Canon station in June 1960 the newspapers for that district were put out at Brampford Speke Halt, the stop being unadvertised. A delivery van would call at the station or halt just before the train was due; the driver would collect the papers and distribute them to the various newsagents. If the van driver was late and it was raining, the guard would put the papers in the waiting shelter.

Only on one occasion was there any sort of mishap with the distribution of newspapers. One dark winter's morning one of the Valley signalmen was travelling to work on a newly acquired motor bike to open up his box for the 6 o'clock. Although the bike was mechanically sound, the petrol gauge was not — unknown to the driver. Approaching Silverton the bike spluttered to a halt, and quick investigation revealed the problem. The only light on anywhere in the village was in the house belonging to the petrol station — a stroke of luck as someone was obviously up and about. Just as the signalman wheeled his dead bike on to the forecourt, the garage proprietor came rushing out of the house pulling on his overcoat and muttering something about not being able to open up yet; being very late; newspapers; and going to the station. Before a reply could be uttered, he had leapt into his van and was tearing off down the pitch-dark road. Arriving back some time later, the man expressed surprise at seeing the motorcyclist still there, and complained that he had not been able to collect the newspapers because the Cadeleigh signalman had not turned up for work and the paper train was consequently delayed. This incident also highlighted the problems in communication that could occur. The Thorverton signalman realised his colleague had not booked on when he got no answer to his 'attention' call on the block instrument. Neither the signalman nor the Cadeleigh station master were on the phone, so the Thorverton man rang 'Control' in Exeter on the internal railway phone. Control contacted the Exeter police, who in turn contacted the Tiverton district, in whose territory Cadeleigh was situated. The duty sergeant at Tiverton then rang the police house nearest to the station and got the village bobby to knock-up the Cadeleigh station master, as he would have a key to the signal box and would be able to accept the train which was still marooned down the line (as was the 06.30 behind it!). All this took such a long time that by the time the paper train pulled into Cadeleigh, the signalman — complete with full tank of petrol — had arrived and booked on.

Apart from the appearance of the paper train, certain pre-war services had yet to be restored. In September 1948 the daily number of departures from Exeter rose by just one, to nine (with an extra late train to Tiverton on Thursdays and Saturdays). It was not until the summer of 1950 that Sunday trains were restored. In September 1954 the number of trains up the valley had risen to ten (with a late Saturday train to Bampton), and nine down, the return from Tiverton being via the main line. The next year, however, saw once again the summer-time complement of twelve trains leaving Exeter on weekdays and five on Sundays. After that, numbers and timings varied slightly, with one or two more trains always running on summer weekdays than in the winter. The timetable extracts show this pattern more clearly than a lengthy written explanation.

In terms of usage, some trains were better patronised than others. The 06.00 and 06.30 from Exeter carried few passengers on the outward run, but were well used on the return leg for travellers to Exeter. Large numbers of schoolchildren were conveyed to and from Tiverton on Mondays to Fridays, while morning trains into, and afternoon trains from, Tiverton on Tuesdays were always busy. A similar pattern existed for Exeter on Fridays and Saturdays, especially the latter. The demand for seating on the mid-morning train was considerable, often more than a two-coach auto train could manage. To accommodate the numbers, the 07.55 from Exeter would have three coaches, lightly loaded on the outward journey but filling up on the return run. The train would leave Exeter and even if all the coaches were auto-trailers and the engine also auto-fitted, it would have to run round at Dulverton. The 'up' late afternoon and early evening trains from Exeter were busy, but as the 'homeward flow' was less concentrated than the morning 'rush' the normal auto-working was quite able to cope. One other busy time was the annual Tiverton 'Mill Holiday', when the workers at Heathcoat's textile mill, the biggest single employer in the town, took their holidays. From mid-July to mid-August special 'non-recognised'

Pannier tank No. 7761 with its train of mixed coaches approaches Blundells Road bridge, Tiverton, on the 'strengthened' 09.45 Saturday working from Dulverton to Exeter on 30th July 1960.
D. Fereday Glenn

(ie non 14XX Auto) workings were arranged. On Mondays to Fridays the 07.55 from Exeter would convey extra coaches, as these would be needed at Tiverton and West Exe Halt on the return (the 'down' train left Tiverton just after ten o'clock in most years). A pannier tank, or even a small prairie, was booked to take this train. After a day on the various beaches of South Devon, the trippers would arrive back at Exeter in the early evening, and find a 'special working' to take them back to Tiverton (departure time from Exeter varied between 18.55 and 19.15).

The early evening train into Exeter on Saturdays was used by those taking an evening out at the cinema, but as the cinemas were in the city centre, a long way from St. David's Station, people always had to leave before the picture finished as the last train left around 9.35 or 9.40 (only in the last two years before closure was this extended to five past ten, but this did not make much practical difference).

Three locomotives were normally sufficient at any one time to operate the daily Exe Valley passenger services from the mid-1920s. Where possible, from 1932, the engines allocated were the auto-fitted Collett 0-4-2 tanks. Exeter's small sub-shed at Tiverton Junction was allocated one 14XX to work the Tiverton Branch and another to work the Culm Valley Branch. Periodically, these engines would return to Exeter for boiler washouts, repairs, and so on, and so the shed would receive another engine in exchange. In this way there was a constant mixing of 0-4-2s between the three lines, and even some transference between more distant sheds.

The shed staff at Exeter St. David's would prepare the locomotives prior to a turn of duty, and clean them out at the end.

Three had to be prepared: for the 06.00, 06.30 and 07.55 departures from Exeter (this pattern of early morning departures existed almost unchanged from 1946). The crew signed on in the shed office. The driver would oil and examine the engine while the fireman would tend the fire. Exe Valley trains usually waited in the bay platform (Platform 2) at St. David's, but with three sets of coaches in the bay, as well as parcels vans detached from overnight trains, the 06.00, and on occasions the 06.30 as well, had to leave from Platform 6 (the 'up'-side island platform). The number of parcels vans backed up to the buffers in the bay meant that passengers for the Exe Valley train had a long walk up the platform. When the train was stabled right up to empty coaching stock, passengers would have to be careful to get into the right part, but the guard was on hand to make sure no-one went wrong.

With the shed and bay platform at opposite ends of the station, the locomotive had to find a route through a very congested area. When ready, the locomotive would move up to the signal protecting the exit from the shed. A whistle would alert the signalman in Exeter West Box, and with the 'road' set and signal pulled off, the locomotive would draw out, bunker first, on to the 'loco spur'. Points were re-set, allowing the engine to move off on to the 'up' goods loop which ran behind the station and so avoiding delays there. Passing the small Exeter (Goods Yard) signal box, protecting the level crossing which took the road from St. David's Hill to Exwick, the locomotive arrived at Exeter (Riverside) box. From here, it would pick its way through a series of slip-points and crossovers to join the 'down' main line at Exeter (East) box, and thence set back to the station and on to its train.

The locomotive always ran 'chimney first' on 'up' branch trains, and would have full tanks (800 gallons of water). If it had not come 'off shed', but had remained in the bay subsequent to arrival with a 'down' train, the tanks would be filled from the water crane near the north end of the bay platform. Between Exeter and Cove gradients were not unduly severe, although the line overall was climbing. North of Cove, however, it was a different matter, the line climbing continuously the 3½ miles at an average gradient of 1:66 (with the steepest section of 1:58 between Bampton and Lower Lodfin Crossing). Water would, consequently, be taken on at Tiverton, and again at Dulverton; there would then be sufficient to allow the train to return, with generally favourable gradients, the 24¾ miles to Exeter without further 'topping up'. If the driver was unable to fill up at Dulverton, he would have to do so at Tiverton: an auto train, with the engine at the rear on the southbound trip would use the water crane at the signal box end of the 'down' platform; a locomotive hauled train would use the crane at the Exeter end of the platform.

The roster allocations were usually distributed within the same group of men, but sometimes involved some work off the branch, as fill-in turns. Most turns simply involved two return trips 'out to the Valley'; others one round trip with shunting/piloting duties at Exeter; and one even involved a changeover of enginemen. The double duty turn on the pick-up goods is described in chapter 7. The 'bitty' change-over turns were not popular with the footplate crews — drivers in particular — who worked the 'second leg' of the turn. The 'first leg' had already set off with the 06.00 train for Dulverton when the 'second leg' crew turned up to take over the locomotive for the 07.55. This they would take as far as Thorverton where they would meet the 06.00 coming back. The enginemen would change over, and move off with their new charges. On arrival back at Exeter at 08.34 the 'second' leg crew would work 'light' over to Riverside Yard to pick up the 10.00 local freight working out the 1¼ miles through St. Thomas to the City Basin with coal for the gas works and freight for the docks and Alphington Road goods depot. After a prolonged spell of shunting the various sidings, the train would return to Riverside about half past one, the crew having to shunt and stable the train before they would return to the shed and sign off. The other part of the turn meanwhile would have worked back to Dulverton and finally from there to Exeter.

Platform allocation for branch trains arriving in Exeter depended on a number of factors. Auto-trains could work straight into the bay providing it was not occupied by an impending 'up' Valley departure. Loco-hauled trains had to arrive in platforms 1 or 3 depending on which was available. The 'down' main platform (No. 1) was preferred for trains going 'off duty' and needing to stable their coaches, as the carriage sheds were off the spur leading directly from that platform. The pattern of operation in the summer was such that two Exe Valley trains would sometimes be in the bay, forming consecutive departures.

Tiverton Branch

The sole function of the line in its earliest days was to provide passengers with connections into main line services at Tiverton Junction. The timings of the trains, therefore, were determined by main line schedules. Being locomotive hauled in both directions, a run-round was necessary at both stations. At Tiverton Junction trains arriving from Tiverton were signalled into the 'up' main platform. The engine would uncouple, run round via the 'down' main line, draw its empty stock back on to the branch, and then shunt back into the covered bay. Departures from the bay were timed more finely with the main line service. The time allowed to complete a journey on the branch was 12 minutes. The number of trains in each direction varied between nine and eleven in broad gauge days on Mondays to Saturdays, and four on Sundays. When the line opened, the fares advertised from Tiverton to London give an insight in the structured nature of travel at the time. The single fare by 'Express' train (boarding at the Junction) was 46/- (£2.30) first class and 35/6 (£1.77½) second class. By 'Ordinary' train it was 42/- first class; 28/6 second class; and 15/3 third class.

From 1876 until the opening of the Exe Valley line in the spring of 1885, some branch trains either worked through to and from Exeter, or conveyed through carriages which were attached/detached at the Junction (the journey time being about one hour). The majority of trains, however, continued to make connections at the junction, some thirteen trains plying each way by the time the branch was 'narrowed' in 1884. The provision of a direct route from Tiverton to Exeter brought about a slight reduction in the branch service. The journey time to the Junction had now been cut to 10 minutes, and at the same time an institution began which continued for almost 80 years; namely, the 'Tuesdays Only' connection with the 05.30 Paddington train. From the end of the 1890s right up until closure, about twelve passenger trains were booked each way, this number only being reduced during and immediately after the two world wars.

From 1884 the Tiverton Branch was invariably worked by a '517' Class tank engine with three of the newly introduced and rather smart four-wheeled chocolate and cream coaches. From 1st May 1885 services were transferred from the old terminus in Tiverton to the new station at the bottom of Canal Hill. Trains from the Junction would arrive in the 'down' platform, the locomotive uncouple, run round its train and then shunt the coaches over to the bay platform on the 'up' side. For many years this manoeuvre was relayed to residents living near the station by way of the whistle 'crow' used by engine crews. Uncoupling from its coaches, the engine would pull out of the 'down' platform. Once on the single line beyond the Canal Hill bridge, the driver would request the signalman at Tiverton South box to change the points by sounding a 1-4-4 whistle sequence (or 'crow'). With this done, and the home signal lowered, a single whistle blast indicated the driver's acknowledgement prior to setting back into the 'up' platform. On a still, frosty evening the whistle could be heard quite a long way off. Trains were still offering first, second and third class accommodation. The new station possessed a First Class Waiting Room on the 'up' platform, as well as the ordinary Booking Office and Waiting Room. At the turn of the century the second class category disappeared, enhancing the differential in price and accommodation between first and third.

The Tiverton Branch continued to operate its 'out-and-back' shuttle, involving the time-consuming and operationally inconvenient process of running the engine round at both ends of the line. The Exe Valley had introduced auto-trains on a regular basis in 1923, but it was not until 1927 that they appeared on the Tiverton Branch and so gave rise to the service so long and affectionately known as the 'Tivvy Bumper' (tank engine and single coach working a push-pull service). In the early days of the auto-working, two-coach trains were run, but with each coach being able to seat 72 people, it was quickly realised that one would suffice. As on the Exe Valley, the coaches were one class only — third — a classification which remained until the re-introduction of second class and deletion of third class after Nationalisation. The coaches, however, remained one class and were segregated solely on the basis of smoking and non smoking saloons. The opening of Halberton Halt in 1927 increased the traffic on the line and although the extra stop put another two minutes on the schedule, the push-pull style of operation allowed very short turn-round times at the termini and a timetable much more responsive to the desirability of connecting with trains to and from the Exe Valley, mainline, and Culm Valley. This fa-

The Adaptable Tivvy Bumper

Above: Most Tiverton Branch trains worked into the 'down' bay. Here, No. 1405 is the locomotive propelling the train into the platform.   *R. E. Toop*

Left: When a connection was made with an 'up' Exe Valley train, the Tivvy Bumper would work out of the 'down' bay providing there was an interval of several minutes to allow passengers to cross the footbridge and walk to the waiting train. Both trains are signalled out together, with No. 1462 getting away first. The instantly recognisable angular outline in the foreground belongs to pannier tank No. 3794 on the Dulverton train. 10th October 1959.

Peter W. Gray

With only three minutes between the arrival of the 10.25 from Exeter (hauled by No. 1471) and the departure of the connection, No. 1451 waits in the 'down' main platform to minimise the walking distance for passengers (much appreciated on this wet morning as they could remain under cover!). 3rd November 1962.

W. L. Underhay

cility was further enhanced by the provision of a 'down' side bay platform at Tiverton — commissioned on 18th May 1931 — and a complete rebuilding of the track layout and station at Tiverton Junction in 1932 (completed in October). The arrival at the Junction locomotive shed of the '48XX' Class of 0-4-2 tanks in the autumn of 1932, now saw the start of the pattern of 'Tivvy Bumper' operation which remained to the end (only the numbers of the locomotives changed when the 48XXs were renumbered as 14XXs just prior to Nationalisation in 1948).

The 'Bumper' was unusual, even by branch line standards, in that it did not have a guard; the driver was responsible for the safe running of the service. It was the job of a member of the station staff — usually a porter — at both Tiverton and Tiverton Junction to give the driver the 'all clear'. The driver then had to keep an eye on his train on the 4¾ mile journey. There was in fact a uniformed member of staff travelling in the coach, a porter, whose sole function was to sell tickets to passengers joining the train at Halberton Halt. This porter, based at the Junction, was just provided with a money box and bus conductor-style hand-held ticket rack; he had no flags, lamp or detonators as a guard would have. Even the item 'money box' was too grandiose. From about 1950 the porter would be given a 'float' of five shillings in the booking office at Tiverton Junction; this he kept in a tobacco tin — much more manageable! The tickets were locked away in a wall-mounted wooden box in the vestibule of the coach, and only occasionally needed replenishing from the booking office. The porter would 'cash up' at the end of his shift, and his relief would set off with his 5/- float. Passengers from Halberton wishing to travel beyond the branch had to re-book once they arrived at Tiverton or Tiverton Junction. The porter would open and close the carriage door at Halberton Halt, but once passengers had alighted or en-trained and he had closed the door, it was the

driver's responsibility to see the train safely away, watching out for late-comers running on to the platform or for any obstruction of the door. This could only be done when the train was running into the halt or leaving 'locomotive first'. When the driver was in the driving compartment of the auto-coach the fireman had to keep a lookout and 'bell' the driver if there was a problem (3 rings on the bell meant 'Stop').

The Tivvy Bumper was a well-used service, not only because it provided a frequent link between the sizeable villages of Willand and Halberton with Tiverton, but also because it took passengers from, and allowed movement within, a much greater catchment. Passengers from Thorverton through to Bampton would 'feed-in' to the line at the western end, while from the eastern end came people from Burlescombe down to Cullompton and Hele on the mainline and from Uffculme, Culmstock and Hemyock on the Culm Valley line. Certain trains were better used than others because of the nature of the connection made. Right up until the closure of the line, school-children from a wide area used the service. The first 'up' mainline stopping train from Exeter brought children (of secondary school age) from Silverton, Hele and Bradninch and Cullompton; they simply crossed the island platform and joined the waiting Tiverton train. At about the same time the first 'down' stopping train of the day from Taunton arrived, bringing in further clientele from Burlescombe and Sampford Peverell, though fewer in number. A few minutes before both of these trains the 'Hemyock Express' — as it was nicknamed by pupils — had arrived from the Culm Valley villages. Pupils spilled out of the single 6-wheeled gas-lit coach and stormed across the footbridge to the Tiverton platform. The nickname, as is so often the case with nicknames, was the very anthithesis of an express, the train taking 37 minutes to cover the 7½ mile route — and that was quick; on the return journey as a

Below: Where connections were very tight, the Tivvy Bumper would occasionally work out of the 'up' bay platform, even though the yard points were not fitted with facing point locks and were protected by a ground signal only. This photograph was taken on 1st July 1963.
R. C. Riley

Right: Following the withdrawal of Exe Valley services in October 1963, the Tivvy Bumper worked into the 'down' main platform and departed from the 'up' main — where No. 1442 is seen here waiting with the 11.40 to the Junction on 4th May 1964.
R. A. Lumber

'mixed' train it would take 58 minutes! The Tiverton train, now ready to depart, was also conveying workers, shoppers, shop assistants and office workers from the mainline trains, as well as having brought out similar people to join these trains. The return 'flow' took place in the afternoon. The Culm Valley line brought more shoppers to the branch in the late morning, with the return from Tiverton on the 16.45. Trains were always busier on Tuesdays, as this was market day in Tiverton. The 05.30 train from Paddington, via Bristol, made a special stop at the Junction on Tuesdays only. The Bumper ran out to meet it as Empty Carriage Stock and returned as a scheduled service; again, 'Tuesdays Only'.

At Tiverton, the Bumper generally ran into the 'down' bay platform, from where it would later depart. However, if a tight connection was to be made with an 'up' Exe Valley train, a different path might be followed. If the 'down' main platform was free, the train would run into that, and stop near the footbridge. Passengers could then get between platforms more quickly. The train would then return to the Junction from the 'down' platform. If the 'up' Valley train was going to take on water, which involved drawing the train well forward in the platform and a long way from the footbridge, the Tivvy Bumper would meanwhile have crossed to the 'up' bay platform so that passengers would just get out of the Dulverton train and walk straight across into the waiting connection.

In every year after the last war — and periodically before it — the last 'up' Exe Valley train on its return from Dulverton would make its way to the Junction and then down the mainline back to Exeter. In some years this was an advertised service, calling at Halberton Halt and the Junction before running non-stop to Exeter. Other times it ran as a scheduled service to the Junction and then continued as Empty Carriage Stock; and on yet other occasions was E.C.S. throughout. The late 'Thursdays and Saturdays Only' Exe Valley train from Exeter to Tiverton (modified later to 'Saturdays Only' Exeter to Bampton), also ran out E.C.S. to the Junction and back down the main line.

Sunday services on the branch were a continuous feature from 1848 right up until 1912. The pattern was generally for two trains to run each way in the morning, and two in the afternoon, with a gap of several hours between the two workings. The function of these trains was to provide connections with main line services at the Junction. As coaching stock was stabled at Tiverton and the locomotive shedded at Tiverton Junction, a light engine ran over in the morning to form the first departure. Two return trips were accomplished, and the locomotive ran back 'light' to the Junction in the late morning. The pattern was then repeated in the afternoon, but with a different train crew. By the time the Exe Valley began summer Sunday working in 1926 the Tiverton Branch Sunday working had ceased. However, from 1949 the last 'up' Valley train always returned to Exeter via Tiverton Junction and the mainline as a scheduled service, and thus provided Halberton Halt with its only Sunday train —

and that either a small prairie or pannier with 3 or 4 suburban coaches! In the summer of 1964, with the Exe Valley closed, a Sunday working was provided to the coast and back, and brought the only regular appearance of a diesel multiple unit to the line. An empty d.m.u. from Exmouth Junction, Exeter, arrived at Tiverton at 09.10, leaving ten minutes later for Exmouth and Sidmouth. It arrived back, from Exmouth only, at 20.07 to return five minutes later as empty to Exeter St. David's. That service finished on 6th September, at which time the line itself had only another month to run.

The daily pattern of train services was remarkably constant over the years, and although the following description is for the period after the last war, it could apply to any year of auto-train operation.

The train crews for the line were based at Tiverton Junction, two shifts covering the turn. The small locomotive shed at the Junction housed both the Tiverton Branch and Culm Valley engines (the Tiverton Junction—Hemyock turn also operated a two-shift rota). A shedman was employed to prepare both engines, the Culm Valley locomotive being first off-shed as it had to collect and arrange wagons for the 05.50 goods (and empty carriage stock) to Hemyock. In the evening, the fireman had to damp down the fire on arrival back at the shed. The early turn crew would sign on about 6 o'clock and prepare their engine to take out the 06.30 goods to Tiverton. The porter, armed with his money box, would travel down in the brake van. The auto-coach was stabled overnight in the 'down' bay platform at Tiverton, and once the wagons had been shunted into the yard, the locomotive would couple up and prepare to take out the first passenger train of the day around about 07.40. The Tivvy Bumper then shuttled to and fro along the branch as its connecting services demanded. The train always worked 'locomotive first' out of Tiverton, and was propelled back from the Junction. Water would be taken on as required at either station.

The train crew (driver, fireman and travelling porter) bringing in the Bumper a few minutes before two o'clock were now coming up to the end of their shift; but, with no return working until three, found themselves at the wrong end of the line. This was put right by the locomotive uncoupling from its coach, collecting the brake van brought over first thing in the morning, and clattering over to the Junction, arriving at ten past two. The late turn shift, having already signed on, took over the train; the early turn locomen walking to the shed to sign off and the porter going to the booking office to pay in his Halberton receipts. The locomotive worked back to Tiverton on a goods train, this shift-change providing an ideal opportunity to convey over the wagons detached from the late morning mainline freight. The shuttle passenger service was then resumed unbroken for the rest of the day. With the last train of the day being an arrival at Tiverton, the crew had to get back to the Junction. This was simply achieved by leaving the coach in the 'down' bay and running back 'light engine' to the shed.

Chapter Seven
The Freight Services

A small prairie No. 4589 arriving at Cadeleigh with the daily pick-up goods from Exeter to Tiverton on 8th July 1959.   *Peter W. Gray*

For the first few months of its life, freight traffic on the Exe Valley was handled by way of a 'mixed' train leaving Exeter at 06.50, running up to Dulverton and returning in the late afternoon, also as a 'mixed' train. A few minutes only were allocated at the stations for shunting purposes. This was clearly not adequate for the increase in traffic that rapidly developed following the line's opening (indeed, freight was the mainstay of the branch, in financial terms, almost to the end of its life), and so from mid-1886 a separate goods train ran the length of the line and back Monday to Saturday. To begin with, the goods roster began at Taunton and ran along the Devon & Somerset line to Dulverton and then down the Exe Valley, returning in the afternoon. After a short time, however, the freight settled into the Exeter-Dulverton-Exeter roster that remained until 1954. Traffic for Tiverton originating outside the valley and parts of the D & S, was routed via Tiverton Junction, while that for Bampton was dispatched via Dulverton if it originated 'up country' from Taunton, and via Tiverton Junction if it came from South Devon and Cornwall. Cadeleigh and Thorverton were supplied from Exeter, except of course for internal local traffic on the branch. Tiverton's freight provision was always more substantial, reflecting the great quantity and variety handled.

The daily goods, calling at all the stations possessing a freight facility, was known as a 'pick-up' goods, but Valley railwaymen simply called it 'The Goods'. The roster remained almost the same for years, so that the following description from the early 1950s could really apply to any year from the turn of the century; only the times varied slightly.

The locomotive had been prepared by the St. David's shed staff and would be nicely simmering 'on shed' when the Valley crew booked on at around 8.20 in the morning. The locomotive was usually a pannier, but very occasionally a small prairie. After the driver had inspected the engine, the locomotive 'whistled up' for 'the road' and set off along the 'up' goods avoiding line to Exeter Riverside goods yard to pick up its train. The train had been made up in the early hours, by one of the Riverside shunters, from wagons off the various overnight main line freights. After setting back on to its train, the guard would inform the driver of what was to be dropped off or picked up, and where.

At nine o'clock the train moved off, clanking along the long 'up' goods loop to Cowley Bridge Junction where it joined the main line to Stoke Canon. The train did not shunt at Stoke Canon, as this station was worked by a main line turn. Eighteen minutes were allowed for shunting at Thorverton and thirteen at

71

Interchange of traffic between the Exe Valley and Devon & Somerset line took place at Dulverton. Standard class '3' 2-6-2T No. 82008 is seen shunting the 'down'-side exchange sidings, while the Valley train awaits its connection. 2nd July 1963.
                                                                                                                                                                R. C. Riley

An eastbound Devon & Somerset freight prepares to leave Dulverton behind pannier tank No. 9670 on 3rd October 1963.
                                                                                                                                                                D. Fereday Glenn

Cadeleigh, with the train booked into Tiverton at 10.15. This was just nicely slotted in between two 'down' passenger trains, although as the first was booked to cross the goods at Stoke Canon a delay was sometimes caused by redrawing the train staff. The custom at Thorverton and Cadeleigh was to do as much of the shunting as possible on the outward journey and transport any up-country empties to Tiverton. The goods did not carry a shunter, the guard having to attend to the coupling and uncoupling of wagons at Thorverton, Cadeleigh and Bampton. If there was no shunting to be done on a particular day, or it was completed ahead of time, the train ran on to the next station and did not keep to the timetable.

On arrival at Tiverton station, water would be taken on from the crane at the far end of the platform while the signalman collected the staff from the fireman — a 'down' passenger train being due in from Dulverton at 10.21, requiring the line to Cadeleigh. The yard in fact was already occupied by another freight, the 03.45 from Exeter, via Tiverton Junction, this having arrived at 07.05 and busied itself in shunting. This train departed at 10.40 for Taunton. The locomotive had generally finished its shunting operations by ten o'clock, or shortly afterwards, and was standing on the line alongside the goods shed. With the arrival of the 'down' passenger train, the Bampton section was now clear, so that, with watering complete, the valley goods would draw forwards until clear of the yard points, and then set back.

With the departure of the Taunton freight, the valley goods locomotive would commence shunting operations. Time on the outward run was limited at Tiverton, so that traffic was simply detached, to be dealt with later. At 11.06 the goods departed for Bampton, following hard on the heels of an 'up' auto-train which had left Tiverton at 10.49. A very generous 34 minutes was allowed for shunting at Bampton, with arrival time at Dulverton being 12.14. Here, traffic from the valley destined for stations to Barnstaple was shunted to await a goods from Taunton (13.30 off Dulverton), while eastbound traffic from Bampton was stabled in readiness for collection by the afternoon South Molton-Taunton freight (13.41 off Dulverton). Any traffic for Dulverton itself was shunted to the small up-side yard. The locomotive then collected wagons for the valley which had been detached off the late morning D & S goods (one to and one from Taunton). The revenue-earning traffic attributed to Dulverton was dispatched via the Devon & Somerset line. The transhipment traffic between the Devon & Somerset and Exe Valley did not figure in the station's accounts.

At 13.15, after the locomotive had taken on water and the crew had managed a short lunch break, the train set off on the return journey. The goods was generally lightly loaded on the Tiverton to Dulverton leg of its roster in the last years of its regular run, but was still required to pull up at the Stop Board three-quarters of a mile south of Morebath Junction on the steep down-grade. The brakes of the trucks had to be 'pinned down' for the short downhill journey to Bampton, where they would be 'taken up' again. It was the guard's job to carry out this manoeuvre. Twenty minutes were allowed for shunting at Bampton before the journey south was resumed. Provision was made for a 'Request Stop' at Cove Siding but this was rarely, if ever, necessary. The short siding was intended for general merchandise, but the traffic had always been slight, and was virtually non-existent after 1945. The train was booked to arrive at Tiverton at 14.05. Rather than run straight into the yard, the goods would give up the 'Staff' at the signal box and run into the 'down' platform, or at least the approaches to it. With the 'down' calling-on signal 'off', the locomotive was able to run round its train, haul it back over to

The Exe Valley goods locomotive, acting as station pilot, is attaching a parcels van for Dulverton to the rear of a train hauled by No. 1466. Vans detached from trains earlier in the day and shunted into the bay would be collected by the 'pilot' and conveyed over to the Junction as 'empties' on the early evening freight.

Lens of Sutton

Pannier tank No. 8783 collecting the wagons brought in from the Junction by the '14XX' class tank sandwiched between the trucks and auto-coach in the 'down' bay.
M. J. Fox; courtesy Tiverton Museum

Large prairie No. 4103 pulls into Tiverton Junction with an unusually short freight from Tiverton on 3rd October 1963.   *D. Fereday Glenn*

No. 1471 shunting 'Insulvans' for the large meat company of Lloyd Maunder at Tiverton Junction.   *W. L. Underhay*

the 'up' line shunt signal and then propel the wagons into the yard. With departure for Exeter not due until 18.35, a new phase in the roster now began.

While the valley locomotive was attending to its duties, the 13.46 passenger from Exeter (arriving in Tiverton at 14.21) had brought out a relief crew to take over from the early turn. Walking from the platform across to the yard, the men — driver, fireman and guard — would take over soon after half-past two. As there was no train to convey the other three men back to Exeter until 4 o'clock, this meant an enforced, but welcome, tea break on the station. On arrival at Exeter, the early turn locomotive crew and guard had to walk to their respective time offices and book off (about 16.45).

The new crew, meanwhile, would be occupied in dealing with a freight over from the Junction. At 14.00, five minutes before the 'down' valley goods had arrived in Tiverton, the 14XX locomotive from the Tivvy Bumper service had, complete with brake van, set off for the Junction to pick up wagons detached from mainline goods and to change crews. This arrived back, with a short freight, at 14.40, working into the 'down' bay platform. The Tiverton shunter uncoupled the locomotive, which then drew forward and coupled up to its auto-coach, ready to form the 3 o'clock to the Junction. The valley pannier moved out of the yard until it cleared the points on the 'up' main line. The points were reset and the locomotive moved into the bay to collect the wagons brought in by the 14XX. These were then taken across to the yard, so clearing the bay for the Tivvy Bumper to resume its usual service.

Once these trucks had been dealt with, the pannier would turn its attention to marshalling the afternoon freight to the Junction, as well as sorting out the wagons left there on the northward journey. As soon as the evening Exe Valley goods had been prepared — time would be short later — the locomotive coupled up to the stock which would form the 17.15 goods out to the mainline. This was often quite a heavy train, with up to 30 wagons. Most of these would subsequently be attached to the evening goods up to Swindon, with traffic arranged in sequence for detaching at intermediate points like Taunton and, notably, Bristol. With a rising gradient of 1:91 commencing immediately

beyond the junction points at Tiverton, a pannier and even small prairie had its work cut out to haul a heavy load. On arrival at Tiverton Junction (at 17.30) the locomotive would run round its train and draw back in readiness to attach wagons to the Swindon goods. This task, and any other shunting completed, it returned light engine to Tiverton, arriving at 18.18, drawing up outside the signal box on the 'down main' in order for the signalman to clear the section and redraw the token for the Tivvy Bumper due off from the 'down' bay at 18.20. There was certainly plenty of activity at Tiverton for large parts of the day!

With the Bumper out of the way, the light engine crossed to the yard to pick up its wagons for the journey down the valley. This operation was not as straightforward as it sounds, however, for the locomotive was attached to the back of the train. Consequently, the trucks had to be drawn out of the yard and shunted over to the 'down' platform. The engine had to run round, but the 'up' platform was occupied between 18.30 and 18.33 by an 'up' Exe Valley passenger train. It was clearly difficult to keep to the 18.35 departure from Tiverton, but with 24-minute stops at both Cadeleigh and Thorverton and relatively little to do there, time was easily made up. The goods had to cross with another 'up' passenger at Cadeleigh, but then had a clear run, the crew often trying to gain some time to get back to the Riverside yard a bit early. Officially, the goods was due back at Exeter at 20.02, where the crew had to stable the wagons ready for the yard pilot before they could take the locomotive back to the shed and sign off at 9 o'clock. This two-shift freight working applied on Mondays to Fridays. On Saturdays the 'up' goods ran to the same schedule as far as Tiverton, where it would shunt and then proceed out to the Junction at 11.50 (this being timetabled as a through working from Exeter; whence it returned by way of the main line).

Until the early 1950s road competition had not been too serious a problem. Indeed, in one sense a rural railway depended on the road, for the stations existed as local railheads to and from which goods were carried by horse and cart and, later, lorry. Traction engines hauling their 'trains' of small wagons regularly plied between Tiverton goods yard and local factories, warehouses and other commercial premises. The appearance of medium and long-distance road haulage firms, however, really spelt the end for the small rural stations as the lorry was better adapted to, and more flexible in dealing with, small loads on a door-to-door basis. Freight handling facilities remained at the stations right up until closure but the book-keeping side of the business was progressively 'zoned', with the goods agency being concentrated first at Tiverton and later at Exeter.

From September 1954 the through freight working ceased. The goods continued to run from Exeter to Tiverton and back on a Monday to Friday basis until early 1962 (retimed to leave Riverside at 11 o'clock); the locomotive acting as yard and station pilot at Tiverton for the whole afternoon until it was required to take the Tiverton Junction freight out at twenty past five. The return from the Junction as a light engine and the subsequent 'down' Exe Valley goods continued unchanged over the years. Bampton was served by the Taunton-Dulverton goods, but from the Spring of 1956 this was cut back to Mondays, Wednesdays and Fridays only. The traffic continued to dwindle, so that after only a further two years the Bampton freight ran 'as required' (the weekday Taunton to South Molton freight locomotive providing the motive power). For the remaining five years of the branch, the sidings at Bampton were usually deserted, except for a little incoming coal traffic and the 'stores' truck. With the virtual disappearance of freight at Cadeleigh around the same time, the

(later 11.40) goods from Tiverton always ran through to Taunton. By the summer of 1962 all the incoming freight was being carried by a single, heavily laden goods first thing in the morning. Apart from the late morning departure there was still a need for an evening train, and so a light engine was sent over from the Junction to take out a train at around 17.20 (this working continued until mid-1965).

Apart from the carrying of general freight, the Exe Valley goods also performed certain specific functions. The most common of these was the station 'truck' service. Parcels traffic for Tiverton and beyond was made up at Exeter St. David's and put into a station truck (a box van) which was shunted by the station pilot to the Riverside Yard and attached to the 09.00 'up' Valley goods. Parcels for Thorverton and Cadeleigh would be unloaded during the booked stops, while the van was detached at Tiverton and shunted back into the 'up' bay platform. Parcels for the town and district were taken off, and those for Bampton, Dulverton and beyond loaded on. Before the goods set off up the valley, the van would be collected and re-attached to the other wagons. A similar arrangement worked on the return southbound trip, but there was rarely any parcels traffic in this direction and thus no need to shunt the wagon.

When the goods ceased running between Tiverton and Dulver-

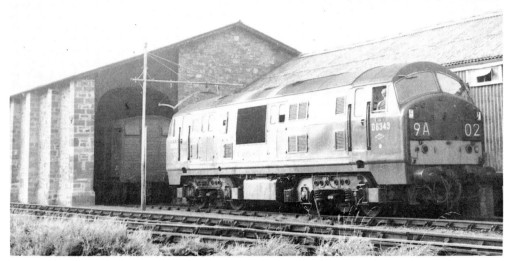

Diesel hydraulic Type 2, No. D6343, waits outside the goods shed in Tiverton yard on 3rd October 1963.

D. Fereday Glenn

need for a daily pick-up goods was diminishing. Tiverton was catered for via the mainline, while the important grain traffic at Thorverton could be dealt with by an out-and-back turn from Exeter. From 1960 the goods was only lightly loaded from Thorverton to Tiverton, and its demise was inevitable. From the Spring of 1962 until closure in October the following year, the goods only ran 'as required', mainly for grain traffic to Thorverton, with just occasional trips with the odd truck or two to Cadeleigh. (Thorverton remained open until 1966 specifically for the mill traffic). Bampton was also served 'as required'; now using the locomotive off the Taunton to Swimbridge roster, but this ceased on the same day that passenger services were withdrawn.

Tiverton too was affected by the drift to the road, but as it had a broader base than the rural stations, continued with a much higher level of freight-train provision. A substantial morning and evening goods departed from Tiverton throughout the 1950s, with most of the incoming freight carried by the two morning services. In June 1962 the early morning through goods from Exeter via Tiverton Junction was replaced by a through working from Taunton, which continued until the final withdrawal of facilities in 1967. Whether from Exeter or Taunton, the 10.40

ton in September 1954, another arrangement had to be made. The station truck was positioned next to the guard's van. On arrival at Tiverton 'up' platform the station truck and brake van were detached, left in the platform for the staff to attend to, and the freight wagons shunted into the yard. The locomotive then returned, collected the station truck (and brake van) and prepared to attach it to the next 'up' passenger train, whose arrival was imminent. Even this could be a tricky operation if the passenger train was hard on the heels of the goods (although the goods commonly arrived early). Ideally, the locomotive would run through the 'down' platform, out on to the single line section, and then draw into the platform and couple up to the vans. Engine and vans would then cross to the 'down' platform to await the 'passenger'. With its arrival, the van was shunted and attached to the rear of the train. The goods engine and brake van would remain in the platform until the 'passenger' had cleared the advanced starting signal, and then work over to the yard. The passenger train would convey the van to Dulverton, where it was detached. Once unloaded, and parcels sorted for intermediate stations between Taunton and Barnstaple, the van would not work back down the valley but, rather, go out to Taunton on the afternoon D & S goods. Following the withdrawal of the Exe

Valley freight between Cadeleigh and Tiverton, parcels for the latter had to be conveyed by passenger train. When the traffic was too great to be accommodated in this way, box vans or parcels vans would be attached to certain northbound trains. On arrival at Tiverton the vans would be shunted into the 'up' bay, to be returned to Exeter later via Tiverton Junction.

A stores truck was also conveyed by the goods, but this was a more infrequent working than the station truck. From time to time provisions at the stations needed to be replenished, and worn out or damaged equipment replaced. The station master would make out a requisition for these items, which was then forwarded to Exeter. Oil for the platform hurricane lamps, the indoor tilly lamps and signal lamps was conveyed in large 40-gallon drums. The stations had to supply hurricane lamps for the halts under their charge, and also oil for the level crossing lamps. The drums were brought up in the stores van — a box van — attached to the 'up' goods. If the crossing keepers required fresh oil supplies they notified 'their' station master, who arranged for a 10-gallon drum to be sent to the crossing; the goods making a special stop there to set it down. Other items more rarely requested include such things as signalmen's dusters, shunters' poles, coal shovels and scuttles, and the delicate mantles and fume-cover funnels for the tilly lamps. The new stock would only be issued when the old or damaged equipment was handed in.

Another function of 'the goods' was to supply the stations with coal. Early in November, a truck load of coal was sent up on the goods. This had to last for a full year, the allocation depending on the size or particular need of each location. Tiverton had the greatest need with a number of offices and waiting rooms, goods office, signal box and water-crane braziers. The other stations required coal for the signal box and station master's office as well as waiting rooms. Some 3 tons per annum was the allocation for the smaller stations. The truck was made up at Swindon and labelled 'Station Coal'. Having worked down from Swindon, the truck was attached to the 'up' valley goods, and was uncoupled and shunted at Thorverton. Here, the signalman had to unload the station's quota as exactly as he could, using the weighbridge in the yard. If he took more than the requisite amount, the station at the end of the chain would go short. In this circumstance an inspector would be sent from Swindon to investigate the short-fall, so keen was officialdom to make sure there had been no misappropriation. If a genuine error had been made, the deficit would be made up. The next day, the goods would collect the truck from Thorverton and take it to Cadeleigh, and so on up the branch. The level crossing huts and ganger's huts did not receive an allocation, as they were only intermittently occupied. On a cold winter's day the line-side gang liked to retire to a warm ganger's hut for tea or meal breaks, so they had to burn anything they could find: old sleepers, dead branches or lumps of loco-motive coal thrown down by sympathetic train crews.

A long, cold winter would diminish coal stocks at an alarming rate, and station staff had to become adept at 'cadging' or ration-ing fuel. Although goods shed offices and weighbridge-houses had fireplaces, the fires were never lit. Similarly, the fire in the station's rear office and general waiting room were never lit in ordinary winters, while the fire in the ladies' waiting room was only lit in exceptional cold to prevent the pipes and lavatory cystern bursting. Despite these economies, and damping down the stove in the signal box well before the end of a shift, coal shortages still arose. Signalmen would resort to asking drivers to let them have some locomotive coal, but you had to know your driver! Some refused point blank while others were very grudg-ing; many men, however, were happy to help the signalmen out — providing he climbed into the bunker and threw down the lumps himself! Locomotive coal was often rather hard, but was better than nothing; briquettes were also sometimes available from the locomotives. The goods was the favourite train for begging coal because it had a longer stay in the stations.

Private owner wagons. *HMRS*

MAXIMUM LOADS FOR BRANCH FREIGHT TRAINS

SECTION From	SECTION To	WORKING LOADS Maximum number of wagons to be conveyed by Steam Engines	14xx Locos Class 1	14xx Class 2	14xx Class 3	14xx Empties	Group A Class 1	Group A Class 2	Group A Class 3	Group A Empties	Group C Class 1	Group C Class 2	Group C Class 3	Group C Empties	Group D Class 1	Group D Class 2	Group D Class 3	Group D Empties	Group E Class 1	Group E Class 2	Group E Class 3	Group E Empties
EXE VALLEY BRANCH																						
Stoke Canon	Tiverton	40	-	-	-	-	17	23	34	43	21	28	42	53	-	-	-	-	-	-	-	-
Tiverton	Dulverton	28	-	-	-	-	12	16	24	30	14	19	28	35	-	-	-	-	-	-	-	-
Dulverton	Bampton	28	-	-	-	-	10	13	20	25	13	17	26	33	-	-	-	-	-	-	-	-
Bampton	Stoke Canon	50	-	-	-	-	21	28	42	53	25	33	50	63	-	-	-	-	-	-	-	-
TIVERTON BRANCH																						
Tiverton Junction	Tiverton	44	12	16	24	30	17	23	34	43	20	27	40	50	26	35	52	65	32	43	64	80
Tiverton	Tiverton Junction	44	12	16	24	30	18	24	36	45	21	28	42	53	32	43	64	80	38	51	76	95

NB. Class 1 : coal, coke & patent fuel
Class 2 : other minerals
Class 3 : general merchandise

DISTANCE M	C	STATIONS etc.	STN. NO.	POINT-TO-POINT TIMES (Mins.)	ALLOW FOR STOP (Mins.)	ALLOW FOR START (Mins.)
-	-	EXETER (ST. DAVID'S)	1552	-	-	1
3	30	Stoke Canon	1546	8	1	2
4	19	Brampford Speke Halt	1627	-	-	-
4	58	Fortescue Crossing	1626	-	-	-
6	11	Thorverton	1625	7	1	1
6	63	Up Exe Crossing	1624	-	-	-
6	73	Up Exe Halt	1623	-	-	-
8	68½	Burn Halt	-	-	-	-
10	18	Cadeleigh	1622	10	1	1
13	40	West Exe Halt	-	-	-	-
14	9	TIVERTON	1620	10	1	2
16	5	Bolham Halt	-	-	-	-
19	18	Cove Halt	1618	-	-	-
21	14	Bampton	1617	17	1	2
22	24	Lower Lodfin Crossing	1616	-	-	-
22	63	Morebath Junction	1597	-	-	-
22	71	Morebath Junction Halt	-	-	-	-
24	54	DULVERTON	1598	11	1	-

M.P. MILEAGE M	C	STATIONS etc.	POINT-TO-POINT TIMES	ALLOW FOR STOP	ALLOW FOR START
-	-	DULVERTON	-	-	1
-	-	Morebath Junction Halt	-	-	-
0	0	Morebath Junction	-	-	-
0	39	Lower Lodfin Crossing	-	-	-
0	61	Stop Board	7	1	1
1	49	Bampton	2	1	1
3	45	Cove Halt	-	-	-
6	58	Bolham Halt	-	-	-
8	54	TIVERTON	17	1	1
9	23	West Exe Halt	-	-	-
12	45	Cadeleigh	10	1	1
13	74½	Burn Halt	-	-	-
15	70	Up Exe Halt	-	-	-
16	0	Up Exe Crossing	-	-	-
16	52	Thorverton	10	1	1
18	5	Fortescue Crossing	-	-	-
18	44	Brampford Speke Halt	-	-	-
19	33	Stoke Canon	7	1	1
-	-	EXETER (ST. DAVID'S)	7	2	-

TRAIN IDENTIFICATION

(a) Destination Letter: Exeter District = C (Passenger)

(b) Train Classification:
Main Line Passenger 1   Goods 9
Local Passenger 2   Light engine 0
Parcels and E.C.S. 3

(c) Route Numbers: 86 Tiverton Junction to Tiverton
87 Exeter to Dulverton

(d) Local Destinations (Goods & L.E.):   AO4 Bampton

A26 Dulverton   A33 Exeter Riverside   A70 Tiverton
A71 Tiverton Jc.   A72 Tiverton Jc. R. & M.   A79 West Exe

EXAMPLES: (i) Pass. Exeter—Dulverton: 2C87
(ii) Goods Tiverton—Tiverton Jc.: 9A71

Following the closure of the line to passengers, the Stoke Canon to Thorverton section was retained for grain traffic (as required). Here, the train is running into Stoke with empties from Thorverton Mill, hauled by 0-6-0PT No. 4655 on 1st May 1965.
R. A. Lumber

Chapter Eight

Signalling

With trains taking anything between 60 and 80 minutes to travel from one end of the line to the other, some provision had to be made for trains travelling in opposite directions to pass each other, if any sort of flexible service schedule was to be operated. Passing 'loops' were provided at Thorverton, Cadeleigh, Tiverton and Bampton stations and also at Morebath Junction, while Stoke Canon Junction and Dulverton could 'cross' Exe Valley trains either separately or in association with main line workings. The need to control movement to and from these loops, as well as to facilitate shunting at the stations, was met by the provision of signal boxes at the above 'control points'. In this way the Exe Valley was divided into a number of single line sections with signalmen communicating with each by way of 'block instruments' to control access to their respective section. There were originally six other signal boxes on the line, but they were unable to accept or refuse trains, only superintending passage through their section. These 'non-block posts' were situated at the five level crossings, namely, Fortescue, Up Exe Crossing, Up Exe Station, Cove and Lower Lodfin, together with another one at Brampford Speke station.

The Signal Box

The first and most eye-catching feature of the signal box was the row of steel levers mounted in a convex, grooved metal frame

Right: Tiverton signal box: front.
Below: Tiverton signal box: rear. *Both D. Vaughan Davies*

located at the front of the box, just in front of the windows. The levers' colours indicated their function: red for 'stop' signals and discs (ground signals); black for points; and blue for locking devices (notably facing point locks which locked — or 'bolted' in railway jargon — point blades when facing an approaching train). The level crossing ground frames had a brown lever for bolting the gates shut and yellow levers for the distant signals. Levers which had been taken out of use were painted white, and referred to on signalling diagrams as 'spare' while in practice redundant levers were usually removed altogether. This removal left a groove in the frame with no lever, and was referred to as a 'space'. When built, some frames were deliberately provided with spaces in case of future expansion. Detonators were set by hand, except at Stoke Canon Junction, so there was no lever for this function. All the levers in use possessed a tag (known as a 'lead') which informed the signalman of their number (related to the signalling diagram), function, and which other levers had to be moved in order for this particular lever to move. This process of moving a lever in the frame was referred to as 'pulling'; the lever being pulled towards the operator. So men would for example talk of 'pulling over number 14.' Where signals were concerned — with their 'stop' ('on') and 'all clear' ('off') positions — signalmen would talk of 'pulling off numbers 2, 3 and 4', or, conversely, 'putting back numbers 2, 3 and 4.' A lever which was 'over in the frame' meant that it had been pulled; while one which was 'back in the frame' was secured in that part of the groove farthest from the signalman, i.e. the back of the frame. Most levers were always back in the frame until they had to perform their stated function, but where facing points had to be negotiated on a running line, the lever would be over in the frame to keep the point securely bolted.

In the locking room beneath the lever frame an individually designed series of short steel rods and 'locking bars' interacted in such a way that signals might only be pulled off when the appropriate points were correctly set. This is known as 'interlocking', and is of great importance when controlling movements from single to double track, and vice versa. Signalmen would refer to 'setting the road', meaning that the appropriate point levers would be pulled over before pulling off the signals. The intentions of signalmen were communicated between boxes by bells worked in conjunction with block instruments. Each bell had to have a different sound in order to be individually recognisable. At Thorverton for example the bell from Cadeleigh was convex in shape with a large diameter and gave a sharp, clear ring, while that from Stoke Canon looked rather like a large cow-bell and gave a flatter, duller tone.

Above the levers was the instrument shelf, suspended from the ceiling. The shelf contained a large, framed diagram of the layout controlled by the signal box, along with the bells, distant signal lamp indicators and, in some cases, signal repeaters. The lamp indicators performed a vital function. It was important at night that a distant signal be clearly visible to the driver of an approaching train. This was especially necessary at the level crossings. If the gates had not been opened for the train and the signal was 'on' the driver had time to slow down and to whistle a warning of his approach. By day the yellow arm with its distinctive V-notch was clear enough, but at night a lamp was necessary. Coloured spectacles set in a frame on the right of the arm would show amber for 'caution, prepare to stop' (signal 'on') and green for 'all clear' (signal 'off'). A lamp fixed behind the spectacle plate provided the necessary light. The 'fixed' distants at the other locations showed a permanent amber light. If the lamp went out for any reason, there had to be a way of letting the signalman know. This was the task of the lamp indicator. On the top of the lamp case on the signal were two thin strips of metal, separated by a tiny gap. The heat given off from the burning paraffin

caused the metal strips to heat up and expand, so coming into contact and completing an electrical circuit. Back in the signal box this registered as 'lamp in' (white capital letters on a green background). If the lamp went out, the metal strips quickly cooled and contracted and broke the circuit. When this happened the display in the lamp indicator window swung anti-clockwise to display 'lamp out' in white capitals on a red background. Simultaneously a bell would start to ring; this usually being mounted on the back wall of the signalbox near the Train Register desk. The bell could be turned off by moving the pointer at the bottom of the instrument to 'bell off'. The next signalbox down the line in the direction of the failure would be contacted so that the man there could warn the driver of the next train. The lamp would have to be relit as soon as it was possible for the signalman to attend to it. The tab on the bottom left of the instrument was for testing to see if the indicator was working correctly. By depressing the tab, the 'lamp out' display would rotate into view and the bell sound.

The signal arm repeaters were used when a signal was not visible from the box. On the Exe Valley these were mostly the distant signals at the level crossings (as the fixed distants remained 'on', they did not require repeaters) and one or two unsighted stop signals. Expansion and contraction of signal wires could affect the angle which a signal arm would adopt when pulled off. If the arm only moved a few degrees from the horizontal it was not always easy to tell whether it was 'on' or 'off'. At night this was more serious because no obvious colour would be showing. A rachet-style wire adjusting handle was located behind the main signals, and the error could easily be adjusted. To show a signalman that an unsighted signal had not pulled off correctly an 'arm repeater' was used, i.e. a miniature signal fixed on a dial on the edge of the instrument shelf behind the lever concerned. This simply repeated the action of the signal. If the miniature arm pointed to 'wrong', the signal would be returned to 'on' and the lever pulled again. If the arm continued to show 'wrong', the tension of the wire would be adjusted.

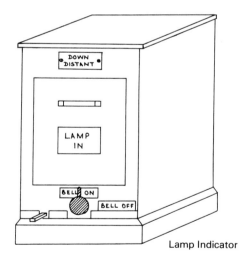

Lamp Indicator

Signal Box Routine

With the exception of Tiverton, the three true Exe Valley signal boxes — Thorverton, Cadeleigh and Bampton — had the lowest classification (Grade 4) and thus paid the lowest wages. They may not have had the glamour and bustle of the more ostentatious boxes like Tiverton Junction or those in Exeter, but they performed a vital task not only in the safe operation of the line but also in the maintenance of the station as a whole. All the Exe Valley boxes were kept clean and tidy, the men taking a pride in their box. A signalman who was too lazy to sweep out the box, let alone attend to the more onerous cleaning tasks, was not appreciated by the others and referred to as 'a dirty man'. The linoleum floor was washed regularly and newspaper put down until dry as protection against the dirty boots of gangers or firemen. The tops of the levers were polished until they shone, even if they were little used. The levers were always pulled over with a duster, as this prevented hands from slipping off the lever and also kept the lever handle bright and shiny. Damp hands would lead to beads of rust on the lever, and consequently it was a heinous crime to touch a lever with bare hands! The stove was regularly black-leaded and the brass fittings polished until they gleamed. At night the tilly lamps hissed and gave off a mellow glow which, combined with the warmth from the stove and the various smells of the fittings, gave the box a characteristic 'branch line ambience'. The tilly lamps unfortunately made the ceiling in particular very dirty; a black film quickly built up, which prompted one of the Cadeleigh signalmen to wash it down. This was successfully accomplished, but streaks ran down the paintwork on the walls, so he had to do these as well. A few days later the District Inspector happened to call in. A man of little outward emotion he clearly noticed the improvement and enquired rather menacingly who had done it. The signalman claimed responsibility and fully expected a 'dressing down' for not having asked permission, but nothing more was said. Then, a few days later, a team of workmen appeared to paint the ceiling — but not the walls!

Apart from his signalling functions the signalman had a number of other tasks to perform, except at Tiverton where operating the box was in itself a full-time occupation. Tiverton not only boasted a Grade 3 signalbox but also gas lamps on the station. The rural stations had been lit by fixed oil lamps until the late 1920s when they were replaced by hurricane lamps. At Bampton tall concrete posts were provided with a lamp-hoist to winch the lamp up to the top; there was even a scheme to install electric

lighting here, but this came to nothing. Elsewhere, hooked posts were provided — generally on the site of, or even as modifications to, the old oil lamps. The lamps were hung on these, and they would withstand quite strong winds for all the flimsy appearance of the arrangement. It was the signalman's job to prepare the lamps, not only for the station but also the halts under the supervision of that station. In mid-summer the lamp duty was not much of a chore, especially on the southern part of the line where the last train up had cleared Tiverton before dark. On Saturdays, and at Bampton during the week as well, trains were still running at dusk and after dark, and so lighting was necessary. In winter, of course, attending to the lamps was a time-consuming business. Other daily duties involved selling and collecting tickets when the station master was off duty and attending to other station business. Waiting rooms had to be swept out and the lavatories kept clean. On occasions the signalman would have to help out in the goods yard or with parcels traffic on the platform, and make visits to the halts to sweep out the waiting huts. Even re-edging the platforms with white-wash was a signalman's duty, albeit infrequent.

To many people, the signalman's existence in his box seemed a lonely one, but at the stations there was plenty to do and people about. Signalmen could always tell who was on duty in the next box by the way the bell codes were tapped out on the block instruments. Personal communication was possible by using the internal telephone. The telephone bell was very much softer than the block bells, and would ring at all the locations on the circuit whenever anybody used the phone. Everybody was conditioned to listen for their own code without consciously attending to every bell. The code was usually only repeated once before it was answered. A public telephone was installed in the station master's office.

To most of the valley men the railway was not just a job, more a way of life. Colleagues rarely met because of the very nature of the job, but when they did there was always much to talk about. The ganger or linesman would call into the signal box for a chat and a cup of tea, while the goods crew might look in for some boiling water for their 'billy' cans. The station master would look in from time to time, one of his duties in this respect being to tell the signalman of any notified goods or parcels traffic, and also to sign the 'Train Register Book'. Even the two signalmen who operated the box would only chat for a few minutes on the change-over between shifts but the box ran smoothly because of the unwritten rules that had grown up: the early turn cleaned the box and did the signal lamps; the late turn did the platform lamps and attended to the station.

Punctuality was another characteristic; the trains were delayed if a signalman was missing, and colleagues would be annoyed if a man was late in taking over the turn. It was extremely rare for a man ever to be late for the early turn even in some of the worst weather. In the heavy snow and ice of the winter of 1962-63, men got through the snow-filled sunken lanes to get to work on time. One man left home at 3 am in order to trudge the 4½ miles to work and open the box at 6 o'clock. Quite often the signalmen would rise very early in the morning to see what the weather was like before having another hour's snooze prior to setting off. Once in the box, and the first train had been accepted, the fire had to be made up in the stove in order to put the kettle on. Water was obtained from a hand-cranked pump at the rural stations, and once 'on', the kettle was rarely far from the boil. The difficulty of transporting milk meant that many men would drink tea without it, a feature by no means peculiar to the Exe Valley. Sandwiches were the staple food, but some men would occasionally indulge in a 'fry-up', and one had a particular penchant for the foil-wrapped 'dinner for one' meal! It was rare for signalmen to move far from their home area, and even if they later became relief signalmen, they always enjoyed a spell of duty on the branch. A number of men started their careers as porters on the mainline at stations like Silverton, Hele and Bradninch, Cullompton, Tiverton Junction and Wellington. Moving to the Signals Department, passing the necessary examinations and applying for vacant posts, men would work their way up either as porter-signalmen interspersed with duty at the tiny boxes like Rewe and Westcott (only open at peak times in the summer); or by learning the box on the branch and passing out as full signalmen. Certain patterns became recognisable. Men would begin on the branch and only move for promotion or to a box nearer home. From Cadeleigh and Thorverton men would move, if a vacancy arose, to Stoke Canon Crossing box on the mainline or even to Stoke Canon Junction box or to smaller boxes on the mainline. From these, men could move on to Tiverton, the busier mainline boxes or become relief signalmen. The signal boxes on the Devon & Somerset line tended to furnish men for Morebath Junction and Dulverton, while from the latter, men would move out to higher grade posts on the mainline. Station masters, by contrast, moved within a wider orbit, made possible by virtue of the fact that a house went with the job. Even so, migration was regional if not local.

Staff' in the late 1860s. The staff was made of wood, about 12 inches long and 3½ inches thick, with a thin metal loop at one end so as to allow it to be hung up on brackets in both the locomotive cab and signal box. A key-like attachment at the other end of the staff was provided for unlocking point levers. There was only the one staff for the branch, and a train could not enter the section unless it was in the possession of the driver. In this way only one train could be on the line at a time, and so the system was known as 'One Engine in Steam'. There was no signal box at Tiverton because with the branch engine shed at the Junction, and the first train of the day always working into Tiverton, the staff need only be kept in the signal box at the mainline. A disc-and-crossbar style fixed distant signal gave advanced warning of the station ahead.

The one engine in steam with train staff mode of operation continued until the end of the broad gauge on the branch. With the beginning of construction work on both the Tiverton and North Devon Railway and Exe Valley Railway from early 1880, there would soon be a need for adequate signalling and train control at Tiverton. A signal box was built at Tiverton to supervise the junction between the Dulverton and Tiverton Junction lines

---

BRITISH RAILWAYS
TRAIN STAFF TICKET

To the driver ....train from ....

to ....

You are authorised, after seeing the train staff for the section, to proceed through the ....

.....................................section and the train staff will follow.

Station ....

Signature of person in charge ....   Date ....

This ticket must be given up by the Driver to the person in charge of the train staff working at the place to which he is authorised to proceed, immediately on arrival.

Single Line Working

On single line railways a means of working had to be devised in order to prevent trains travelling towards each other on the same stretch of line at the same time. Signalling in the early days of the Great Western was somewhat primitive, with trains being given a fixed time allowance to get between control points — like stations, junctions or tunnels. These control points were manned by policemen, the fore-runners of signalmen (and in some areas signalmen were still referred to as 'bobbies'). These men had no way of contacting one another except by messages carried by the train crew. The problems and shortcomings of mainline operation, however, did not really affect the Tiverton Branch, opened in 1848. The trains ran on an out-and-back schedule, being allowed 12 minutes to complete the journey point-to-point. With this style of working there were no problems providing the timetable was followed rigidly. By the mid-1850s the electric telegraph system came into use, so that Tiverton Junction could inform the station staff at Tiverton when a train had left. Points were changed by a hand-operated capstan-style switch adjoining the point itself.

Train Staff

Although strictly speaking there was no great need for signalling on the Tiverton Branch, the Bristol & Exeter Railway Company replaced the telegraph system of communication with the 'Train

with both the old terminus station and the new 'through' station then under construction. With the narrowing of the Tiverton Branch on 29th June 1884, and the possibility of exchanging traffic with the Dulverton line, a new system of signalling came into being, namely, the 'Train Staff and Ticket System'. This was an extension of the idea of the simple train staff, and would allow greater flexibility of operation. The opening of the line through to Exeter in May 1885 necessitated the construction of a second signal box to cover the southern end of the single line into the station, the distance from the original box being too great for mechanical leverage. The box at the end of the 'down' platform was known as Tiverton South and that at the junction, Tiverton North. With double track between these two boxes there was no need for staff and ticket. The new staff had much the same overall dimensions as the old one, and in case the shape was not adequate identification, the names of the signal boxes at either end of the section were included on a name plate. With only one staff per section, a driver's possession of the staff gave him complete safety to travel through that section, but as the staff had always to be at that end of the section where it was next needed, the ticket could be used as authorisation instead. In the months following the line's opening, two trains left Exeter before one returned: 06.50 passenger and goods to Dulverton and 09.45 passenger to Tiverton. To overcome this problem, (2 trains, 1 staff), the Stoke

Canon signalman would fill out the details of the 06.50 on a printed paper ticket. The tickets were kept in locked boxes attached to the signalbox wall and which could only be opened with the key on the end of the staff, so signalmen at either end of the section could not issue tickets simultaneously. The ticket was only valid, however, when it was issued in conjunction with the staff; the driver of the 06.50 would be handed a ticket but only shown the staff by the signalman. The 09.45 train was booked to cross the returning 06.50 at Thorverton, and so the Stoke signalman would give the staff to the driver of the 'up' train. This would be handed in at Thorverton and then reissued to the driver of the 'down' train who would bring it back to Stoke Canon Junction. This system would work smoothly providing trains ran to the timetable and all the 'crossing arrangements' were printed in full. The signal boxes were in contact with each other by means of block instruments, a bell alerting a signalman to his neighbour's intentions and indicating whether an 'up' or 'down' train was 'in section'.

Electric Train Staff

Unless trains between signal boxes operated on an out-and-back principle, the staff and ticket system was not very efficient. In the late summer of 1907 the Webb-Thompson Electric Train Staff was introduced on the Exe Valley (the Tiverton Branch for the moment keeping the wooden staff and ticket system). The raised 'rings' on the staff were spaced so that they would fit corresponding grooves in the instrument to prevent them falling out; and as they would only fit that machine it was not possible for a staff to be wrongly placed. Just in case that was not clear, the names of the signal boxes were etched at the end of the staff. The easiest way to explain its operation is to examine the procedure followed when an 'up' train had left Exeter. As the train passed Cowley Bridge signal box the signalman would send 2 beats on the block instrument to Stoke Canon Junction (train entering section). The Stoke man would acknowledge this and then turn to the Webb-Thompson machine to gain permission to send the train on to Thorverton. On the right-hand side of the machine was the 'ringing key'. This was tapped down once, to gain the attention of the Thorverton signalman and ask him if the section (Stoke Canon to Thorverton) was clear. The Thorverton man would return the single beat, transmitted as a single ring on the bell fixed on the instrument shelf. The Stoke man would now tap out the code 3-1 (ordinary passenger train) which would be duly answered. On the last beat, the Thorverton man would hold down his ringing key which would release the electric locking device on the Stoke machine and allow the man there to draw out the staff. In the middle of the instrument was a dial containing a centrally pivoted vertical needle, which flicked every time the bell rang. When Thorverton held down his ringing key, the needle would lie obliquely, telling Stoke that he could draw a staff. There was a hooped carrier into which the staff could be fixed to make it easier for the fireman to catch, but he had to be careful as the staff could swing back. Generally, this was not a problem as the exchange usually took place when the train had stopped in the station (although a relief signalman at Thorverton was once hit on the head when accepting the staff at track level). Having drawn the staff, the pointer on the left of the machine was turned to 'up staff out', and this would be repeated on the display instrument in the keeper's hut at Fortescue level crossing. With the train booked to take only a few minutes to cover the distance from Cowley Bridge, the signalman at Stoke would have already set the road, i.e. changed the points to take the train from the 'up' main line to the branch platform line; a 20 m.p.h. speed limit subsisting on this route. The signals controlling entry to a single line section were interlocked with the staff machine; only when a staff had been drawn could the signalman pull off the signals.

With the staff out, the Stoke man pulled the appropriate levers, but not the distant signal due to the low speed limit, and the need to safely obtain the staff. As the train approached, the signalman held the staff upwards and outwards to be taken by the fireman. The fireman then had to show it to the driver as it gave him the right to occupy the line ahead. Even if the signal showed 'all clear', a train could not proceed unless the staff was on board. Having secured the staff on the footplate, the fireman could resume his duties and the train would begin to curve out over the meadows towards Brampford Speke. The Stoke signalman then sent a beat of 2 (train entering section) to Thorverton, who similarly replied. The Thorverton man would now have to ask 'line clear' of Cadeleigh; and so on up the line as the train progressed. On arrival at Thorverton, the fireman would give up the staff, which the signalman then replaced in his machine and gave the

Webb-Thompson electric train staff instrument.   *British Rail/OPC*

code of 2-1 (train out of section) back to Stoke Canon. The Stoke man acknowledged this, and turned his dial to 'staff in', entering the time of the clearance, as with all other times, in his Train Register Book. Once back in the machine, at either end of a section, the signals and machines were now locked. Only one staff could be drawn at a time, so that it was impossible to have two trains in a section at once.

Electric Token

In the summer of 1948 the electric key token system was introduced on to some sections of the Exe Valley. The token had actually been in use on other parts of the Great Western from the beginning of World War One. The key token was much more manageable for exchanging on a moving train: it was just under

8in. long and only weighed 8 ounces (being made of aluminium, although earlier ones were made of iron and consequently weighed more). At first the token was restricted to the Thorverton-Cadeleigh section, the staff being used elsewhere. On the 14th January 1953 the token was provided on the Tiverton-Bampton section, and in August 1957 on the Bampton-Morebath Junction section. The token had been used for some time on the Morebath Junction-Dulverton line, as token exchange apparatus had been installed on the Taunton-Barnstaple route to allow the exchange of tokens at higher speeds than the 15 m.p.h. permitted on the Exe Valley. When this apparatus was in use, signalmen could pull off the distant signal, otherwise it would be left 'on' to caution drivers to slow down. All tokens looked the same, and so had the names of the signal boxes at each end of the section stamped out on one of the faces, and also were painted in different colours. Thus the token from Thorverton to Cadeleigh was blue; from Tiverton to Bampton, yellow; and from Bampton to Morebath Junction, green.

The token machine operated in exactly the same way as the staff machine, except that the ringing key was replaced by a bell plunger. The token replaced the old train staff and ticket on the Tiverton Branch in 1932. Except for the occasional freight, the normal pattern of this line was still the 'out-and-back'. Although the Tivvy Bumper ran a shuttle service, with sometimes only a wait of 2 or 3 minutes before returning, the token had always to be given up to the signalman at Tiverton or Tiverton Junction, put back in the machine, cleared, and asked for, and drawn again. The locomotive crew were often busy taking on water, so that the travelling porter (there was no guard on this service) would take the token to the box. At Tiverton Junction the token was given back to the porter or handed to the crew on the platform, while at Tiverton it was sometimes handed up from track level. When the token was introduced on the Tiverton branch the catching hoop was very large, with the token placed in a leather pouch at the base. Very soon, however, this was replaced by a more substantial spring-clip holder. This device facilitated the installation of lineside token exchange apparatus, which was installed at Tiverton, Bampton, Morebath Junction and Dulverton. Situated on the left-hand side of the direction of travel, the first piece of equipment encountered was an arm projecting from a post, and backed by a square-mesh rope net. The fireman would hold the token-equipment out, hoop first, so that it engaged the arm pointing towards it. A few yards further on was a second post, bifurcated at the top; the arm pointing away from the track supported a lamp, while the shorter arm pointing towards the track held the token for the section about to be entered. The fireman would catch this with his arm in the usual way. The apparatus was most used at Morebath Junction, where trains were running through; the signalman could retrieve the token from the 'horn' once he had sent the 'train entering section' code to Dulverton. The equipment existed for 'up' trains only at Bampton, where the signal box was some yards from the station, and for 'down' trains only at Tiverton. In both places, however, the exchange was usually made on the platform, even when crossing trains. At Tiverton, a fireman or porter would go to the box to hand in or collect a staff or token during busy periods when the signalman was dealing with three trains at once.

One feature of single-line working on the Exe Valley was the 'up-line migration' of staffs and tokens on the Stoke Canon-Tiverton and Tiverton Junction sections. In most years up to 1946 the numbers of 'up' and 'down' trains balanced but then the last train up in the evening returned from Dulverton to Tiverton and then ran back to Exeter via Tiverton Junction. In addition to this, on Saturdays, a late train ran up to Tiverton or Bampton and also returned to Exeter via the Junction and main line. The last evening summer Sundays train up to Tiverton actually ran out to the Junction and back down the mainline as an advertised train. Each signalbox had a stock of staffs or tokens contained in their respective machines, but in the course of a week in mid-summer there would be an up-line migration of 8 staffs or tokens (this did not happen between Tiverton and Morebath Junction because the trains were 'balanced'). It was one of the jobs of the lineman to remedy this imbalance every now and again. The Exe Valley lineman was based at Dulverton, and he would travel down the branch by train to attend to the matter. He had a key which would unlock the instrument and allow him to remove the surplus tokens/staffs and take them to the respective signalboxes. The rule was that however many he removed, it had to be an odd number, never even.

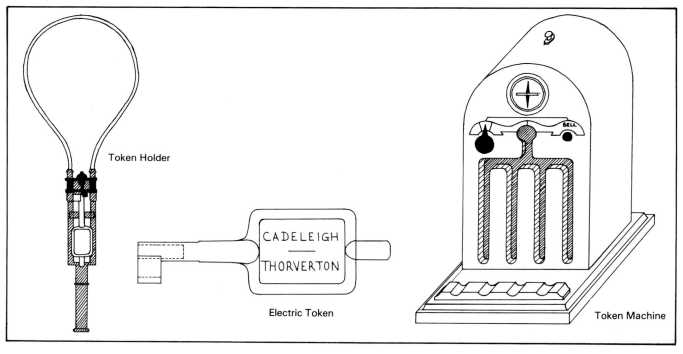

Token Holder

Electric Token

CADELEIGH
—
THORVERTON

Token Machine

The Crossing of Trains

One of the most interesting maneouvres to watch was the passing of trains at a crossing station. Following a spell of quiescence, there would be a flurry of activity before quiet once again descended on the scene. The procedure followed will be described for Thorverton.

Because of the curve of the track, southbound trains were concealed from the signalman's view by the down-side station buildings. 'Up' trains, by contrast, could be seen a long way off as whisps of steam came out of the trees at Nether Exe, and the train came into view on the long straight that led into the station. For this reason, 'down' trains were generally timetabled to arrive first — providing the train was on time! To combat the danger of over-running the starting signal, it was not permitted to signal the 'down' train straight off the single line into the platform. The points would be set for both trains to enter their respective platforms, but the home signals were left 'on'. With both trains 'on line', the first the signalman knew of the 'down' train's impending arrival was a shrill whistle as the train rumbled over the river bridge near the mill. The signalman would be able to see the final approach to the home signal and, if the 'up' train was still a long way off, he would wait until the 'down' train had slowed to a crawl and then pull over the signal lever. Opening the regulator, the driver would bring his train in over the facing points, mill siding connection and road bridge and into the platform. On 'down' auto-trains the locomotive was propelling its coaches and so was a long way from the signal box. Meantime, the signalman

Above: No. 1451 on a 'down' train at Thorverton waits for No. 1450 to arrive with an Exeter–Tiverton train. Signalman Bill Mears waits by the alcove, while No. 1451's fireman looks out of the cab ready to exchange staff and token when the two locomotives are alongside. 13th April 1963.

Peter W. Gray

Right: This time the 'up' train has arrived first, with the southbound locomotive running in with decidedly 'foreign' stock on 17th September 1963.

R. A. Lumber

having lowered the home signal, would leave the box and walk down to where the engine would stop. Collecting the token from the fireman, he would return to the box, put back the 'down' home to 'on' and change the points to set the road for the 'up' train. The token would be replaced in the machine and 2-1 tapped out to Cadeleigh. On acknowledgement, 1 and then 3-1 would follow to allow the Thorverton man to immediately redraw the token for the 'up' train. Once obtained, the 'up' home, starting and advanced starting signals would all be pulled 'off'. Crossing over the line to the platform, the signalman would collect the Stoke Canon staff from the fireman of the 'up' train and give him the Cadeleigh token; then back to the box to repeat the procedure followed for the 'down' train. With the 'down' starting and advanced starting signals 'off', the staff had finally to be taken to the fireman of the 'down' train before it could continue on its journey to Exeter. As soon as both trains pulled past their respective starting signals and moved out on to the single line section, the bell code of 2 beats was sent to the appropriate boxes, and the signals returned to 'on' once the train had passed them. All the times were then logged in the Train Register Book.

This operation sounds fine in theory, but in practice could be a far from leisurely activity. Trains had a habit of arriving simultaneously, so that the 'first to the (signal) post' was allowed to draw in first. By the time the signalman returned to his box from the 'down' locomotive, the 'up' train was already well on its way, and so the 'train entering section' code would be somewhat after the event! Some firemen exchanged the token/staff between the cabs when the locomotives stopped alongside each other. If a passenger and freight had to cross, the passenger was given precedence, the freight being held at the home signal.

An illustration of the terror a District Inspector could inspire in a young signalman was illustrated when the said Inspector was travelling up to Tiverton on the 10.25 from Exeter whilst a pannier was performing its shunting duties at Thorverton at an unusually slow pace. Having propelled a number of empty grain wagons out on to the Cadeleigh section to pick up the brake van — the 'down' home showing 'off' — the two-coach 'up' auto-train appeared and 'whistled up'. The Stoke Canon signalman had seen the Inspector on the train, and telephoned up the line — the Inspector was in charge of signalmen and porters, and it would not do to have his train delayed by shunting! The goods guard seemed to take an age to hook up the brake van, and as his train was straddling the points the signalman could not pull off the 'up' home signal. As the Dulverton train whistled again — in that insistent way they had — the freight began to move, albeit painfully slowly. As soon as the brake van was clear of the points, the 'down' home went back and the 'up' home lever was pulled over — just as the auto-train was 'blowing-up' for the third time and about to stop. Nothing was said about the incident afterwards, but at the time the crew of the freight thought the signalman's predicament funny.

Facing Points

When making reference to changing the points it has to be borne in mind that where single lines led into double track stretches at stations or directly face into sidings or loops, a system of securely locking the points has to be employed. The passage of a train over facing points might cause the point blade to move as the train passed over it, or it might not have been quite firmly closed up beforehand (a piece of ballast or something being lodged against

Above: The signalman holds the token aloft for the fireman of the 14.50 to Tiverton Junction on 26th September 1964. *R. A. Lumber*

The fireman collects the Train Staff for the section to Cadeleigh from the lineside apparatus outside Tiverton signal box. The tracks and hut-cum-store for the Ganger's trolley are clearly seen in the left-hand foreground. *Eric Chorley*

the rail). To prevent this, and to interlock with the signal covering the point, the 'facing point lock' was employed. The locking mechanism was in fact a square-sectioned metal bolt which fitted into a matching notch cut in the transverse bar on the point blade, and thus effectively wedged the blade tight up against the outside rail. When an 'up' train was approaching Thorverton the point was arranged to run through to the 'up' platform, but the facing point lock lever had to be pulled over in the frame to lock the point. Unless this lever was pulled (No. 7 on the signalling diagram) the home signal and yard disc signal could not be moved. This interaction between points and signals is known as 'detection', and is achieved by means of slide bars. The operation of slide bars is best shown diagrammatcially, suffice it to say that these small, carefully machined pieces of metal were extremely effective in preventing signals being lowered to 'clear' when the points were wrongly set. Sometimes the points were not switched right over, so that the grooves in the slide bar did not have a perfect alignment, and thus the facing point lock could not be pulled. Alternatively, a facing point lock might not register exactly, and the signal lever could not be pulled right over in the frame. When this happened, the offending lever would be returned in the frame and pulled again — usually with some vigour — and then the signal lever would be tried again. If a facing point lock was particularly sticky, it might have to be pushed and pulled three or four times before the signal would respond. Tiverton had a double-bolted facing point lock, locking points immediately on either side of it: on the station side was the point leading into the 'down' bay and dock road, and on the junction side was a crossover leading to the 'up' main line. The bay line point was facing to both 'down' valley trains and the Tivvy Bumper working into the bay. The crossover, 'trailing' to the valley train was facing the Tivvy Bumper as it ran back out of the bay to rejoin its own branch.

Thus both points had to be locked whichever way trains ran over them. This lock was the dreaded lever number 19; so much else was interlocked with it that its malfunction caused problems (it locked 15 other levers!). As one Tiverton signalman said: 'If something won't go; it'll be No. 19'. If there was a problem with points and point-rodding the ganger would be notified to attend to it, while the correct operation of signal instruments, cables, signals and telegraph wires was the province of the linesman, who usually worked with an assistant.

Trap and Catch Points

The points assemblage at Morebath Junction contained both trap points and sprung run-back catch points. The trap points here protected the exits from the loops to the single line sections of the Taunton-Barnstaple line. The trap point lever together with its facing point lock lever had to be pulled before the starting signal could give the 'all clear'. The catch points were not operated by levers, and were in a 'trailing' direction. They were set against the train, but as the wheels passed over them, the point blade would be forced over, only to spring back afterwards. Their function at Morebath Junction was to 'catch' runaway wagons before they could roll back down 1:66 gradients either to Morebath or Bampton, and they were situated just inside the loops.

Ganger's Occupation Key

One vital piece of single-line signalling practice involved the Ganger's Occupation key. The ganger had to make regular checks along the branch and sometimes undertake lengthy work somewhere between signal boxes. He used a small, noisy petrol driven inspection trolley, while the full Tiverton gang used the large trolley. These men had to have safe occupation of the line and at

The Ganger Ganger inserting the occupation key into the instrument housed in the Telephone Hut, while his men lift the trolley on to the grass verge.
British Railways/OPC

The Bampton Gang before the First World War. The Ganger, Alfred Saffin, is on the extreme right, his team consisting of (from left to right): Jim Wilton, Bill Gadd and Jim Hancock. In the centre is Mr. White, one of the station staff. *R. J. Kingdon collection*

The Tiverton Gang's trolley was kept in the corrugated hut next to the signal box. *British Rail/OPC*

the same time minimise disruption to service schedules. This was assured by the Occupation Key system, which was similar in principle to the Electric Token but rather more complicated in operation. Two instruments were needed to operate the system: the Ganger's Key Instrument and the Control Instrument. Every signal box possessed the former, as it was designed to lock the block instrument on each section. In order to understand its mode of operation, it is necessary to know the patterns of movement on the Exe Valley. The stretch of line from Stoke Canon Junction to, and including, Bampton was serviced by the gang from Tiverton (the hemi-cylindrical corrugated iron shed next to the signal box housed the ganger's trolley). The wooden marker board delimiting their boundary was just beyond the points at the north end of Bampton station. The Bampton-Morebath Junction stretch was worked by the Dulverton gang.

Before post-war rationalisation, Bampton had its own gang, who came under the Barnstaple Branch administration, and worked from Morebath Junction almost to the junction points at Tiverton. The Tiverton Gang was also responsible for the Tiverton Branch (excluding the Junction). The operation is best explained by describing a journey from Thorverton to Cadeleigh. Both Thorverton and Cadeleigh had a key instrument, (Thorverton alone possessing a Control Instrument) but there was only one brass key for this section, and this was presently locked into the machine at Thorverton. In order to obtain the key, the Thorverton signalman would have to have the co-operation of the Cadeleigh man. A phone call would be made to the latter, in which he would be asked to 'hold down' on the plunger of the Electric Token Instrument (i.e. keep the plunger pushed in). This action unlocked the 'slides' on the Control Instrument. The slides were square-sectioned horizontal bars with handles on the end. Thorverton now pulled out the slides as far as they would go, which unlocked the Key Instrument but locked the Control. It was now possible for the Occupation Key to be taken out of the instrument and given to the ganger. By turning and removing the key, the similar instrument at Cadeleigh was locked as were the token machines at both stations. In this way it was impossible for a token to be drawn and a train enter the section while it was occupied by the ganger. The time of this operation was entered in the Train Register Book as for a normal train. On reaching Cadeleigh the ganger would insert and turn the key in the Key Instrument there and ring up Thorverton to inform him of that. By replacing the key, the slides at Thorverton were now unlocked and would be pushed back in. The token machine was then tested to ensure it was working correctly, and the time entered in the register.

Sometimes the ganger would want to stop en route, and so intermediate telephone huts were positioned to allow him to clear the section. These were spaced at roughly one mile intervals on the Exe Valley. The large white box fixed to a telegraph pole contained a Key Instrument and a telephone to the adjacent signal boxes. The ganger would insert the key — so unlocking the token instruments — and ring up Thorverton to inform him of his action and also say where he was (so that the signalman could warn a train crew to look out for him working on the line). The slides were pushed back in and the token instrument tested. When the ganger was ready to move on, he needed to get the key out of the instrument, the key having been locked in. He would ring up Thorverton who in turn would ring up Cadeleigh to ask the man there once again to 'hold down' on the token instrument. This time only the left-hand slide was pulled out at Thorverton (the slide labelled 'Control') and the button on the machine pressed firmly. This latter action unlocked the Key Instrument in the lineside hut and allowed the ganger to withdraw the key. This procedure happened every time the ganger stopped for more than a few minutes at a new site. Before the key was replaced, the

trolley had to be lifted off the track; in some locations rails set at right angles to the running line were provided. The light petrol trolley could be manhandled by the ganger alone, while the whole gang would be needed to lift off the big trolley. On arrival at Cadeleigh, the same clearing sequence was followed to allow Thorverton to replace the single slide.

For various reasons, the gang would usually need to be working in between telephone huts. On these occasions the key was inserted at the nearest hut and the men would then move on to the site. Sometimes the ganger forgot to replace the key, and the problems this caused can be imagined! On one occasion the men were cutting back long grass in a cutting between Cadeleigh and West Exe, and had not replaced the key. The Cadeleigh signalman did not know exactly where they were, and was becoming anxious because an 'up' train was due and the staff instrument to Tiverton was locked. When Thorverton asked 'line clear' for the train, some sort of action was required. Fortunately the Cadeleigh signalman had come to work on his motorbike, so the station master said he would man the box while the signalman tried to find the gang and replace the key. For most of the journey between Cadeleigh and West Exe, road and railway ran close together, and the men were spotted on the trackside near Ashley Court. Profound apologies were uttered and the ganger went back to the telephone hut. By this time the train had arrived at Cadeleigh, but it was only delayed for a few minutes before the staff was unlocked from the machine and drawn by the station master. The train heading north then passed the signalman driving south!

MOTOR TROLLEY SYSTEM OF MAINTENANCE

The maintenance of the sections of line shewn is under the control of Engineering Gangs with headquarters at Tiverton and Bampton. The Bampton Gang will be responsible for the section 0m. 0ch. to 8m. 36½ch; the Tiverton Gang for the section 8m. 36½ch. to 19m. 20ch.

Small petrol motor driven inspection cars are provided for the use of the Gangers. Each Gang is provided with one petrol motor driven trolley, capable of carrying men, with a small quantity of tools. A trailer is also available for conveyance of materials and tools.

In order to avoid sending out Handsignalmen in accordance with Rules 215 and 217, when it is necessary to run trolleys along the line, or to carry out operations which would render the running of trains unsafe, telephones and Occupation Key Boxes are fixed at places named below.

SECTION MOREBATH JUNCTION TO BAMPTON
No key boxes. Standard working will apply.

SECTION BAMPTON TO TIVERTON

$ Group No. 11 (One Key)

Bampton Signal Box:	m.	ch.
Key Box No. 41	2	48¾
Key Box No. 42	3	47¾
Key Box No. 43	4	60½
Key Box No. 44	5	55¾
Key Box No. 45	6	67
Key Box No. 46	7	62¼

Telephones in this Group communicate with Bampton. $

SECTION CADELEIGH TO THORVERTON

* Group No. 3 (One Key)

Cadeleigh Signal Box:	m.	ch.
Key Box No. 10	13	39
Key Box No. 11	14	20
Key Box No. 12	14	75
Key Box No. 13	15	60
Thorverton Signal Box.		

SECTION TIVERTON TO CADELEIGH
(For Group No. 1 see Tiverton Branch)
* Group No. 2 (One Key)

Tiverton Signal Box:	m.	ch.
Key Box No. 6	9	19
Key Box No. 7	10	10
Key Box No. 8	11	1
Key Box No. 9	11	70
Cadeleigh Signal Box.		

SECTION THORVERTON TO STOKE CANON

* Group No. 4 (One Key)

Thorverton Signal Box:	m.	ch.
Key Box No. 14	17	42
Key Box No. 15	18	40
Stoke Canon Junction Signal Box.		

$ Part of Barnstaple Branch maintenance.
* Telephones in Group 2 communicate with Tiverton; 3 & 4 with Thorverton.

The Signals

By the time the Exe Valley line opened, Great Western signalling practice was more or less established uniformly throughout the system, although minor changes continued to be made. Except at Stoke Canon, Tiverton and Dulverton, there were no radical changes to track layouts on the branch but rather a series of small amendments: a siding removed or lengthened, facing points realigned, and signals renewed or repositioned. The only exception to the localised nature of change came with the role and style of distant signals and ground signals. When the branch opened, all the distant signals were of the 'working' variety. When the arm was in the horizontal position at 'caution', drivers could expect to pull up at the 'stop' signal ahead. If the arm was down in the 'all clear' position, then all stop signals ahead were 'off' and the train had a clear run. The signals themselves were the standard square-post design with a 'fishtail' notch on the free end of the arm. The arm was painted red, with a vertical white

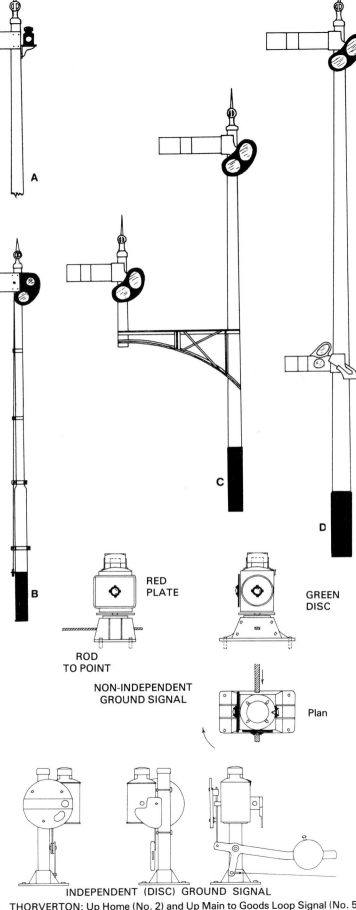

stripe on the front and showed a red light when at 'caution' and nothing at all when at 'all clear' (implying no problem ahead at night as no light would be seen). A solid spectacle disc would move over the lamp when the arm moved, so obscuring the light. The backlight (facing the signal box) was green, but was obscured by a blinker plate when the arm was 'off'. The lever in the signal box controlling the distant was green in colour. At night, it was not possible to identify the difference between the red light of a stop signal at 'stop' and a distant signal at 'caution'. Although a green light was added for 'all clear' from the early 1890s (which meant that the backlight was changed from green to white), this anomaly remained. In the early days on the Exe Valley the speed restrictions imposed on the trains approaching stations were severe, 10 m.p.h., and as low as 5 m.p.h. over the junction at Tiverton. This, together with the need to slow down for staff-exchanging purposes or even to stop at a station, made the purpose of working distants somewhat superfluous. By 1907 all the distants had been fixed at 'caution', with the exception of the level crossings. The signals retained their red arms and lights right up until about 1930 when they were repainted in their familiar colour of yellow with a black 'V' on the face of the arm, and white with a black 'V' on the back. The filter on the fixed distants was changed to amber while an amber spectacle replaced the red at the 'working' crossing distants. The levers were changed from green to yellow.

Another change was in the nature of ground signals, although this time the old structures managed to survive in a few places. Ground signals were widely employed to control movements to and from sidings, and thus needed to be distinguished from the semaphore types on the running lines. In the 19th century all the ground signals on the branch were of the non-independent type, that is they were connected directly to the point and would change when it changed. The signal consisted of a lamp case with two coloured metal plates attached to, and set on, the case at right angles to each other. The 'stop' plate was a red-painted rectangle with a small red lamp showing in the centre, and this faced the train when the points were against it (and a white backlight showed in the opposite direction). When the point was changed a rod attached to the point blade moved laterally and swivelled the signal through 90 degrees, turning a green disc with green centre light towards the train, giving it the 'all clear'.

The ubiquitous independent disc signal found its way on to the mainline earlier this century, but only penetrated the Exe Valley when signalling alterations were made. Indeed, at Bampton with its noted lack of ground signals, the three original swivelling

A FIXED DISTANT: found at all Branch Stations and Junctions
B WORKING DISTANT: restricted to controlled Level Crossings
C THORVERTON: Up Home (No. 2) and Up Main to Goods Loop Signal (No. 5)
D TIVERTON: Down Main Home with co-acting arm (No. 40)

RED PLATE

GREEN DISC

ROD TO POINT

NON-INDEPENDENT GROUND SIGNAL

Plan

INDEPENDENT (DISC) GROUND SIGNAL

Attractive wooden square post signal with wooden arm and weighted metal spectacle plate. Stoke Canon's branch platform 'up' starting signal.　*W. L. Underhay*

discs remained until the line's closure. Thorverton possessed an unusual double ground signal of this type, also right up to closure. This had two red and two green faces and controlled entry to and exit from the goods shed loop line at the north end of the station. The independent ground signals comprised a white disc with horizontal red bar and red light on the face and a white backlight. When the signal was changed to 'clear', the whole disc rotated until the red bar became oblique (sloping down to the left when viewed from the front). A small green light would show forwards, and a blinker plate would revolve at the back to obscure the backlight. These signals, known as 'dolls' to valley signalmen, were worked by their own lever in the signal box, although the slide-bar arrangement interlocking with the point prevented them from showing 'clear' if the points had not been set.

Junction bracket signals, Tiverton. Modern steel tubular posts with pressed steel arms (and integrated spectacle plate).　*D. Vaughan Davies*

There were none of the gantries of signals or multi-directional signals on the branch that one would find on the main line, but each station had its own assemblage of signals which identified that particular location. Morebath Junction kept its elegant and superbly-proportioned wooden square-post signals; and also a signal frame (of McKenzie & Holland manufacture) in which the levers came so far over when pulled that if a man of average height took up the usual stance, the lever-tops came over into the stomach! Bampton also retained all but one of its square-post signals, the 'down' distant and 'down' home signals being sited on the tops of deep cuttings in order to give better visibility. The possession of outer and inner home signals on the 'up' line, and starting, intermediate starting and advanced starting signals on the 'down' line marked out the layout at Bampton as different from the other two rural crossing stations. Cadeleigh was unique in that all the signals, including the distants, were renewed with modern tubular steel posts and pressed steel arms (between 1954 and 1958). At Thorverton all but two 'stop' signals were replaced with tubular types, but the two wooden ones that remained had eventful lives! Both were short, square-post pine signals of considerable age. The 'down' home signal went 'walk about' in the late 1950s when it was moved to the other side of the track to give better visibility, but then obscured the 'up' advanced starter and so a year or so later was moved back. The 'down' advanced starter was bought for firewood after the line's closure and on close examination was seen to have the inscription 'Second hand, 1917'.

Some of the signals at Tiverton deserve closer attention as they were out of the ordinary for this particular branch line. The 'down main outer home' signal (i.e. the first one reached from Bampton) had a 'co-acting arm'. The line approached Blundells Road bridge on a sharp curve from the Cowleymoor district of Tiverton. As this signal protected the junction with the Tiverton Branch, it was important for it to be visible some way from the bridge, while the bridge itself would obscure some signal of normal height. Thus the signal post was extremely tall. As a train approached the bridge it would be increasingly difficult for the driver to look up at the arm (especially from his compartment in an auto-coach), and so another 'repeating' arm was positioned

Tiverton's 'down' starting signal with 'calling-on'-style shunt signal beneath.

M. J. Fox;
courtesy Tiverton Museum

much lower down the post; indeed, it could be seen as the train went under the bridge. A rod connected the two arms, so that when the signal wire pulled off the one, the other co-acted with it. The height of the post — nearly 40 feet — warranted a lamp-hoist to obviate an unpleasant ladder climb, although the lineman would still have to venture to the top on occasions. On the same side of the track (wrong-sided) and hard up against the bridge abutment was the 'up main advanced starting' signal. This was another square-post structure, and beneath the main arm was a subsidiary shunting signal arm: a 3-foot feature with a large white letter 'S' fixed to it. A driver was allowed to pass the signal when 'off' for shunting purposes only, usually to draw wagons out of, or shunt them back into, the up-side sidings. He would not need the Bampton token to move on to the single line, and neither was the signal locked by the token instrument, but under no circumstances could he take his train on to the next station. (A similar signal existed beneath the 'down' advanced starter at Cadeleigh, but both arms were removed in December 1954). Controlling the junction points at Tiverton were three junction-bracket signals;

all modern tubular constructions put up in February 1958 as replacements for the earlier wooden versions. At the departure end of the 'down' platform was the 'down' starting signal and beneath it the short arm of a 'calling-on' signal (both signal arms were renewed in August 1956, but unusually the original wooden post was retained). The enamelled short arm had a red-white-red alternation of horizontal stripes (when in the 'on' position). When pulled 'off' a white pane with a black letter 'S' was revealed; this was illuminated from the back at night. This was the same as the 'shunt' signal discussed above, and was not locked by the Cadeleigh staff instrument. As this signal was 190 yards from the signal box and unsighted, it had an arm-style repeater to tell the signalman that it had responded correctly (the 'up' home likewise). The centrally pivoted signals shown in one of the track plans disappeared with the alterations and resignalling of Tiverton in 1912. They were used because of the limited visibility a normal signal would impart on a tight curve, while the distants were a useful guide to the state of the road ahead.

Non-independent ground signal; north end of Thorverton goods yard.

R. A. Lumber

Chapter Nine

Special Workings

Running parallel with the Great Western main line from the Devon-Somerset border to Exeter, the Exe Valley was a useful emergency diversionary route. Of all the most usual causes of diversions — breakdowns, engineering work and flooding — it was the latter which most frequently pressed the Exe Valley route into service. The main problem area was in the Culm Valley between Cullompton and Stoke Canon, a distance of 10 miles in which railway and river kept close company. In normal conditions the Culm was a placid river meandering its way in a shallow channel through a flat-floored floodplain. The Culm and its tributaries rise on the high ground on the Somerset-Devon border, which includes the Blackdown Hills. Heavy rain in this area can cause the river level to rise very quickly, so that the shallow channel combined with adjoining level ground is a recipe for flooding. The first place where the railway was affected was generally in the vicinity of Hele and Bradninch station. In steam days, trains could splash their way through a few feet of flood-water, but sometimes the floodwater was over the tops of the platforms at Hele, and it was not safe to attempt to get through (especially as the ballast had a habit of washing away). It was on these occasions that trains were directed via the Exe Valley. Northbound trains from Exeter simply took the Exe Valley branch at Stoke Canon and could run without any problems to Tiverton, where they would take the Tiverton Branch to Tiverton Junction, running straight out on to the 'up' main line again at the north end of the station. For southbound trains the journey was not as easy via Tiverton Junction because of the need to reverse from the 'down' main line across to the Tiverton Branch platform. Consequently, provision was made for 'down' trains to work via Dulverton if necessary as this would remove the need for

shunting a train full of passengers. Trains would work over from Taunton into the 'down' platform at Dulverton and another locomotive or locomotives would couple to the other end of the train and haul it off down the branch.

These diversionary arrangements sound fine in theory, but take no account of the restrictions on motive power on the branch. With a route availability classification of 'Yellow', the heavier more powerful locomotives normally rostered for main line express passenger work were not able to use the line. Under normal operating conditions the only engines permitted on the Exe Valley were the 14XX and 58XX classes of 0-4-2 tanks; all the 0-6-0 pannier tanks (except the 94XX and 15XX classes); the 22XX class of 0-6-0 tender engines; and the 45XX class of 2-6-2 tanks (the small prairies). The small prairies and 57XX panniers were the most powerful locomotives regularly at work on the branch, being classified as 'C' on the Great Western power scale (which went from 'Unclassified' through A to E with E being the most powerful). These engines, singly, were under-powered for heavy passenger work, and so special emergency regulations were applied to meet the problem. Under these exceptional circumstances the large prairies were allowed on the branch, even though they possessed the higher 'Blue' route avail-ability coding. These engines, however, had to work unassisted. Alternatively, the 43XX moguls could be used; also 'Blue' engines. If double-heading was necessary then either two small prairies would be assigned or, on the heaviest trains, a mogul and a small prairie, providing the mogul acted as pilot. These loco-motives were substituted at Exeter or Taunton.

The last time the Exe Valley was called on before its closure was on Saturday October 1st 1960. The Culm burst its banks at

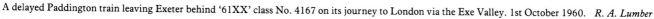

A delayed Paddington train leaving Exeter behind '61XX' class No. 4167 on its journey to London via the Exe Valley. 1st October 1960. *R. A. Lumber*

Hele in the early afternoon and overwhelmed the tracks to such a depth that the line was declared unsafe. Moguls and large prairies were quickly pressed into service, but this took time to organise and trains began to queue up at Exeter and Taunton. Once again the branch played host to such illustrious named expresses as the 'Torbay Express' and 'The Royal Duchy', as well as north of England and South Wales expresses, while its own services were greatly disrupted. By early evening one track through Hele was brought back into use, and trains were switched back to the main line. Ironically, the Exe Valley having done its bit, now suffered its own flood problem when the River Lowman burst its banks at Tiverton and covered the station and yard in a two-foot deep sheet of water.

plain and both Western and Southern tracks. By late morning trains were still managing to get through, albeit moving cautiously, but the water level continued to rise and even flooded St. David's station to a depth of almost three feet. The first Exe Valley train of the afternoon approached the junction warily, but with the ballast giving way beneath the train and with the imminent danger of water washing on to the footplate, the driver decided that the best course of action was to expeditiously reverse!

On December 4th serious flooding occurred again, once more washing away ballast at Cowley Bridge and flooding St. David's station. It is hardly surprising that a massive flood prevention scheme was born of this experience.

Cowley Bridge Junction under water. October 1960.   *F. H. Clarke; courtesy Tiverton Museum*

The autumn of 1960 was exceptionally wet. The floods of October 1st were repeated later in the month, this time further south, at Cowley Bridge (there had already been trouble here, when on September 30th the Southern Railway's river bridge had been swept away, leaving the tracks draped over a yawning gap). Serious flooding at this location affected Valley trains as well as those on the main line, and was one of the rare causes of severe disruption of services on the branch. Apart from being a railway junction, Cowley Bridge is also a junction of two rivers: the Exe and Creedy. As both rivers originate in high rainfall areas one or the other, or both, were liable to periodic flooding. On Thursday 27th October the rivers burst their banks, covering the flood-

The Exe Valley line was of much value as a diversionary route during World War Two. The main line from London and the north to Plymouth was to be kept clear for essential military traffic, with through passenger expresses severely reduced. Local services continued much as usual, with eight 'up' Exe Valley trains leaving Exeter on Mondays to Fridays and an extra one on Saturdays (and an equal number returning). Non-military freight, parcels and some mainline passenger trains were sent along the branch, working right through to Dulverton and then on to Taunton so as to clear the entire main line section. The increased traffic in the valley, together with the unpredictable and irregular nature of wartime traffic, meant that from the end of 1939 until well into 1945 all the Exe Valley signal boxes were manned continuously.

The branch did not suffer any direct damage by enemy action, although in the Baedecker raids of May 1942 the Riverside yard in Exeter was bombed, with an air raid shelter there taking a direct hit. In 1944 a delayed-action bomb was dropped on the mainline at Hele, and caused all traffic to be diverted on to the valley. This caused a unique event at Bampton when the 'up' and 'down' 'Cornish Riviera' expresses crossed. Both trains had a Churchward 2-6-0 as pilot with a small prairie as the train engine.

Royal Train

Following the coronation of 1953, there was to be a royal visit to Exeter and district, which involved the overnight stabling of the Royal Train. For security reasons it was thought better to keep the train outside Exeter. Thorverton was chosen as the venue.

Shortly before the visit, the Exeter Divisional Office learned that there was a chance that Prince Philip would sleep on the train. Administrative wheels quickly began turning. The station master at Thorverton was given a week's leave, and an inspector was deputed to look after the station — higher status to befit the occasion! The man had to be on duty all night during the train's visit. Arrangements were made to clip all the points at the station so that no other train could possibly run into the Royal Train. It was realised with horror that the station needed a lick of paint, and so a team of painters was dispatched poste-haste. A feverish session began of painting anything that would be visible from the train. Even the point rodding between the platforms was painted — in silver! With the 'down' platform wooden fencing looking quite respectable, a start was made on the 'up' platform, beginning at the Exeter end. Word then came through that the Prince would not after all be sleeping on the train. By this time, the painters were well along the platform; indeed, they had done the southern half and had started on the final section beyond the alcove. The order came to stop immediately and return to Exeter. This they promptly did and left behind a prepared but unpainted section of fencing that remained in that condition until the line closed!

Excursions

Before World War Two, Sunday School outings by train were a feature of a town or village's calendar. One such was organised by St. Paul's Church, Tiverton, for Thursday 27th June 1912. The outing, by special train to Teignmouth, in itself was nothing out of the ordinary, except for the emphatic request printed at the foot of the publicity hand-bill. Train times are given, complete with detailed instructions of how, when and where to assemble; from whom to purchase tickets; and the various costs for intending travellers. Then comes the stricture that, 'it is particularly requested that children and friends will not purchase any shellfish during the day'. A train of swaying non-corridor coaches full of children eating shellfish on top of sweets and other seaside delights does not bear thinking about!

ST. PAUL'S, TIVERTON.

Sunday School Excursion,

THURSDAY, JUNE 27TH, 1912.

SPECIAL TRAIN

Leaves Tiverton 9.10 a.m.   Leaves Teignmouth 7.45 p.m.

SCHOLARS OVER 14	1/6
SCHOLARS UNDER 14	1/-
*PARENTS' & VISITORS' TICKETS	3/-
(including Tea).	
*MEMBERS OF CHOIR *MEN'S BIBLE CLASS *MOTHERS' MEETING	2/6 each (including Tea).

*These Tickets are limited in number and should be purchased not later than TUESDAY, JUNE 25th, from the Churchwardens, the Verger, and Teachers.

TIVERTON

St. Paul's Sunday School

TREAT

At TEIGNMOUTH, June 27th, 1912.

DIRECTIONS.

Children to assemble in their respective Schools at 8.30 a.m.

The Children and Adults are to enter the Station by the doorway adjoining Wilcombe Road, and to be at the Station not later than 8.50 a.m.

That part of the Ticket marked "Railway" will be collected in the Train at the Station, the other part at the Tea Table.

Children will not be permitted to go out in a boat without permission from their Teacher or Superintendent, and in no case without a proper boatman.

The Teachers and Children will meet at the Pier Entrance at 3.45 o'clock. Tea at 4 o'clock, on the Pier.

The Tea for Teachers, Visitors, and Bible Classes will be at 5 o'clock, on the Pier.

Teachers and Scholars to meet at the Pier at 7.25 p.m. punctually, to proceed to the Station.

Parents and Visitors to be at the Station at 7.35 p.m.

☞ It is particularly requested that Children and Friends will not purchase any Shell-Fish during the day.

Poster; St. Paul's Church Outing. 1912.   *Tiverton Museum*

Having travelled up the Exe Valley from Exeter, an enthusiasts' 'special' starts away from Tiverton, hauled by two '45XX' class prairies. Note the track-side token-exchange apparatus. 24th February 1963.   *H. Ballantyne*

At Tiverton Junction the special was taken over by A4 pacific No. 60022 *Mallard*, a rare bird indeed on GW tracks!   *H. Ballantyne*

Chapter Ten

Epilogue

As soon as the closure of the line was announced, rail tours were arranged so that enthusiasts could say farewell; regular users, though equally nostalgic, had to give urgent thought as to how they would travel in future. Photographers became increasingly prominent at the stations at weekends, in their endeavour to capture memories of a line which so many held in affection.

The last day of passenger operation, Saturday 5th October 1963, brought an unpleasant surprise for the people along the line who turned out in their hundreds during the day. The 14XX tanks with their auto-coaches were replaced by Class 22 diesels with ordinary coaching stock. The last train, the 22.05 from Exeter to Bampton, had six corridor coaches to accommodate the expected crowds, and was booked to work back as a 'special' down the Valley instead of running as Empty Carriage Stock to Exeter via Tiverton Junction. The normal timetable was altered to enable the last train to call at all the halts in addition to the stations. All week, people had been taking their last ride up the Valley, and all the trains on Saturday had been busy.

The last train, diesel hauled or not, was going to get a good send-off. As the train stopped at each station and halt more people boarded. A number of passengers got on at Up Exe Halt, some of whom danced 'The Twist' while others accompanied them on guitars. Crowds of people piled in at West Exe Halt some of whom proceeded to hang toilet roll streamers from the carriage ventilator windows. The 'up' platform at Tiverton

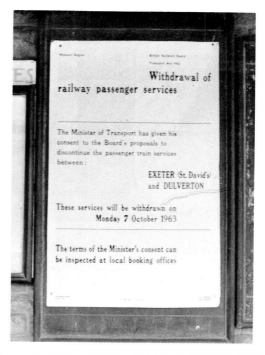

Literally the 'End of the Line'. '43XX' class mogul No. 7337 on the 11.25 ex-Taunton passes the former connection with the Exe Valley line at Morebath Junction on 3rd August 1964.

R. A. Lumber

Up Exe Crossing after closure; looking south.
F. H. Clarke;
courtesy Tiverton Museum

Left: Up Exe Halt and North Crossing; looking south.
F. H. Clarke; courtesy Tiverton Museum

Below: Sadness and desolation at Tiverton; 1968.
A. Demellweek; courtesy Tiverton Museum

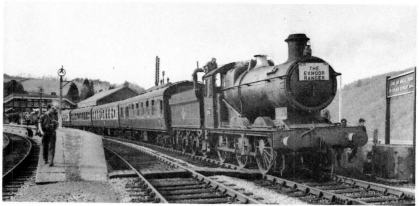

An enthusiasts' special on the D & S at Dulverton on 27th March 1965.

R. A. Lumber

was thronged with people and the train, now running late, was cheered and waved out. At Bampton everyone had to leave the train and cross to the 'down' platform while the locomotive ran round and transferred its coaches. A brass band was playing on the now packed 'down' platform, while the road bridge at the northern end of the station was lined with local residents. As the guard gave the 'right away', the band struck up, 'will ye no come back again' and detonators went off as the train pulled out. At each stop on the return journey many people got out of the train for a last glimpse of the station or halt. The train was now somewhat animated; people were thronging up and down the gangways in the coaches so that they could get off at a halt, and each of the stops got longer, aided no doubt by the fact that the rain which had been falling on the outward journey had now stopped. Crowds left the train at Tiverton and West Exe Halt, and as the rest of the journey continued the train subsided into a quiet mood. At Thorverton the station master could not bring himself to come out on to the platform to see the train away, and as people alighted at Brampford Speke Halt and the train moved off, the realisation came that, with the approach to Stoke Canon Junction, passenger trains would never again traverse this Devonshire valley.

With the 'clearing back' of the last train, the stations and signal boxes at Cadeleigh and Bampton closed for good. Freight trains continued to run 'as required' with grain traffic for Thorverton Mill, and the signal box remained open there until Saturday 4th April 1964, by which time buffers had been installed on the single line 300 yards north of the station and thus allowed the section from Stoke Canon to be worked as 'one engine in steam'. The station master at Tiverton superintended the removal of station fittings and the winding up of paperwork at Bampton, while the station master at Thorverton did the same for that station and Cadeleigh. This done, the latter station master was allowed to retire a year earlier than usual, a small ceremony taking place at the station on his last day, Saturday 7th March 1964 (Tiverton's last station master, H. J. Vinnicombe, retired in December 1963, after which time the station was supervised by Tiverton Junction). The closure of the signal box a month later was accompanied by the removal of the 'up' platform line and short dock siding, so that locomotives had to run-round through the goods shed. On the day after the Thorverton signalman closed his box for the last time, the layout at Stoke Canon station was altered to allow the branch to be worked in effect as a siding. The facing points leading off the branch were clipped so that the goods had to work in and out of the 'up' platform line. Buffers were installed at the Exeter end of this platform, so that trains had to work by reversing to or from Stoke Canon Crossing signal box. The points leading from the 'up' main to the 'up' platform loop and Exe Valley platform together with the trailing crossover were clipped and their levers taken out of use. Within a month the Junction signal box was closed, and the redundant track lifted. The goods continued to run until the announcement that this facility would

be withdrawn on and from 30th November 1966. The track lingered on, unused and rusting, until it was finally removed in September of the following year.

At the northern end of the branch, trains were continuing to run over the old Devon & Somerset line. Soon after closure of the Exe Valley, however, the junction points were removed at Morebath Junction.

A re-structuring of services on the Devon & Somerset, together with the loss of the branch, removed the need for the Junction signal box, and so the 'up' loop was taken out of use and the signal box closed after the last train on 29th April 1964. Passenger services continued between Taunton and Barnstaple until October 1966, with Dulverton reduced to a single platform and a pale shadow of its former glory.

DMU at Dulverton on 29th August 1966 with the 16.40 from Taunton. The signal box was now closed, the points clipped, and all trains were using the 'up' platform.

R. A. Lumber

Tiverton, outwardly, changed least of all. The Tivvy Bumper continued to run, though obviously under sentence. The Exe Valley line was blocked by buffers on both sides of Tiverton station; the first set near the Blundells Road bridge giving a headshunt for the yard, and the second set just short of the bridge over West Exe Road, the intention here being to operate a grain unloading facility direct from rail to mill, but this came to nothing. With the Valley line now sealed off into two isolated sections, Thorverton to West Exe and Tiverton to Morebath Junction, the demolition contractors moved in during the summer of 1964. They had a specially designed jeep which was fitted with rail wheels to enable it to drag the cut-up rail sections back to the nearest station yard for removal by road.

On Saturday 3rd October 1964 the inevitable happened, and the people of Tiverton and Halberton said farewell to the Tivvy Bumper, which travelled the line for the last time in the late eve-

The Tivvy Bumper in transit to Tiverton Museum on Saturday 14th October 1978. '14XX' class No. 1442 had been bought by Lord Amory, who presented it to the Town in 1965. Its first home was in Blundells Road, opposite the goods yard, but being in the open air it was subject to depredation both meteorological and human. Its removal to the covered 'Railway Gallery' in the Museum provides a fitting environment, enhancing both engine and other exhibits.   *D. J. Chivers; courtesy Tiverton Musuem*

ning. The locomotive rostered for the last day was 0-4-2 tank No. 1450. It worked with its single auto-trailer (W228W) as usual until the early afternoon, from which time it was 'strengthened' by a second trailer (W225W). The last train left Tiverton Junction at 9.28p.m., exploding detonators as it moved on to the branch. It whistled its valediction all the way to Tiverton, from whence it returned empty carriage stock to the main line. With the Junction sending back the 2-1 'train out of section' code on the bell, the signalman shut up shop for the last time, the branch to be worked from Monday as a 'one engine in steam' line.

The wholesale removal of superfluous track began, leaving only the 'up' and 'down' platform lines for a run round and the goods shed line and sidings on the site of former Bristol & Exeter terminus. A morning freight now sufficed, usually diesel hauled (the Class 22s), until that too was withdrawn early in June 1967.

The demolition crews moved in once more, and by the summer of the following year all tracks had been lifted, leaving a site of dereliction and desolation, which has only slowly been improved or developed in recent years.

Tiverton Junction struggled on with the thinnest of main line train services, with a connecting bus service run out from Tiverton. The arrival of the M5 and the opening of the Tiverton section of the North Devon 'spine road' led to the announcement at the end of May 1984 that a new 'Parkway' style station is to be built near the junction of these two roads where they cross the main line at the site of the old Sampford Peverell station. Simultaneously with the opening of this station will come the closure of Tiverton Junction, the old Bristol & Exeter 'Tiverton Road' of 1844, and with its demise will go the very last link with the Company whose plans brought trains to the Exe Valley.

Part Two

Gazetteer of Stations and Locations

South end of Stoke Canon station in 1921, looking towards Exeter.
L&GRP; courtesy David & Charles

Stoke Canon

When the Exe Valley branch opened on 1st May 1885 it formed a junction with the Great Western main line at Stoke Canon, 3½ miles north of Exeter. The original station built by the Bristol & Exeter Railway was a quarter of a mile further north, by the level crossing on the road from Stoke Canon village to Nether Exe. This station, with its 'staggered' platforms, had been built some time after the opening of the broad gauge Bristol & Exeter. As part of a gradual move towards gauge standardisation and greater flexibility of working, a third rail had been added to the track by the late 1860s, enabling Stoke Canon to be served by both broad and narrow gauge trains. The main line stopping service consisted of about six trains each way a day, with a sprinkling of freight. By providing a new station actually at the Exe Valley junction, the village would receive a much better service, but it was not until the 1st July 1894 that a station opened in this location, some two years after the broad gauge had been

Looking north; 1910.
Mowat collection

STOKE CANON — 1905

MAP AND TRACK — PLAN SYMBOLS

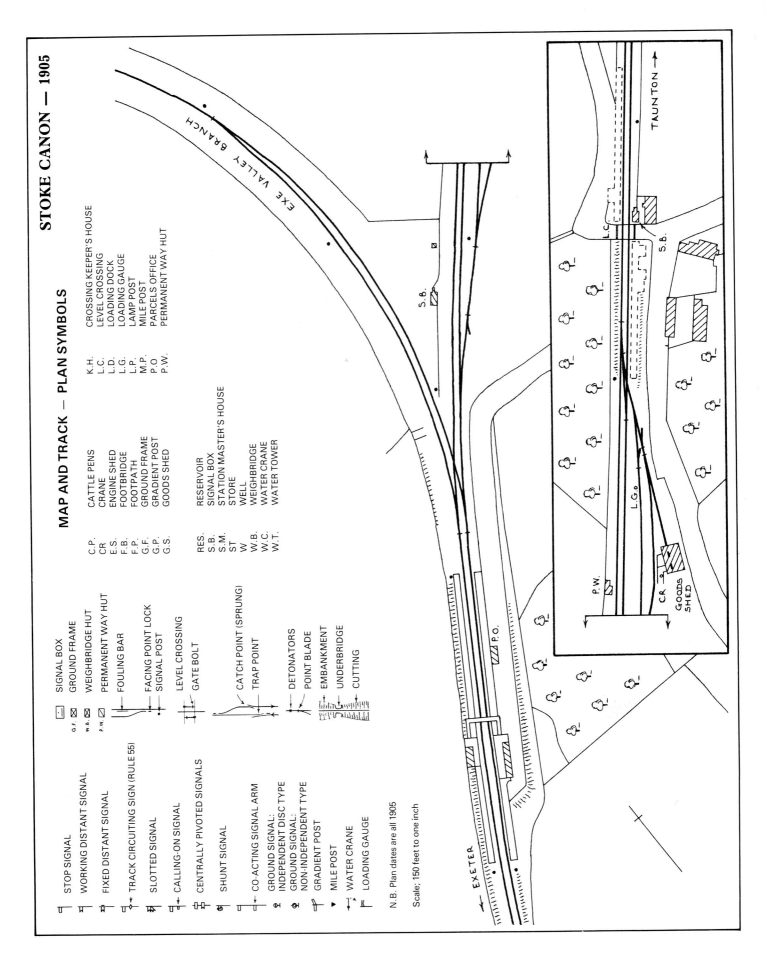

	STOP SIGNAL	G.F.	SIGNAL BOX	
	WORKING DISTANT SIGNAL		GROUND FRAME	
	FIXED DISTANT SIGNAL	W.B.	WEIGHBRIDGE HUT	
	TRACK CIRCUITING SIGN (RULE 55)	P.W.	PERMANENT WAY HUT	
	SLOTTED SIGNAL		FOULING BAR	
	CALLING-ON SIGNAL		FACING POINT LOCK	
			SIGNAL POST	
	CENTRALLY PIVOTED SIGNALS		LEVEL CROSSING	
	SHUNT SIGNAL		GATE BOLT	
	CO-ACTING SIGNAL ARM		CATCH POINT (SPRUNG)	
	GROUND SIGNAL: INDEPENDENT DISC TYPE		TRAP POINT	
	GROUND SIGNAL: NON-INDEPENDENT TYPE		DETONATORS	
			POINT BLADE	
	GRADIENT POST		EMBANKMENT	
	MILE POST		UNDERBRIDGE	
	WATER CRANE		CUTTING	
	LOADING GAUGE			

C.P.   CATTLE PENS   K.H.   CROSSING KEEPER'S HOUSE
CR   CRANE   L.C.   LEVEL CROSSING
E.S.   ENGINE SHED   L.D.   LOADING DOCK
F.B.   FOOTBRIDGE   L.G.   LOADING GAUGE
F.P.   FOOTPATH   L.P.   LAMP POST
G.F.   GROUND FRAME   M.P.   MILE POST
G.P.   GRADIENT POST   P.O   PARCELS OFFICE
G.S.   GOODS SHED   P.W.   PERMANENT WAY HUT

RES.   RESERVOIR
S.B.   SIGNAL BOX
S.M.   STATION MASTER'S HOUSE
ST   STORE
W   WELL
W.B.   WEIGHBRIDGE
W.C.   WATER CRANE
W.T.   WATER TOWER

N.B. Plan dates are all 1905

Scale; 150 feet to one inch

EXE VALLEY BRANCH

TAUNTON →

← EXETER

Work on quadrupling the GW main line through Stoke Canon necessitated the remodelling of the Exe Valley junction layout and a complete rebuilding of the station. The first stage, early in 1931, was the construction of the 'up' island platform. In this picture, taken at the end of 1931, the 'up' main/Exe Valley island platform has been finished, while work continues on the 'down' loop and platform. The new signal box opened in July 1931. The new station was fully commissioned in March 1932.

British Railways/OPC

abandoned. Despite the narrowing exercise, the track layout remained remarkably similar. The old trackside goods shed was demolished and a new facility provided by converting the small engine shed. A crane was installed on the loading dock and the pointwork modified at the level crossing end of the yard.

The new station possessed two platforms, directly opposite and of equal length (475 feet overall although this was later cut back to 400 feet). The main station buildings were on the 'down' side as before, with a footbridge connecting the platforms. The early 1930s saw considerable modification of layouts and rebuilding of stations between Taunton and Exeter, partly as a reflection of, and precursor to, improvements in train services, and partly

Station layout, looking north; c.1933. *British Railways/OPC*

Main station building, from the approach road; c.1933. *British Railways/OPC*

ornate platform canopy valancing, barge boards and fencing of the late 19th century station. With the modification of the junction, a new brick-built signal box was provided, this being of the standard type that could be found anywhere on the Great Western at this time. If the main line was occupied, a 'down' branch train could run into the branch platform line and wait; while the crossing of Valley trains could also take place by using both sides of the island platform (the 'up' train would be signalled into the 'up' main platform line, while the 'down' train would work into the branch platform line). A speed limit of 20 m.p.h. was placed on the branch platform line, and 15 m.p.h. over the 'up' platform line to the branch connection.

By virtue of its history, operation and very appearance, Stoke Canon cannot be considered an Exe Valley station in the full sense, but was tied up — in part at least — with the daily life of the branch. The Exe Valley provided a better passenger service to Exeter than did main line stopping trains, while the station staff were responsible for the welfare of Brampford Speke Halt and Fortescue Crossing. The small village of Stoke could not possibly support the level of service that was available after the modernisation, and in any case had a direct and reasonably regular bus service from the centre of the village almost to the centre of Exeter. Despite this, all branch trains continued to call at the station until the end of the summer service in September 1954, after which date trains called at peak times only. Passenger services were withdrawn on and from Monday 3rd June 1960, the branch trains then just slowing down to receive or relinquish the train staff as they passed through. The 'up' and 'down' platform loops remained in situ for goods trains, while the station buildings remained in use for a time by the permanent way and signalling departments. Goods facilities, always attended to by main line rosters, were withdrawn from 3rd May 1965 and although freight working up the Exe Valley to Thorverton continued until November of the following year, the station layout had been drastically altered, the Junction signal box closed and the goods sidings removed.

as a form of direct works in a time of high unemployment. Stoke Canon was completely transformed. The station was rebuilt yet again as it had to be with the quadrupling of the track and alteration of the junction. Branch trains had their own platform and now joined the main line at a point farther south than formerly. The 'up' and 'down' main platforms were of equal length, although the Exe Valley side of the island platform was several yards shorter. This third Stoke Canon station, opened in March 1932, was a plain, even austere, red-brick construction lacking the

Looking south; c.1933. *British Railways/OPC*

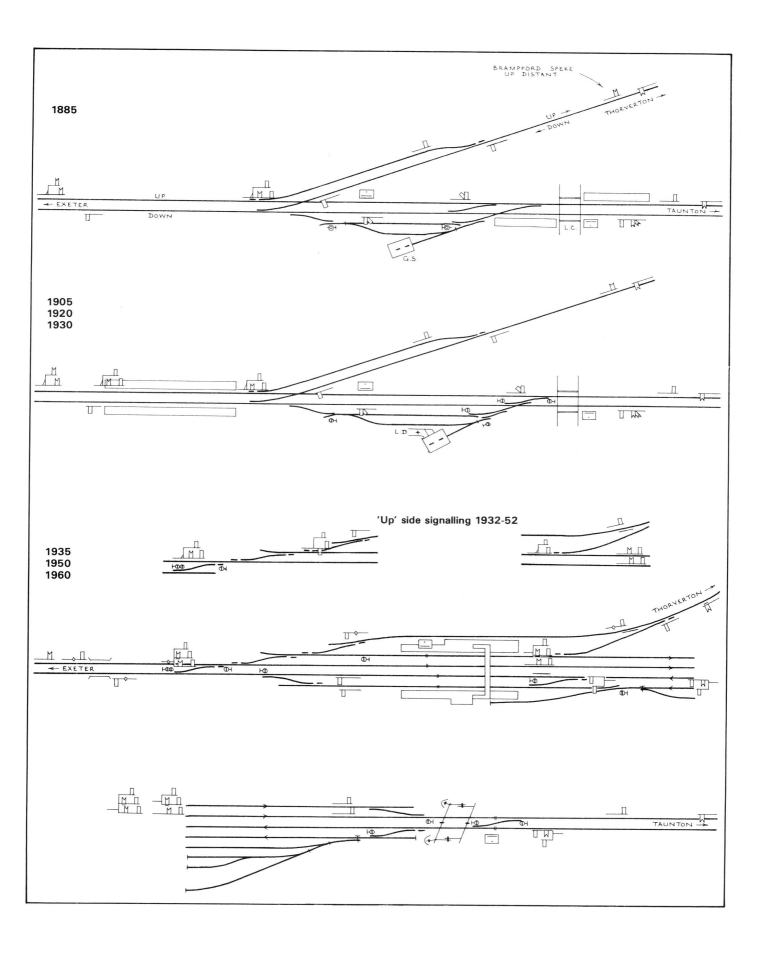

1885

BRAMPFORD SPEKE
UP DISTANT

THORVERTON

UP
DOWN

EXETER

UP

DOWN

TAUNTON

L.C.

G.S.

1905
1920
1930

THORVERTON

L.D

'Up' side signalling 1932-52

1935
1950
1960

THORVERTON

EXETER

TAUNTON

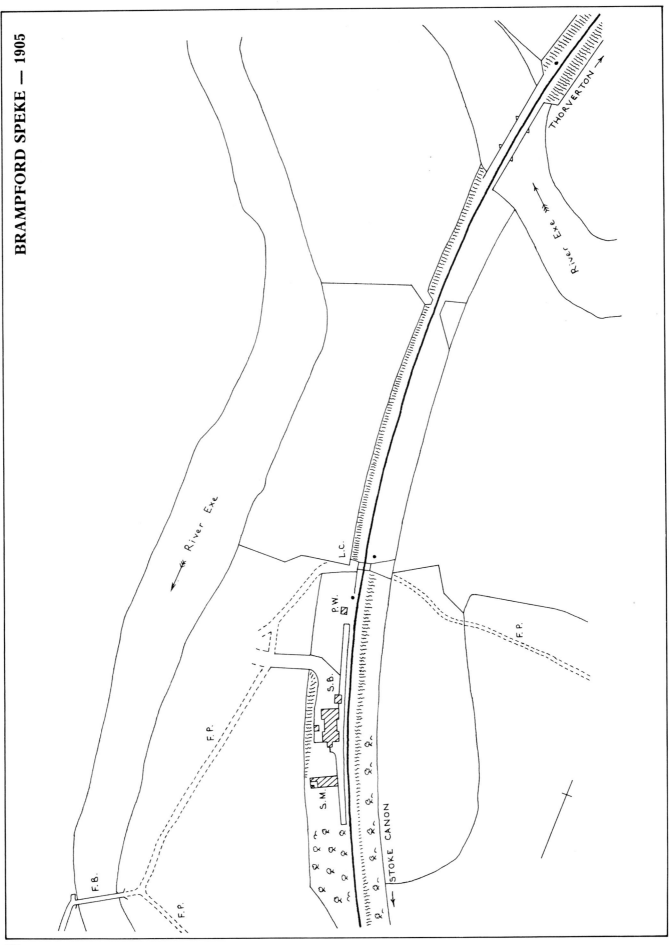

BRAMPFORD SPEKE — 1905

THORVERTON →

River Exe

River Exe

L.C.

P.W.

F.P.

S.B.

S.M.

F.P.

STOKE CANON ←

F.B.

F.P.

Brampford Speke

Early view of the station, c.1900. Together with Up Exe, this was the most lowly graded of manned stations on the line, the station master being paid 27/- a week in 1914 (compared with Thorverton and Bampton's 35/- and Stoke Canon's 40/-).
Lens of Sutton

At 4 miles 19 chains from Exeter, Brampford Speke was the first station on the Exe Valley. Situated on the water-meadows of the Exe floodplain, the station was on a lower level than the village (which was a short distance away on the other side of the river). A footpath led from the village down a steep wooded slope to an iron lattice-girder footbridge across the river. Leading to the right was a trodden grass track to Stoke Canon village, while to the left was a narrow metalled path leading to the station. There was a perfunctory bus service right from the centre of the village to Exeter, although 'service' is hardly the right word with only two buses a day, the journey taking about 25 minutes (compared with 10 minutes on the train). The only advantage of the bus was that it went to the centre of the city (Paul Street and, later, Paris Street), while St. David's was at the bottom of a steep hill, over half a mile from the High Street. As most villages on the line had either no bus service or a very poor bus service, this inconvenience was accepted. Brampford Speke was thus quite a well-used station and all trains stopped there. The only train not advertised to stop was the 06.00 from Exeter, although it did in fact call to put out newspapers.

The station opened on Friday 1st May 1885 as a full station with station master and two porter-signalmen. The 300ft. long platform on the west side of the track possessed a centrally located station building which was built to the same pattern as all those on the southern portion of the line.

As with all staffed stations, Brampford Speke handled parcel traffic as well as passengers, but had no freight facility. The purpose of the signal box is difficult to explain: it was too close to Stoke Canon Junction to be useful as a section break; had no sidings to control; was not a block post; and to begin with did not even cover the occupation crossing (a footpath leading from the village across to Rewe). An 8-lever frame signal box controlled a distant, home and starting signal in each direction, with two spare levers. The point of interest here is that the home and starting signals in both directions were on the same post, an occurrence which was unusual in signalling. By 1902 the signalling had been rationalised, with just one stop signal in each direction but with these protecting the crossing. The crossing gates continued to be opened and closed by the user, but the signals gave warning of approaching trains. The signal box closed in the late summer of 1907, and was subsequently demolished. In 1917 Brampford Speke was closed as a wartime economy measure, the only station on the branch to do so, while the comparatively little used Up Exe remained open.

There had been a time when it seemed as though the village might have lost its station permanently. Early in 1892 the G.W.R. announced its decision to build a new station at Stoke Canon junction, on the completion of which Brampford Speke was to be closed. The villagers were dismayed at this news, as the long walk to Stoke Canon would be inconvenient to say the least. A letter of petition was sent to the Company on 27th April 1892 asking for the station to be retained. After due consideration, the Railway decided to grant a stay of execution after the opening of Stoke Canon (1st July, 1894) in order to see how the presence of the new station affected traffic. In the event, the villagers' case proved well-founded, for traffic levels at Brampford Speke were maintained. In July 1896 the G.W.R. officially declared that the station was to remain open.

As passenger and parcels traffic had not come up to expectations, the station was downgraded to a halt in late 1923. Stoke Canon took over responsibility for maintaining the platform, posting notices, sweeping out the waiting hut, and putting up lights at dusk. Passengers had to buy tickets from the guard and re-book at Exeter if they were going on a longer journey. With the station building closed, life on a winter's morning suddenly became spartan: no sheltered waiting room with its coal fire — and no toilets! A small corrugated hut containing a bench was built on the site of the former signal box — a poor substitute. The 100 yard-long grey stone-edged platform began to show signs of neglect at its extremities, as most trains from the mid-1920s were 2-coach auto-trains, requiring less than half this length. The station house continued to be lived in, and the former station buildings were eventually sold and converted into a house, so the halt did not develop the air of decay which so often befalls un-manned stations. In the years after the last war, the passenger traffic was mostly commuters going into Exeter to work, school or shop, but any assessment of its scale is impossible to ascertain as the records are 'zoned' with and undifferentiated from Stoke Canon.

The last train called at the halt on Saturday 5th October 1963, but freight trains with grain for the mill at Thorverton continued to run through until 30th November 1966. The track was lifted in September of the following year, but station and station house remain today in a little-altered form.

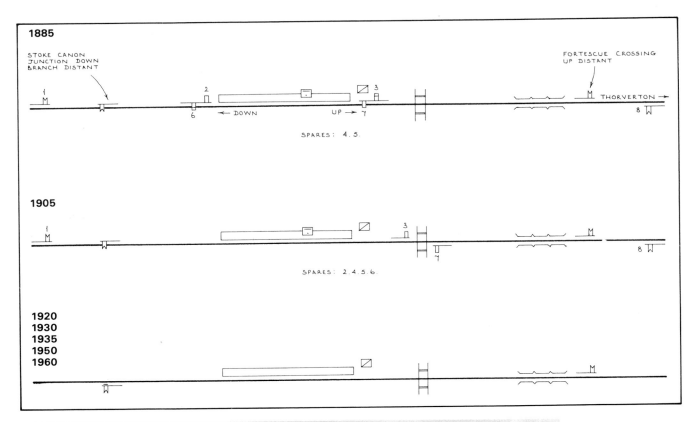

No. 1451 leaving with an Exeter – Tiverton train on 15th June 1963.

Peter W. Gray

Crossing and ground frame.
Tiverton Museum

Fortescue Crossing

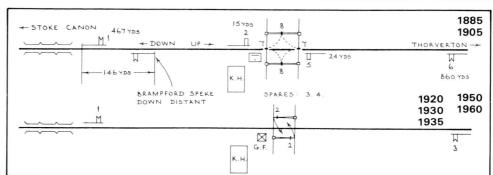

Crossing keeper's house. *Tiverton Museum*

Northbound auto-train.

R. Alford; courtesy Tiverton Museum

Nether Exe

River and Railway in parallel.

Tiverton Museum

Thorverton

Opened on 1st May 1885, 6 miles 11 chains from Exeter St. David's, Thorverton was the first crossing station on the line. The village of Thorverton is very old; it can certainly be traced back to Saxon times. For centuries the village remained nucleated around the meeting of seven lanes well above and to the west of the Exe floodplain. The arrival of the railway encouraged a ribbon of development the half-mile along the road from the village centre to the station.

The main station building, as at Cadeleigh and Bampton, was on the 'down' platform. The external design of Thorverton's buildings is identical with those shown for Cadeleigh, the only difference being that the stone used here had more of a blue-grey hue. The stone-faced platforms had an overall length of 324 feet,

The oil drums for the platform and signal lamps were kept at the back of the southernmost store-room. Water for the station was brought up from the old mill leat by a hand-cranked pump situated against the back wall of the gents.

The routine at the station went on almost unchanged for 80 years, with only small external changes to acquaint the observer with the passage of time. The points at the southern end of the station were altered to provide a smoother run in for 'up' trains, the new pattern being officially brought into use on 3rd January 1934. By this time the spur at the northern end of the goods yard had been removed, while most of the revolving non-independent ground signals had been replaced by the ubiquitous disc signal. Other signalling changes are referred to in chapter eight.

View looking south, c.1960.   *Nelson Collection; courtesy OPC*

while a board-walk for passengers to cross the line was provided at the north end. The goods shed possessed a 30 cwt crane, while the yard crane with its wooden jib was a 5-ton version. The cattle pens and loading dock were joined to the south side of the goods shed. A gangers' hut/workshop was situated on the southern margin of the yard.

The wooden sleeper-built hut behind the signal box housed the station coal and a corrugated iron hut next to it was the lamp store. Unlike Cadeleigh, all the back rooms in the station building at Thorverton were office storerooms, the shelves being stacked with tied-up bundles of papers, notices and regulations.

Until the closure of the line, Thorverton had no bus service. Buses on the Exeter-Tiverton main road stopped at the Ruffwell Hotel a mile and a quarter from the village, where not even a bus shelter was provided. The railway therefore was always well supported. It is difficult to form an estimate of station usage, especially with the opening of the halts, but with a careful analysis of the figures it is reasonable to suppose that whereas 65 to 70 people a day were boarding trains at Thorverton in 1925, this had risen to 80 or 90 in 1930, 100-120 in 1938 and then to a peak of 170 plus in 1953. Numbers then fell off slowly but progressively after that, settling at the 85 to 90 mark in 1960. Incoming parcels

View looking north. 2nd July 1963.   *R. C. Riley*

No. 1466 on 17.15 from Dulverton crosses No. 3659 on the 17.48 from Exeter on 8th June 1963.   *Peter W. Gray*

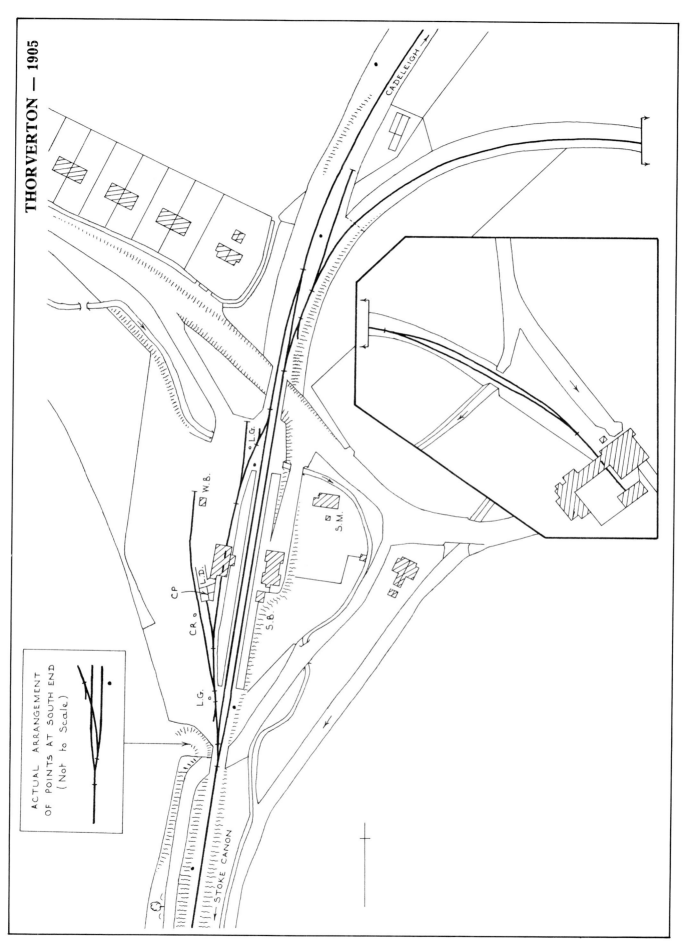

THORVERTON — 1905

ACTUAL ARRANGEMENT
OF POINTS AT SOUTH END
(Not to Scale)

CADELEIGH

STOKE CANON

L.G.

W.B.

C.P.

L.D.

C.R.

L.G.

S.B.

S.M.

No. 1471 with a Dulverton train in the 'up' platform. Signalman Bill Mears attends to the train while station master Reg Cole characteristically watches the proceedings from outside his office on the 'down' platform.
W. L. Underhay

traffic held up extremely well, with as many being handled in the late 1950s as at any time before. There was a catastrophic fall in outgoing parcels in the mid-1930s, while general freight held up well until the late 1940s. The nearness of the village to Exeter combined with its residential desirability made it an easy target for car owning commuters, although as the figures above suggest there remained a substantial degree of rail-dependence. The majority of the tickets sold were day-returns, or season tickets, to Exeter, the northbound trains conveying schoolchildren and workers to Tiverton every weekday morning with a small number of miscellaneous travellers at various times throughout the day.

In 1925 almost 78% of the revenue taken at Thorverton was for freight, and although revenue declined gradually over the years in total, its relative value remained more or less at this level. To the mill at Thorverton the coming of the railway was a blessing; a siding leading directly into the mill was laid in August 1898 at a cost to the owner, Mr. Coomb, of £1,697 — quite a sum of money in those days.

The grain wagons — or 'granos' as they were known — had worked down from Avonmouth Dock to Exeter overnight, and made up a significant portion of the 'up' Exe Valley goods. From the early days, right up until 1962, the pattern of working the mill was the same. Engines were not allowed to pass through the gate into the mill siding, and yet it was some 300 yards into the mill itself. In post-war times, the mill owned a specially adapted tractor which straddled the rails. A thick wooden buffer, complete with hook, was built on to the front. This vehicle would shunt the mill site and then loose shunt the empty vehicles close up to the siding gate, where their brakes would be pinned down.

The method of shunting the granos depended on the preference of the train crew and the other work to be carried out at the station. In any case, the locomotive would propel its loaded granos 'wrong way' through the 'down' platform and into the mill siding. The guard, armed with shunting pole, had in the meantime opened the gate and was awaiting the train. The full wagons were pushed slowly past the gate until they buffered-up to the waiting empty ones. The guard coupled them up, and the train chuffed vigorously up the bank to rejoin the main line. Once in the platform, the signalman changed the points and indicated that the driver 'had the road' by pulling off the 'down' home signal. The whole train was pushed out over the road bridge until the empty granos were clear of the mill siding points, where they were uncoupled. The shortened train then drew back into the platform, points were changed, and the full wagons propelled into the mill siding. The locomotive would stop short of the gate, the guard pinning down the wagons' brakes and then uncoupling them from the engine. This accomplished he climbed into the cab and the locomotive moved back to the mainline to collect the empties, draw them right through the 'down' platform out on to the single line, and then propel them into the 'up' platform to join the rest of the freight. Late in the morning the mill tractor would couple up to the granos pull them further into the siding, close the gate across the track, and draw them slowly down to the mill. The empty granos were always taken up to Tiverton, rather than picked up by the evening 'down' goods. This was a more satisfactory arrangement because they would go out of Tiverton on the 17.20 freight to Tiverton Junction, where they would be attached to the 'up' evening Swindon freight which conveyed them to Bristol,

Main station building and signal box.

Tiverton Museum

where they were detached and subsequently taken on to Avonmouth. With the 'down' Valley goods not due off Thorverton until about 19.40, and shunting necessary at Riverside, the Tiverton route was more immediate. The granos came up the branch three or four times a week, the numbers of wagons varying from three or four at a time up to seven or eight.

The mill traffic was typical of a sizeable part of the freight handled at Thorverton: loaded wagons in and empties out; this applied particularly to livestock, coal and coke. Of the 7,628 tons of traffic handled at the station in 1947, some 76% of it was 'received', while the less significant livestock trade showed the same pattern: twenty one wagons brought in but none forwarded. This 'loaded in/empty out' predominance was also to be found at Cadeleigh and, to a lesser extent, Bampton, although with certain important local variations in traffic type. The large annual cattle fair in the village which produced much traffic, was not continued into the present century, while the importation by rail of beef cattle for fattening was also dying away by World War One.

The poor roads and hilly terrain to the west of the village made Thorverton a rail head for the farms in the immediate vicinity and the agricultural nature of its traffic remained to the end. Two-hundredweight 'West of England' sacks (made in premises off Queen Street in Exeter) were kept in the office attached to the goods shed for farmers to buy at harvest time to 'bag-up' their produce, regardless of whether or not it was intended for dispatch by rail.

On the Monday after the branch closed, buses were diverted to call at Thorverton. The buses were now extremely full, the peak periods requiring 'duplicates' to run, in the terminology of the Devon General Bus Co. Double-deckers could not be run right up to the village because of the low railway bridge, which had to remain as the line was still in use by goods trains to the mill. Once the track had been finally lifted, by the autumn of 1967, the bridge was subsequently demolished. By the time this happened, however, the need for double-decker buses had gone; the poor service had persuaded people to use cars instead. Today, the station house remains, as does the main station building, in a somewhat modified form, also as a house. The signal box continues to serve a useful purpose, giving warmth to one former Exe Valley railwayman as a life-time's supply of firewood!

Reg Cole, station master from 1959 to 1964. Photograph taken on 5th October 1963.   *Author*

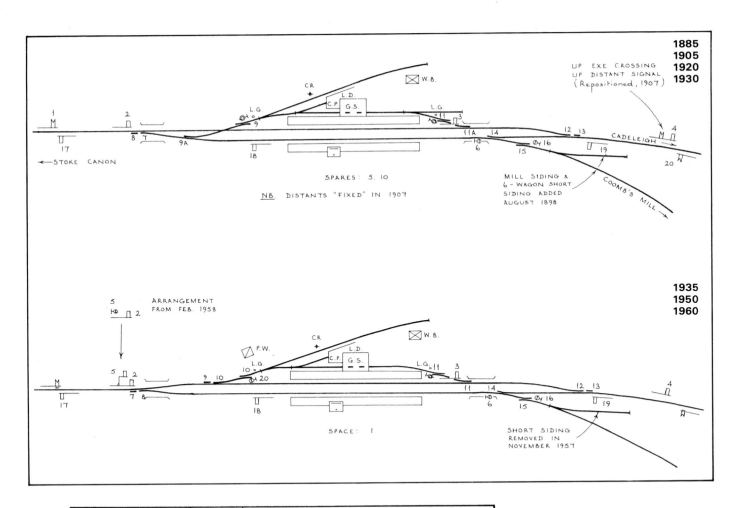

LEVER NO.	DISTANCE FROM BOX (IN YARDS)	HEIGHT OF SIGNAL (IN FEET)	LOCKING TABLE		
			LOCKED NORMAL	LOCKED REVERSE	RELEASES
1	853	20		2. 3. 4	
2	150	22	11. 13. 14. 15. 17	8.	1
3	70	16	11. 9	9. 12	1
4	290	22	11. 12. 13. 19	11. 12. 13	1
5					
6	119	Disc	16. 18	15	
7	134		8		9. 18
8	136		7. 16. 19		2
9	56		11. 15. 18. 19	7	
9A	120				
10					
11	75		2. 3. 9	12	
11A	114				
12	180		13. 14		3. 11
13	182		2. 12		19
14	120		2. 12. 15		19
15	157		2. 14. 19		6. 16
16	158	Disc	6. 8	15	
17	300	16	2. 7. 8. 9	7. 8. 9	20
18	57	16	6. 9. 15	7. 15	20
19	193	25	4. 8. 9	13. 14	20
20	810	20		17. 18. 19	

THORVERTON SIGNAL BOX 1905

SPARE LEVERS : 5. 10

ELECTRIC REPEATER : 20

Right: View looking south; c.1962.
Lens of Sutton

Below: No. 1405 approaching the North Crossing with the 15.45 from Exeter on 17th August 1957.
Peter W. Gray

Up Exe Halt

In many ways this was a less well-used version of Brampford Speke. The station building followed the stereotype shown for Cadeleigh, the stone being of the blue-grey variety. The station master's house was on the other side of the line, and later on became the residence of the keeper at Up Exe North Crossing. Located at 6 miles 75 chains from Exeter, the station was built on the east side of the line to serve a cluster of farms and cottages, but was clearly intended to draw from a wider catchment as the station opened as 'Up Exe and Silverton'. A station called simply 'Silverton' in fact already existed on the Great Western mainline, but was 1¾ miles from the village, whereas Up Exe and Silverton was about a mile away, in the opposite direction; a useful differential if people had to walk! In 1905 the name was abbreviated to 'Up Exe', but it retained its full station status, traffic justifying the continued manning of the station. In 1907 the signalling pattern, connected with the level crossing on either side of the station, was rationalised. The signal boxes were rebuilt as ground frames on the opposite (west) side of the track, jointly controlling the distant signals which remained to protect the gates. In late 1923 Up Exe was reduced to a halt, the guard issuing tickets to passengers who joined the train, while the responsibility for looking after the halt passed to the station master at Thorverton. Soon

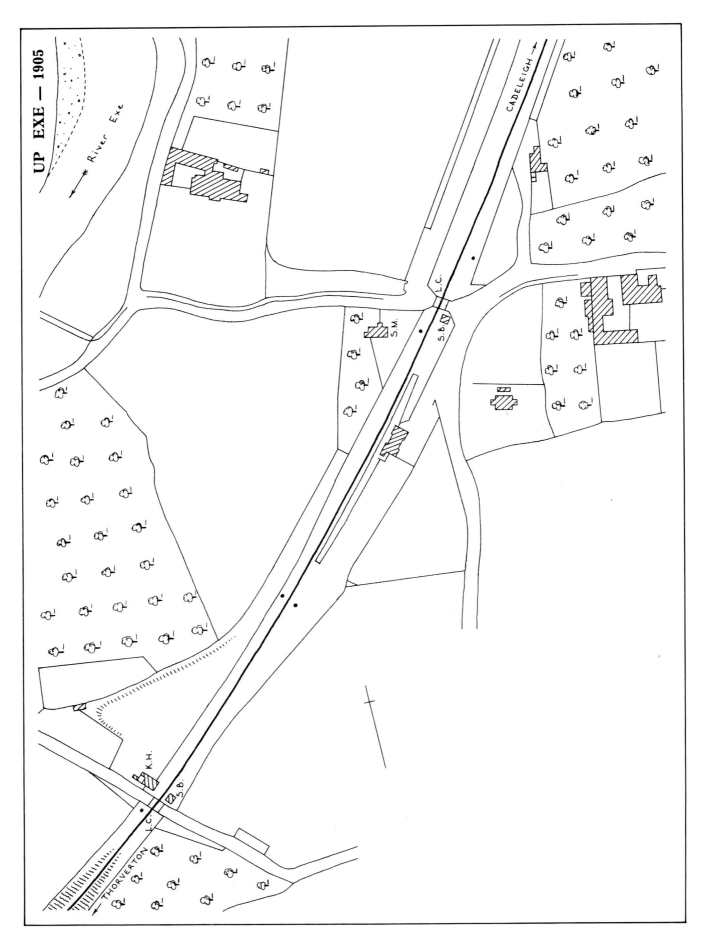

UP EXE — 1905

River Exe

CADELEIGH

L.C.

S.M.

S.B.

K.H.

S.B.

L.C.

THORVERTON

Right: Large prairie No. 5183 sets a brisk pace through Up Exe Halt with the 'Sundays Only' 08.30 Exeter to Tiverton on 2nd August 1959.

D. Fereday Glenn

Below: Up Exe North Crossing; looking north; c.1962.

Lens of Sutton

after this, the station building was converted into a house while a corrugated iron waiting shelter had already been installed at the north end of the platform.

The 326 foot long platform was more than adequate for the one or two-coach auto trains which became the mainstay of the passenger traffic after 1923. Indeed, as at Brampford Speke, it was the introduction of these trains, with a conductor-guard, that made the on-train sale of tickets easy. The open saloon nature of the auto-trailer gave the guard an access to passengers which had been denied by the former compartment-style coaches. All trains continued to call at Up Exe until September 1954 when peak time trains only were booked to stop. The least trodden part of the platform became mossy, while grass began to encroach from the fencing at the back, and this gave the halt a somewhat forlorn appearance in its last years. It was, however, regularly used by schoolchildren and shoppers, and continued to draw people over from Silverton as the Exe Valley line provided them with a better service to and from Exeter than did the local trains on the main line to Silverton station.

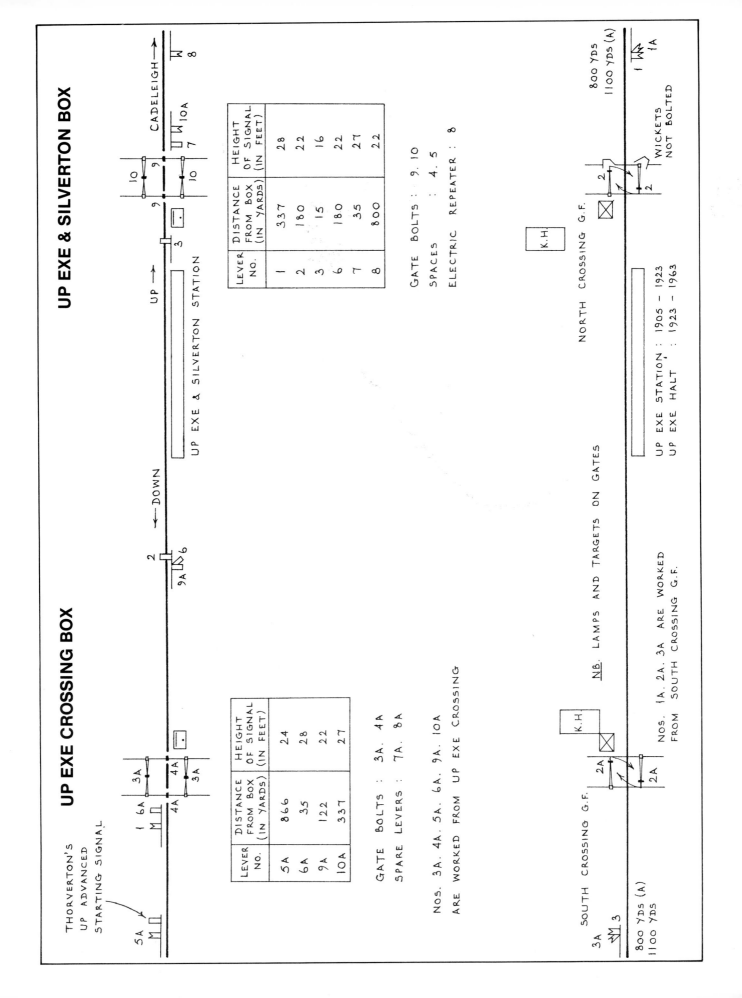

UP EXE & SILVERTON BOX

CADELEIGH →

UP →

← DOWN

UP EXE & SILVERTON STATION

LEVER No.	DISTANCE FROM BOX (IN YARDS)	HEIGHT OF SIGNAL (IN FEET)
1	337	28
2	180	22
3	15	16
6	180	22
7	35	27
8	800	22

GATE BOLTS : 9. 10

SPACES : 4. 5

ELECTRIC REPEATER : 8

800 YDS
1100 YDS (A)

WICKETS
NOT BOLTED

K.H.

NORTH CROSSING G.F.

UP EXE STATION : 1905 - 1923
UP EXE HALT : 1923 - 1963

UP EXE CROSSING BOX

THORVERTON'S
UP ADVANCED
STARTING SIGNAL

LEVER No.	DISTANCE FROM BOX (IN YARDS)	HEIGHT OF SIGNAL (IN FEET)
5A	866	24
6A	35	28
9A	122	22
10A	337	27

GATE BOLTS : 3A. 4A

SPARE LEVERS : 7A. 8A

NOS. 3A. 4A. 5A. 6A. 9A. 10A
ARE WORKED FROM UP EXE CROSSING

NB. LAMPS AND TARGETS ON GATES

NOS. 1A. 2A. 3A ARE WORKED
FROM SOUTH CROSSING G.F.

SOUTH CROSSING G.F.

K.H.

800 YDS (A)
1100 YDS

Right: A view looking South.

Lens of Sutton

Below: Bound for Exeter, pannier tank No. 3659 glides through Burn Halt without stopping on a misty morning in April 1962.

D. Fereday Glenn

Burn Halt for Butterleigh

Burn itself was just one farmstead, while Butterleigh was really just the ecclesiastical parish, this being a collection of scattered farms. A footbridge over the Exe, adjacent to the halt, gave convenient access to a few farms on the right bank.

Opened on January 26th 1929, the halt was situated on the east side of the line, 8 miles 68½ chains from Exeter, and was reached by a short fenced footpath from the main Tiverton road above. The 109-foot long platform was faced with reconstituted stone blocks surmounted by four-inch thick edging slabs. If the platform possessed an air of solidity, this was offset by the crude wooden waiting shelter located mid-way along it. Its walls were made of wooden cladding, while the backward-sloping roof was of corrugated iron.

The halt was intended to tap trade from the nearby farms, but this never came up to expectations and traffic was occasional rather than regular. Latterly, only six trains in total were booked to stop, giving schoolchildren a service to Tiverton in the morning and back after school; shoppers a morning train to Exeter and back after lunch; and two 'up' early morning trains which were designed to get mill workers to West Exe. In fact, the halt was little used, except by courting couples who found the waiting hut either more private than a local lane, or somewhere to shelter when it was raining! The stops here were unpopular with drivers on northbound trains because they were on an up grade and had a relatively straight run; to stop would make more work. If they knew there were no passengers wishing to alight they would sound the whistle as they approached, slow down somewhat and keep a lookout for anyone on the platform. If, as usual, there was no-one about they would open the regulator and head for Cadeleigh, the station under whose supervision Burn Halt was placed.

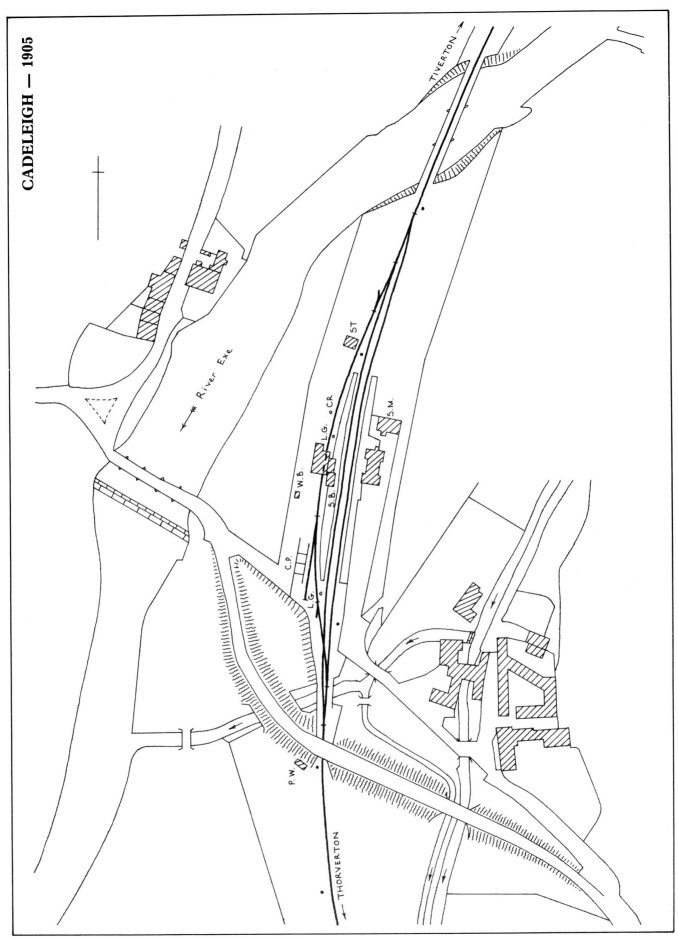

CADELEIGH — 1905

River Exe

TIVERTON →

ST

L.G. ○CR

S.M.

W.B.

S.B.

L.G.

C.P.

L.G.

P.W.

THORVERTON

Cadeleigh

The station opened on 1st May 1885 as 'Cadeleigh and Bickleigh', a name which it retained until 1st May 1906, from which date it was known simply as 'Cadeleigh'. The track layout was a straight-forward affair: 'up' and 'down' platform lines and a goods loop with short cattle dock siding at the south end. The original platforms, 10 miles 18 chains from Exeter, were 322 feet long and faced with stone. The remodelling of the point-work at the south end of the station in the early 1930s brought about a rebuilding of the platform faces and edges, using regular blocks of reconstituted stone for the faces and concrete slabs for the edges. The platforms were also slightly shortened at the south end.

The main station building was on the 'down' platform with a waiting alcove and signal box on the 'up'. A few yards south of the signal box was a gate in the platform fence which gave out on to steps which led down to the goods line and yard. Passengers who lived on the west side of the river used these steps to leave the station, to save a detour of several hundred yards via the 'official' station approach. The goods shed contained a 30 cwt crane while the yard crane, originally 5-tons, was replaced by a heavier version in order to deal with the lifting of timber. The wooden hut at the northern end of the goods shed loop was an agricultural supplies store. With the lengthening of the goods loop (it was brought into use on 11th November 1929) the hut was moved and rebuilt at the north end of the yard. The southern end of the goods shed loop was also altered, a few years later. The cattle pens were now adjacent to the loop rather than on their own siding, and a bracket signal was installed to cover the entrance to both 'up' platform and goods line. This modification was commissioned on 20th October 1934, and the layout remained unaltered until closure; only a few signals being renewed. A gangers' hut/workshop was situated immediately to the south of the road overbridge.

Cadeleigh served a thinly-populated part of the Exe Valley and was the least financially successful of the stations, showing almost continuously falling passenger, parcel and freight receipts from the late 1920s. Being right alongside the A396, bus competition was a factor from this time, and by 1957 only about twenty people a day were regularly boarding trains at the station.

Another illustration of the economic menace of road transport is seen in the former cattle auction held every April. The auction was held on the large flat area now occupied by the car park of the 'Trout Inn', on the other side of the river from the station. Once business had been concluded, the cattle were dispatched by rail, the station staff having to assist in the man-handling of the beasts into the wagons. This traffic was gradually siphoned off by cattle lorries after the last war, although the auction itself did not last much longer. By one of those twists of fate, the road was the direct cause of the survival of the station buildings. Soon after the closure of the line the building at Thorverton was converted into a house, while at Bampton and Tiverton all buildings were demolished. Devon County Council took over the Cadeleigh station site as a road depot; today, salt is stored in the goods shed, the 'down' platform is adorned with road-side litter baskets and the yard is full of mounds of assorted road-stone. The buildings have been left untouched.

General view from the Exeter – Tiverton road, looking north; c.1950.   *S. J. Dickson*

Looking north, c.1934. Note the oil lamps.   *L&GRP; courtesy David & Charles*

View north from the cattle dock, showing the unusual double-sided station nameboard in 1958.   *S. J. Dickson*

North end of the station and yard; c.1960.   *Nelson Collection; courtesy OPC*

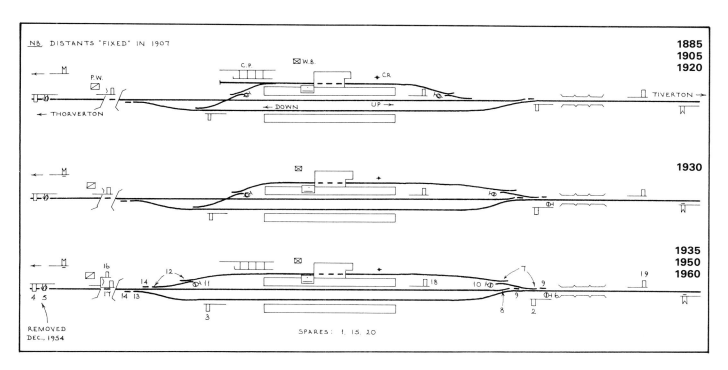

No. 7761 leaving Cadeleigh for Exeter on 8th August 1959. *Peter W. Gray*

Southbound train pauses at Cadeleigh on 28th September 1963. *H. Ballantyne*

Cadeleigh earned the least revenue of the stations on the Exe Valley, but considering the low wages paid to employees an annual freight earning of over £2,000 right down until 1936 made it cost effective. Just over 80% of the takings at Cadeleigh were for freight, although as totals were considered low, the goods

agency was zoned with Tiverton from 1st July 1948. Despite this move, however, quite valuable traffic continued to be handled for the next ten years or so. There was a two-way traffic in livestock, but more was always dispatched.

Sugar beet was regularly sent out, as was timber. Just after the last war a local farmer began to send timber out from Cadeleigh by rail. The yard crane — the standard 5-ton crane found all along the branch — was not able to cope with this timber, and so a new, 'heavier' crane had to be installed. The overall pattern, however, was for more traffic to be received than dispatched, with coal and coke predominating, followed by general merchandise.

The goods yard at Cadeleigh was the simplest on the branch; with the removal of the cattle-dock siding before 1920, it was simply a goods shed loop behind the platform. This loop was extended northwards and brought into use on 11th November 1929, while the trailing point connection at the south end was changed into a facing point on 20th October 1934. The method of shunting this layout was to draw into the station, uncouple the requisite wagons, draw forward and shunt back into the loop. Empties or outward bound wagons would be drawn out first, rather in the fashion of the mill siding at Thorverton. From the late 1940s freight was almost completely dealt with by the 'up' goods; outward traffic being taken on to Tiverton. The little used southern connection continued to be protected by a bracket signal (which even had a repeater on the loop arm), but the 'down' advanced starter with its shunt signal were superfluous and were removed in December 1954. This economy was a minor irritation from Spring 1962, because with the 'request' freight stopping at Cadeleigh, the southern connection to the yard was used rather than the northern, and in any case the engine needed to run round. As the 'down' starter and yard disc signal were locked by the token instrument, the Thorverton signalman had to be contacted to allow access to the single line.

West Exe Halt

West Exe Halt was opened in March 1928 to serve the growing housing development in the West Exe district of Tiverton. Although it was only 49 chains (about five-eighths of a mile) from the main station it cut out the long walk up and down hill through the town centre and gave level access not only to the houses but also to Heathcoat's Mill, the biggest employer in the town at the time. The original structure comprised a 109-foot long platform — built of wooden facing and edging boards — on the north side of the embanked track which crossed the Exeter road just beyond the halt. The access footpath led down to near the junction of Exe Vale Terrace with West Exe South. The usual wooden waiting shelter was provided.

It very quickly became apparent that the heavy usage the halt was receiving justified an extension to the platform. This would then allow passengers to leave the train from both carriages of a non-auto train, without having to be in the coach conveying the guard. With the numbers coming back from Saturday and market day outings to Exeter and from day trips to the coast on Summer Sundays, a longer platform would be much more suitable. The extension was commissioned in May 1937, having cost £160 (£12 less than the original construction). The extension was made out of pre-cast concrete platform and edging slabs, and doubled the length of the platform (in the Tiverton direction). Timetable-cum-notice boards were put up both on the platform — near the name board — and at the top of the steps and path leading to the platform. At busy times, Tiverton would send down a porter to collect tickets and it was as a refuge for him that a hut was built at the top of the approach path.

West Exe was certainly the best patronised halt on the branch, but any estimate of its usage is impossible to arrive at because it was grouped with Tiverton for administrative purposes. All trains stopped at the halt, except the first 'up' train of the day, which only really ran to get newspapers up the branch and provide the stock for the well-used return working. The halt provided one interesting working which ran on Saturdays only from the end of the war until 1960. A train was booked to leave Dulverton at around 11.30 to run to West Exe. This it did sometimes as

Looking towards Tiverton; c.1962. *Lens of Sutton*

Bank holiday passengers gathering for the mid-morning train to Exeter on 5th August 1963. *Peter W. Gray*

an advertised train to Tiverton and then 'empty' and sometimes 'empty' all the way. Its main function was to get a train to West Exe to provide a return working to Dulverton for Saturday morning shoppers.

View towards West Exe from St. Andrew Street overbridge. The stately GWR signal is Tiverton's 'up' distant, beyond which is the four-arch stone viaduct over the River Exe. As the picture was taken in 1913, West Exe Halt — which was situated on the curve beyond the road bridge — does not appear (it was not built until 1928). *Tiverton Museum*

A northbound auto-train leaving West Exe Halt. The ticket hut was only staffed during busy periods, notably in 'high summer'. *Peter Slater*

Tiverton

The terminus station built by the Bristol and Exeter Railway occupied a flat, low-lying site to the east of the town centre. It possessed two platforms, with passenger trains mostly departing from the shorter northern one. Both platforms were covered at the buffer-stop end by a wooden overall roof 48 feet wide, this great width being necessary to span platforms as well as broad gauge tracks. Entrance to the station was through a canopied doorway, on the northern side of the trainshed, leading off Station Road i.e. the original Station Road (the present road of that name dates from the opening of the new station in 1885, at which time the name 'Blundells Road' was applied to the former). A wagon turntable sited behind the north platform allowed trucks to be moved, individually, into one or other of the two short loading docks and into the goods shed. The coal yard was entered

and clerestory glass roof. All the main buildings were on the 'up' platform, their function being advertised by large enamelled signs consisting of blue capital letters on a white background. Apart from the 'First Class Waiting Room', these signs survived until closure. The inability to control points at a distance from a signal box meant that two boxes were required to cover the new layout: the 25-lever North box at the junction end of the station and the 9-lever South box at the Exeter end of the 'down' platform. Water for the water cranes and also for non-drinking purposes at the station came from a tall water tower on a grass bank above the north end of the 'down' platform. This tank was gravity fed from the Grand Western Canal basin 80 feet up the hill side. Apart from the water tower, all the buildings and platforms were made of stone obtained from quarries just a few miles away.

Early view of the 'new' station, from the approach road; c.1900. *Lens of Sutton*

through a gate at the southwest corner of the station building, in close proximity to which was the weighbridge.

By the early 1880s the new station, in association with the Exe Valley Railway, was well under construction. It was being built to the south of the coal yard, the railway's approach from Exeter involving a considerable amount of engineering work, from the spanning of the Exe and Lowman rivers, to the demolition of houses in St. Andrew Street, the digging of a cutting below Deymans Hill and the construction of a bridge beneath Canal Hill. The new station comprised two platforms, 'up' and 'down', each 350 feet in length, with a 145 foot bay on the 'up' side for Tiverton Junction trains. The 'down' platform possessed a general waiting room and gents' lavatory, both buildings being set back behind the line of the stone wall which formed a back-support for the attractive wooden canopy with its etched valance

The growth in freight traffic, together with the desire to 'ease-out' the facing points leading off the three single line sections, brought about a modification in the track layout in 1912 (the alteration at the south end involving a slight shortening of the platforms). A shunt spur was added to the goods yard, as was a new long siding connected to the existing network by a double-slip point. A new brick-built signal box was erected on the 'down' side main line in a central location for the station, yard and junction. The scheme and new signal box were commissioned on 6th May 1912, at which time the old North and South boxes closed. The massive improvement in Exe Valley services from the late 1920s, together with the use of auto-trains on both Valley and Junction services gave the impetus for a further modification in track layout in 1931. The removal of the need for the Tiverton Branch locomotive to run round made the provision of a 'down'

No. 1450 takes on water before propelling its two coaches to Exeter. No. 1451 waits in the 'up' bay with its single trailer, ready to run out to the main line at Tiverton Junction as soon as passengers have transferred from the Dulverton train, hauled by pannier tank No. 9635. 24th July 1962.   *D. Fereday Glenn*

View towards West Exe; c.1960.   *Nelson Collection; courtesy OPC*

View towards the junction; 1960.   *Nelson Collection; courtesy OPC*

Above: View through the station; c.1930

L&GRP; courtesy David & Charles

Right: Footbridge and south end details; 1958.

Peter Slater

Left: Miss Hine, the Manageress of Wyman's bookstall, at her place of work on the 'up' platform; 1930.

Tiverton Museum

Right: Original enamel signs (blue on white); 'up' platform; 1964.

D. Vaughan Davies

Tiverton goods yard. The line on the left runs to Goodland's Yard. *D. Vaughan Davies*

bay sensible, this being the side on which the trains worked in. The opportunity was taken not only to put in a new bay but also to provide a new loading dock line near the water tower. The 'up' bay and dock lines were altered, the original connection with the 'up' main being removed and access now being gained by way of the double-slip point in the yard. Although this point was protected by a ground signal instead of the original semaphore, the Tivvy Bumper could, and did, work from this bay on occasions. The 40-lever signal box now controlled the layout which was to remain until the station closed; only a few signals being renewed and/or repositioned in the period after 1931.

Tiverton was a busy station throughout the post 1885 period in terms of train movements; numbers of passengers and parcels; and volume of freight. In a period of static fares, prices and wages, the station was producing more passenger revenue in the 1950s than at any time before. In 1959 for example, 1,055 season tickets were sold and 52,592 individual tickets, while 13,174 parcels were dispatched. The actual number of passengers boarding trains at Tiverton peaked just before the last war, but recovered to almost the same level afterwards and remained there until at least 1960 (the passenger figures include takings at West Exe and Bolham Halts, the former certainly providing a sizeable return). A large staff was always employed at Tiverton. Up until 1956 there had always been a staff of at least thirty (1950 was the peak year with thirty eight), and even after that the numbers fluctuated by twos and threes, being never far from the mid-twenties. Unlike the other Exe Valley stations, Tiverton's station master was not provided with a house.

As might be expected, Tiverton dominated the freight scene in the Exe Valley. In 1925, the first year for which records are available, some 77% of the line's freight by value was handled at Tiverton, this representing just over 74% of the total revenue collected at the station that year. The peak year was 1930, and although receipts fell slightly after that they maintained very high levels. The vast bulk of the town's freight both inward and outward was carried by the Tiverton Branch. Traffic from Exeter and southwards was marshalled at the Riverside Yard from main line trains calling overnight. For decades, the departure time never varied between 03.45 and 04.00, with a lengthy time spent shunting the mill at Hele and Bradninch on the main line. Three heavy freights — one from Paddington Goods Depot, one from Bristol and one from Avonmouth — called at Tiverton Junction between about 04.00 and a quarter to six to detach wagons for Tiverton. With the arrival of the Exeter goods just after six, there was a considerable amount of traffic waiting to be transferred to Tiverton. The ruling gradient of 1:86 (falling then rising) at the eastern end of the line limited the number of wagons carried on a freight — depending on the power of the locomotive and the class of traffic. Right up until the late spring of 1962 the pattern was for the Exeter locomotive to shunt at the Junction, and make up two trains, the heavier of the two it would haul itself. The 0-4-2 tank shedded at the Junction overnight would collect the shorter of the two trains, and depart at 06.30, arriving at Tiverton 15 minutes later. It would arrive in the 'down' platform, the locomotive would uncouple and run round and draw the trucks to the yard in the manner described for the 'down' Exe Valley goods. With the trucks well clear of the double-slip at the 'throat' of the yard, the locomotive would cross to the 'down' bay platform

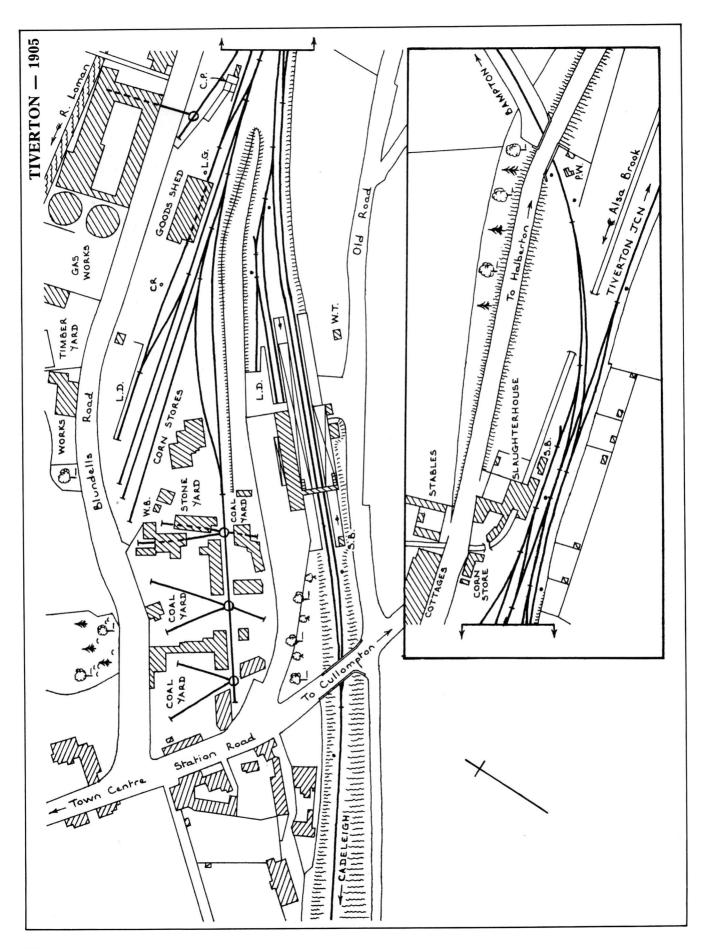

TIVERTON — 1905

R. Loman

C.P.

o.L.G.

GOODS SHED

GAS WORKS

TIMBER YARD

WORKS

Blundells Road

C.R.

L.D.

CORN STORES

W.B.

STONE YARD

COAL YARD

COAL YARD

COAL YARD

Station Road

Town Centre

To Cullompton

CADELEIGH

W.T.

L.D.

S.B.

Old Road

BAMPTON

To Halberton

P.W.

Alsa Brook

TIVERTON JCN

STABLES

SLAUGHTERHOUSE

S.B.

CORN STORE

COTTAGES

and couple up to the auto-coach left there overnight (this forming the 07.13 Tivvy Bumper). With the line to the Junction now clear, the Exeter goods departed — at 06.50 — to arrive in Tiverton at 7.05. The train arrived in the 'down' platform, but the locomotive had to wait until the 07.11 'up' Dulverton and 07.13 Junction trains had gone before it could run round and convey its wagons to the yard. It would then shunt as required until it departed for Taunton at 10.40. The afternoon freight and light engine workings have been described earlier, being part of both Exe Valley and Tiverton Junction rosters.

The type of traffic handled at Tiverton was varied, reflecting the wide, though agriculturally related, base of the town. The main incoming commodities were coal, coke, timber and building materials, together with a whole range of general merchandise. The outgoing traffic was much less in quantity and with no dominant commodity; amongst the more important were meat, varied livestock, stone and textiles. Only just over 15% of the tonnage handled at Tiverton in 1950 was recorded as 'forwarded', illustrating clearly the railway's role as a net 'importer'. Only with livestock was the picture reversed, with 760 wagons sent out and only 30 received. The tonnages, handled at the station by volume, reflected the expansion that occurred after World War Two. From a total of just under 64,000 tons in 1945, traffic built up quickly, achieving over 88,000 tons between 1948 and 1951 inclusive, but as road competition began to grow these figures had diminished to just over 46,000 tons in 1955. From 1st July 1956 Tiverton's receipts/invoices were absorbed into Exeter's, and no further objective assessment may be made of the state of trade. Freight, however, continued to be the major revenue earner and a service continued until June 1967.

Coal and coke played a large part in the composition of trains inward bound for the town. A number of coal merchants had 'staithes' of coal between the goods yard spur and Blundells Road, but the biggest importers were Heathcoat's Mill, Goodland's yard and the gasworks. Heathcoat's received a shipment by rail every weekday. The coal was unloaded directly from truck to factory lorry. In the early days, traction engines hauling a few four-wheeled trucks of coal would ply between the station yard, Gold St., Fore St. and down the short but steep Angel Hill and on to the mill. The brewers Starkey, Knight & Ford also used traction-engine hauled wagons to move barrels to the station. The wagons in Goodland's yard were loose shunted, running back slowly until

Above: 'The Queen of Devon' in the station yard; c.1910. *Below:* Starkey, Knight & Ford's steam wagon in the goods yard.   *Tiverton Museum*

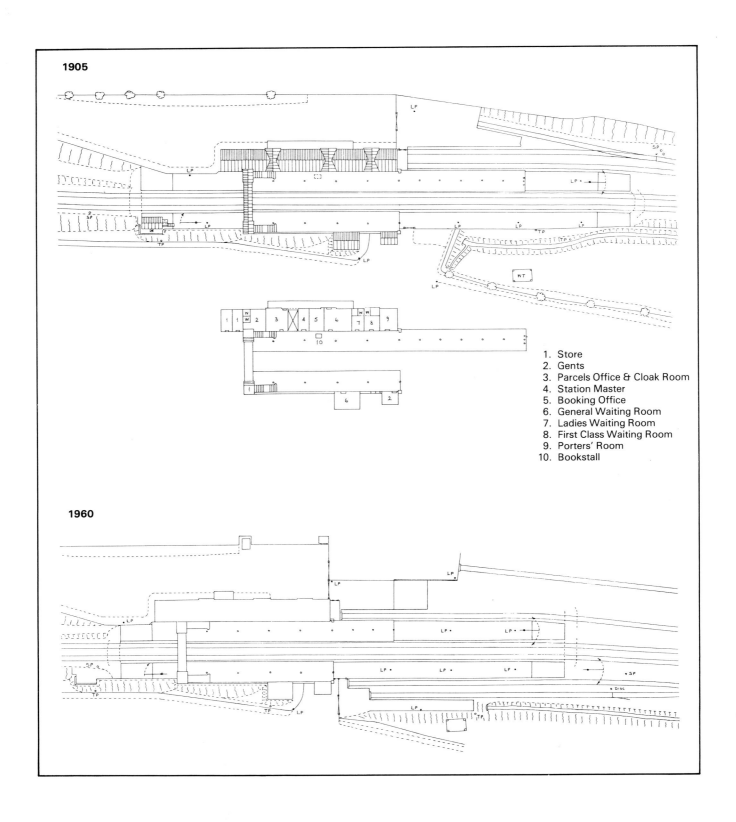

1905

1960

1. Store
2. Gents
3. Parcels Office & Cloak Room
4. Station Master
5. Booking Office
6. General Waiting Room
7. Ladies Waiting Room
8. First Class Waiting Room
9. Porters' Room
10. Bookstall

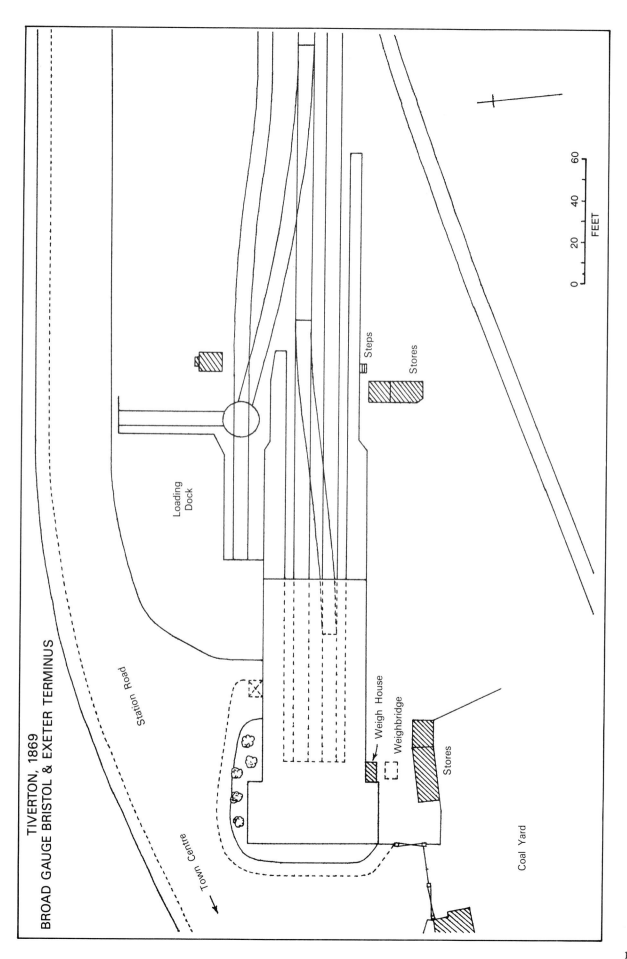

TIVERTON, 1869
BROAD GAUGE BRISTOL & EXETER TERMINUS

Town Centre

Station Road

Loading Dock

Steps

Stores

Weigh House

Weighbridge

Stores

Coal Yard

0   20   40   60
FEET

137

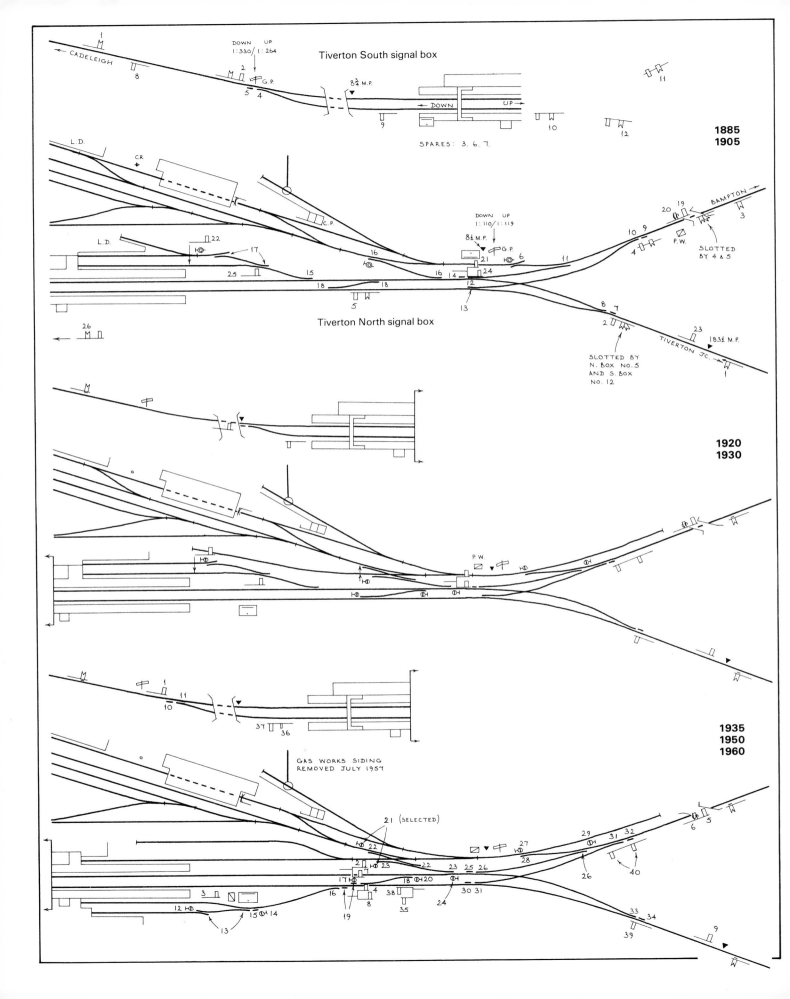

they were brought to a stand on one of the small turntables which fed off two sidings into various sections of the yard. The wagon would be turned and then manhandled into the required position. In the late 1950s a newly appointed employee was killed when, failing to hear the wagon gliding into the yard, he was crushed against the buffers. The turntable mode of operation was also used to supply the gasworks. Wagons were shunted, one at a time, on to the wagon turntable near the cattle pens. From here a line led out the short distance over Blundells Road and into a covered section of the gasworks yard. When the gasworks line was taken out in 1957, the other turntables and their related sidings were removed and replaced by two conventional sidings.

Timber was imported in quantity by two merchants in the town. The saw mill on the north side of Blundells Road unloaded the timber from the dock which was once part of the old Bristol & Exeter terminus station, the wood then being taken across the road on trolleys. Goodland's received much of their timber from Totnes. It was loaded directly on to trucks from the riverside storage sheds on the quay, and then brought by rail right into their yard. This arrangement stopped in 1959 when one consignment took three weeks to make the 48-mile journey, and then arrived in a sodden and poor state because it had not been covered by tarpaulins. Plaster was brought in from Stoke-on-Trent, and cement was also railed directly into their yard.

The slaughterhouse off Blundells Road — built over the Alsa Brook — generated a good deal of meat traffic in the days before refrigerated lorries. The loading doors of the building opened straight out on the railway at platform height to facilitate easy transference of carcasses. The financial importance of this traffic may be gauged by the fact that the Tiverton Branch opened specially for an hour or so on a Sunday afternoon to move out this traffic. This was referred to as the 'Meat Train', and it ran from the summer of 1929 until 1936. From Mondays to Fridays the meat vans would go out on the evening goods, but on Sundays — when the meat would be needed for the Monday morning wholesalers — special provision had to be made. An engine and brake van worked over from the Junction sometime after 5 o'clock, and marshalled and attended the vans for about 20 minutes before returning, with train, to the Junction, where the Exeter to Acton meat train was waiting. The vans were attached to this train which then continued its journey. The pork butchers Lloyd Maunder also had a large factory development at Tiverton Junction from which, until quite recent times, a train-load of insulvans of meat would be sent out every day.

The brewers Whitbread also made use of the railway, until road transport took away the trade in 1950. Indeed, draught and keg beer had always gone by dray-lorry, but bottled beer was sent out by rail to distribution points within the region. Most went to Paignton and Barnstaple, and a further small amount to Taunton. This was a popular consignment with the yard staff because the brewery drivers would sometimes have the odd spare bottle which would act as a token of appreciation for giving precedence to the brewery traffic when loading the morning goods! Petroleum came in between the wars to supply the small depot built near the station approach, a working which increased from the late 1940s. In addition to all of this, the multifarious 'Collected and Delivered' accounted for a very large tonnage, especially on the incoming side.

The problem at Tiverton, as with the other Exe Valley stations, was that operating costs were beginning to rise from the late 1950s and the enormous and vitally important revenue from freight was falling away. Many people locally were convinced that if diesel multiple units could be introduced, along with the unstaffing of all the stations except Tiverton, the service could have been restructured and made to pay — or at least the line south of Bampton could. Whatever the arguments, the swinging of the Beeching Axe seemed unstoppable in the early 1960s and, indeed, in two closely spaced stages one of the bigger and more commercially vibrant towns in Devon found itself without a railway.

Blundells School

The original School (founded in 1604) was very close to the station, but in 1880 moved to a new site about three-quarters of a mile along the road towards Halberton. The start and finish of academic terms produced a distinctive form of traffic on the railway. Vans were shunted into the 'up' bay for the loading or unloading of anything from 400 to 500 trunks and tuck boxes, and 200 to 300 bicycles.

To celebrate the Tercentenary of the School's foundation, the Superintendent of the Line requested the station master at Tiverton, Mr. L. Harvey, to decorate the station and station approach for the two-day event (29th and 30th June 1904). The GWR provided the flags and bunting.

Tiverton Museum

Station Personnel

Right: Presentation to Guard Slee in the General Waiting Room at Tiverton, on the occasion of his retirement in February 1922. Mr. Slee had worked on the Tiverton Branch for 35 years, and was well-known to passengers on account of his voice. When a train from Exeter pulled into Tiverton's 'up' platform he would be standing near his own train in the 'up' bay and would loudly proclaim: 'This way for Tiverton Junction.'
Tiverton Museum

Below: Head Porter Davey (left) and Station Master Harvey pictured outside Tiverton station in 1908.
Tiverton Museum

Above: Lionel Adams with the station delivery van; 1930.
Tiverton Museum

Right: Porter Swatridge. The work in progress on the 'down' side is in connection with the addition of a bay line and loading dock siding (commissioned in May 1931).
Tiverton Museum

Bolham Halt

Bolham Halt opened at the same time as West Exe Halt in March 1928. Despite this similarity, and indeed the geographical proximity, the halts were quite different in construction and appearance. The disparity in halt style is another illustration of the variety of detail which so characterised the Exe Valley. Bolham was 16 miles 5 chains north of Exeter, and occupied the east side of an embankment overlooking the village. The platform was a sectionalised, all-concrete structure, more reminiscent of the L.S.W.R. than G.W.R. The 109 foot long platform (inclusive of ramps) was backed by a 6-strand wire fence with concrete posts. An unusual feature for the Exe Valley was the incorporation of the lamp and name-board posts with the fence posts. The waiting shelter was an open-fronted corrugated iron affair with a wooden bench along the back wall. Facing west into the prevailing rain-bearing winds, the term 'shelter' was something of a misnomer, but it was better than nothing at all! A sloping footpath led up to the platform.

The maintenance of the halt came under Tiverton, this being less than two miles away. Bolham was only a small settlement but the halt was situated in the middle of the village and consequently was very convenient for market-day and Saturday shoppers as well as for schoolchildren. In most years all trains were scheduled to stop at the halt with the greatest booking of passengers to and from Tiverton. The first 'up' train, the 06.00 from Exeter, called at Bolham — not so much to pick up passengers as to put off newspapers. After climbing to a summit point at the Chettiscombe road bridge, drivers used the subsequent short descent beyond the curves to gain speed for the 1:103 upward haul through Bolham. Stopping at Bolham when there were no passengers was irritating and some train crews bent the rules in order to make life a little easier on this train. A shrill whistle would alert anyone on the platform, and if no-one emerged from the shelter the driver would 'open up' the locomotive to maintain its speed. The guard would open the vestibule door on the auto-trailer and, at the precise moment, launch the bundle of newspapers into the shelter. Fortunately, the papers were well-secured and protected and, also fortunately, the guards always seemed to have a good aim!

Hauling a single trailer, 0-6-0PT No. 3659 slows to walking pace prior to stopping at the halt on 21st April 1962.
D. Fereday Glenn

Right: General view, looking south; c.1960.

Lens of Sutton

Below: Cove Crossing, looking north; c.1960.

Lens of Sutton

Cove Halt

Cove Halt served the adjoining hamlet of Cove and a thinly spread number of farms. Being a bridging point on the River Exe — albeit for a very minor road — Cove had access to a moderately sized if sparsely populated hinterland. This fact had been realised by the Tiverton & North Devon Railway Company who had provided a siding next to the level crossing to provide a more immediate facility than that available two miles to the north at Bampton. Cove Siding could only accommodate five wagons, with a further two on the 'spur', and was little used. Freight trains were always booked to call by request only; with no run-round facility, shunting of more than two trucks could not be performed on 'up' freights. From 1884 until 1923 the siding and level crossing at Cove were fully signalled, even though the signal box was not a block post. In July 1923 the signal box was reduced to ground frame status, and although the stop signals were removed, the box remained outwardly unchanged, even keeping its 'Cove Siding Signal Box' nameplate until closure in 1963.

In March 1923 a 'low platform' (ie. at ballast level) was installed at Cove; it was sited to the south of the level crossing, on the east side of the line, 19 miles 18 chains from Exeter. As auto-working became more widespread, a number of these platforms were built with a view to tapping potential traffic at a minimum of expense. In a report on branch lines, published in 1926, the Great Western's Assistant Superintendent of the line, W. L. Wilkinson, commented:

'A striking example of the success of this scheme is Cove Siding Halt on the Exe Valley line, where new passenger business has been obtained to such an extent that the adjustable steps on the trailer for use at low platforms are now inadequate to cope with the traffic, and . . . the cost of erecting a platform of standard height will have to be considered.'

Soon after this statement the conversion was indeed authorised, and a more substantial halt built. The platform was a solid structure made from reconstituted stone blocks, surmounted by

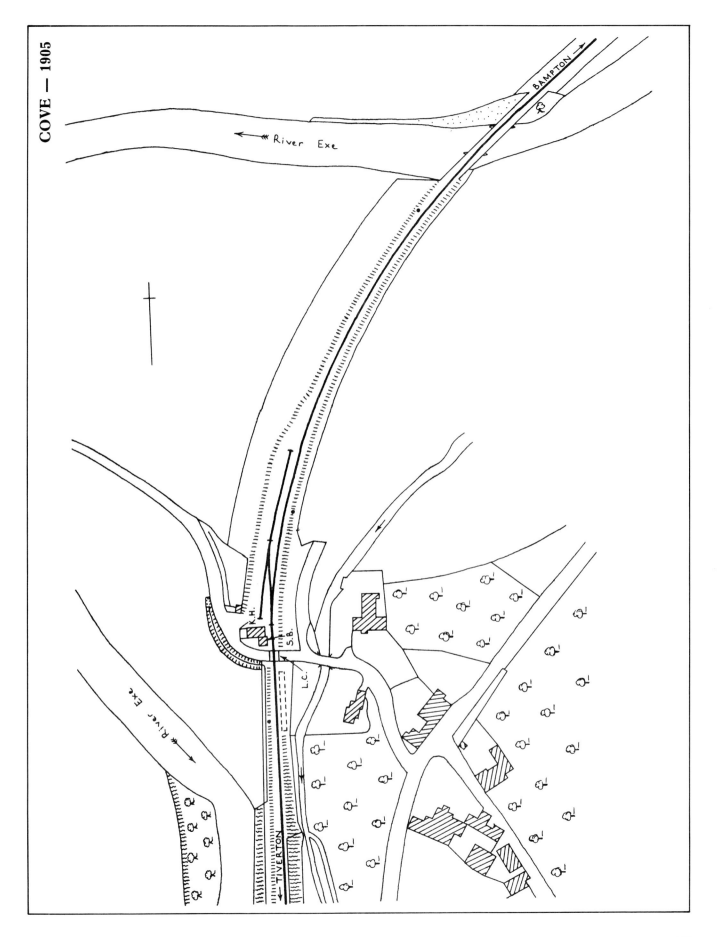

COVE — 1905

River Exe

BAMPTON →

River Exe

H.
S.B.
L.C.

TIVERTON

4in. thick edging slabs and with a 12in. overhang between platform edge and platform face. The overall length of the platform was the standard 109 feet. The access to and from it was through a wicket gate next to the level crossing, while the ubiquitous concrete posts and wire provided the back fencing. The original glass-top oil lamps were replaced by a single cylindrical post near the name board on which a hurricane lamp was hung. This lamp, together with other matters of routine, was the responsibility of Bampton. The most characteristic feature of Cove was undoubtedly its corrugated iron pagoda-style waiting-room, the only one on the line. This substantial shelter afforded a much more commodious facility than the other halts could provide. The halt had a steady trickle of passengers through the day but could never be said to be busy. Most of the tickets sold — by the guards — were to Tiverton, with the peak numbers on Tuesdays — market day — and Saturdays. Cove, along with Bolham to the south, did not suffer the drastic cut-back in services in 1954 that was the fate of Burn and Up Exe.

In 1933 quarrying of the tough roadstones began at Holmingham, just to the north of Cove and the lorries had to use the level crossing to reach the site. Despite the proximity of the railway and the bulky nature of the product, the siding at Cove was not used by the quarry company. The crushing and screening plant were geared up to road haulage, and despite a massive expansion in quarrying after the last war, the railway was ignored. Indeed, instead of a possible expansion in the siding capacity at Cove, a contraction took place in the little it already had: the short spur was removed sometime between 1916 and 1920. The river bridge at Cove was left in place after the closure of the line because it carried a gas main, and its decking was modified to give direct road access to the quarry. The quarry itself closed in 1982 but the bridge remains, as does the crossing keeper's house and signal box, making Cove one of the few locations north of Tiverton to possess reminders that a railway once flourished there.

No. 1450 entering the halt with an 'up' train on 15th June 1963. *Peter W. Gray*

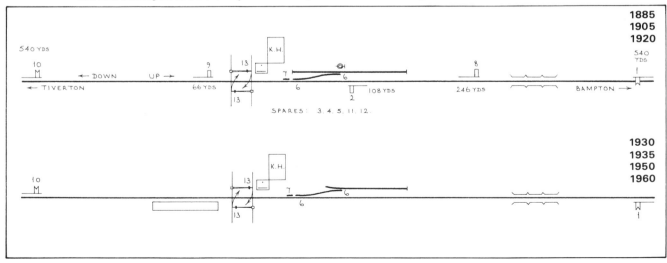

View of Bampton station from the road bridge, circa 1910. An 0-6-0 saddle tank is engaged on shunting duties.

R. J. Kingdon collection

Bampton

To the casual observer Bampton might seem much like all the other Exe Valley stations, but in a number of respects it was very different. For a start, the station was part of the Tiverton & North Devon Railway, and although in practice it was operated by the Great Western, it opened on 1st August 1884 nearly a year before the section south of Tiverton.

The initial train service was very sparse — only four trains each way a day — until the full Exe Valley route opened the following May. For many years, all trains on the northern section worked through to Dulverton, but from the 1920s Bampton became the terminus for market day trains from Tiverton, and, later on, other trains from Tiverton and Exeter. From June 1911 the station appeared in timetables as Bampton (Devon), just in case it should be confused with the other Bampton in Oxfordshire!

At 21 miles 14 chains from Exeter, Bampton was the northern-most crossing station on the branch. The station was con-veniently situated on the western fringe of the small, compact town and was narrowly confined within a cutting south of the bridge connecting High Street with Luke Street. For this reason, the goods yards was built beyond the station and not behind it as at Thorverton and Cadeleigh. The platforms were both 326 feet. long, the main building being on the 'down' platform. The tall platform lamp posts with their hoists were a most individual feature. The signal box was some distance from the station in order to give the signalman site of shunting operations as well as the station. For a time the points at the north end of the station were considered to be too far from the signal box, and so a ground

frame was provided beyond the end of the 'down' platform to control these points (the levers being interlocked with the 'up' starting signal and 'down' home). While all the other Valley layouts were losing their revolving ground signals in favour of the standard disc signals in the early 1930s, Bampton did not get this treatment, leaving its non-independent ground signals to control exits from, rather than access to, the sidings. The signal box in fact had about half as many spaces in its lever frame as levers in use (15 in use, with 7 spaces).

Access to extensive quarry workings was installed in 1898, this yielding much stone traffic. In July 1910 the double track section to the south of the station was extended by some 40 yards, but apart from this Bampton experienced the least layout alteration of all the Exe Valley stations. The ground frame ceased its role in November 1927, the points coming under the direct control of the signal box. After that date, no further change took place in the station's mode of operation. The goods facilities were similar to those of other Exe Valley stations, although the siding accommo-dation was more extensive.

The traffic pattern in terms of numbers of passengers and value of parcels points out another difference. Before World War Two the passenger usage of Bampton remained at a constant if rather low level, somewhere between 60 and 70 people boarding trains each weekday, and mostly travelling to Tiverton. The dispatch (and receipt) of parcels, however, was markedly higher than any other station except Tiverton, and this greatly boosted the station's revenue earning potential. Only after the war did

No. 1442 on a train for Exeter.   *Tiverton Museum*

South end details: signal box, goods shed and yard; c.1960. *Nelson Collection; courtesy OPC*

passenger traffic begin to pick up, as witnessed by increased sales not only of individual tickets but also season tickets. From the low figures of 60 to 70 a day (the lower figure being nearer the mark for the 1930s), some 200 a day were boarding trains in the peak years of the early 1950s. The numbers fell gradually away after that, but never sank to the pre-1939 levels.

Freight, however, was the opposite story. The dispatch of stone traffic, general merchandise and livestock was an important source of revenue for the first 50 years of the station's life, but was beginning to fade even in the late 1930s. The war held the decline in check because of restrictions on road vehicles, but it continued again from 1945. One other facet of Bampton's individuality lies in the fact that it was the only one of the three rural stations to show annual receipts for 'cab rents' and 'W.C.'!

In an area of poor roads, the convenience of the train was much appreciated as a realistic rival to the bus for regular weekday commuters. The loss of the line was a particularly unpleasant blow for the town, but they gave the last train a specially rousing send-off. Even after closure, Bampton conspired to be different from the other rural stations. In every case the station building still stands, except at Bampton, where all the buildings were demolished and the cutting substantially filled in. The railway bridge remains, just recognisable as such, while the station area and goods yard have been dramatically altered and act as hosts to a car park and light industrial units.

The dominance of freight over passenger, in financial terms, was somewhat less obvious at Bampton, the former accounting for just under 60% of the total receipts. The dispatch of general merchandise and receipt of coal and coke was enhanced by a once considerable volume of stone traffic. The toughness of the Carboniferous rocks in this part of the Exe Valley, combined with their well-defined bedding, serves to make them ideal material for the quarryman. Latterly, much of the limestone went as roadstone or aggregate. In mid-December 1898 an agreement was made to provide direct rail access across the main road into the quarry complex that was developing south east of the town. This was known as Scott's Siding, and possessed a Stop Board to prevent engines working beyond the confines of the goods yard. A network of narrow-gauge tramways developed to connect the quarries with the Exe Valley branch, and for many decades a prosperous traffic in stone flourished. The restrictions placed on train size by the climb to Morebath Junction, caused this traffic to be moved south to Tiverton and thence out to the mainline. The geological and landscape limitations placed on the early quarries near the town, saw many of them scale down their production after the last war. Competition from the road was also becoming a problem, with the newer quarry development to the south being geared solely to road transport. Although several hundred tons of stone were still being moved out by rail in 1945, this was a pale shadow of the earlier quantities. By 1950 this traffic had all but ceased, with a number of the quarries now 'worked out' or looking to road haulage.

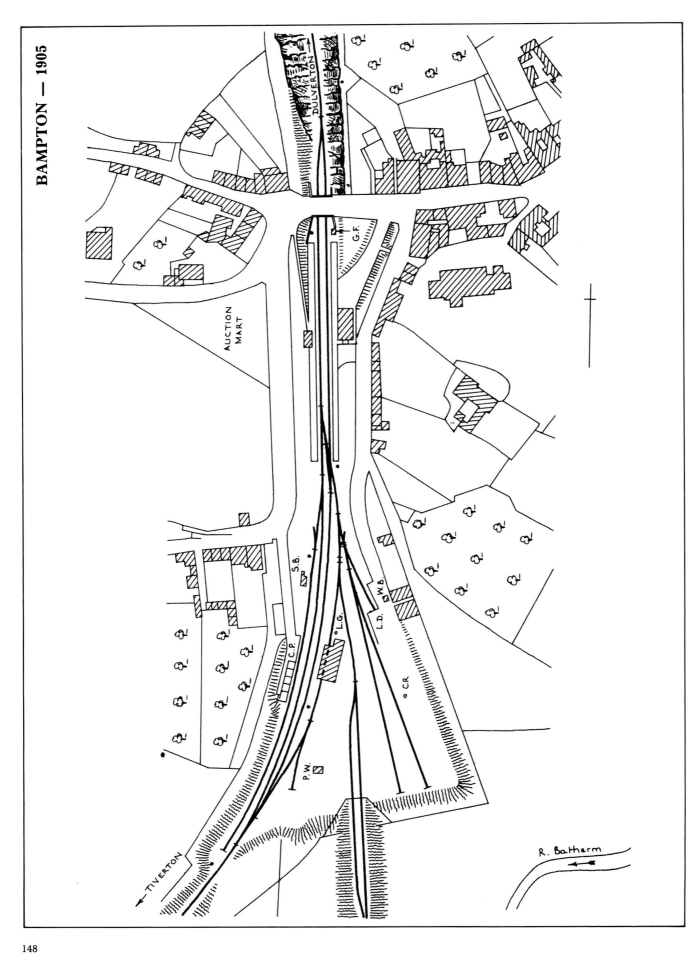

BAMPTON — 1905

DULVERTON

AUCTION MART

G.F.

S.B.

C.P.

L.G.

L.D.

W.B.

CR

P.W.

TIVERTON

R. Batherm

Looking south through the station; c.1960.   *Nelson Collection; courtesy OPC*
View north; c.1960.   *Nelson Collection; courtesy OPC*

Bampton goods yard; c.1960.　*S. J. Dickson*

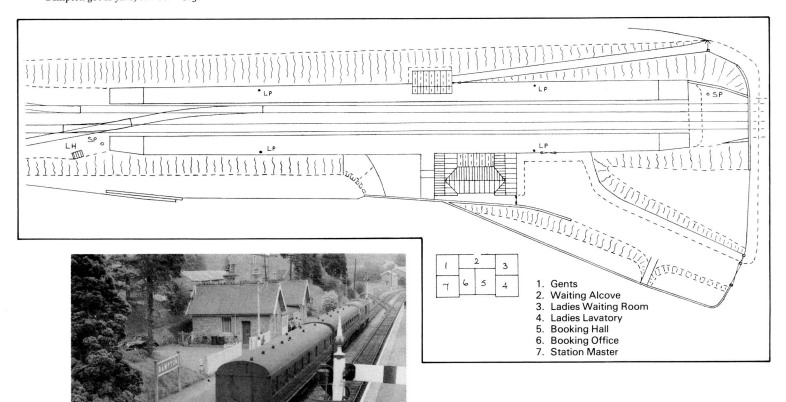

1	2	3
7	6	5	4

1. Gents
2. Waiting Alcove
3. Ladies Waiting Room
4. Ladies Lavatory
5. Booking Hall
6. Booking Office
7. Station Master

D6318 waiting with a 'down' train at Bampton. The locomotive had arrived with the 14.08 Exeter to Bampton service, and had run round and transferred its coaches prior to this picture being taken on 28th September 1963.
　　　　　　　　　　　　　　　　　　　　R. A. Lumber

Bampton Fair Day; c.1910.   *R. J. Kingdon collection*

The wholesale seasonal movement of animals by rail was a feature of the Exe Valley for many years. Only at Bampton did the tradition remain with its famous Pony Fair. At the end of the summer, ponies rounded up on Exmoor were — and are — taken to Bampton Fair for sale. The Fair took place in the second week of October and every day for about a fortnight beforehand the pick-up goods from Exeter would carry a few empty cattle wagons up to Bampton. These were shunted back into the 'up' (cattle dock) siding by the signal box. This siding would hold 25 wagons, so as others continued to arrive they were stabled in the two sidings between the loading dock and Scott's Siding. By the day of the Fair, there would be from 40 to 50 wagons waiting, and the Exeter Shed sent a light engine up to shunt the yard and convey the wagon loads of ponies to Tiverton where they were further marshalled and dispatched. This traffic flourished up until the last war, but was then very quickly supplanted by road transport from about 1947.

A small trade in other livestock continued, but the diminution in freight traffic was such that regular daily services ceased from September 1954. From that date, Bampton was serviced from Dulverton, through which station all traffic had to be routed. The move towards centralisation of freight agencies had already zoned Bampton into the Tiverton district from 1st February 1947, while East Anstey, Morebath and Dulverton (on the Devon & Somerset) were added from 1st August of the same year. Although Tiverton now acted as the 'clearing house', there was no direct freight between there and the northern half of the branch from 1954, a reflection of the sad reduction in traffic.

View looking south, circa 1910. Note the horse and cart transport awaiting their loads.   *Paul Karau Collection*

The signal box at Bampton was some way from the platforms, making it less easy for the signalman to deal with station traffic when the station master was off duty, as well as attend to his signalling duties. Thus Bampton possessed a porter as well as a station master, underlining further its individuality. The porter — known along the line simply as Wilf — was 'good at parcels', and it was to this function at Exeter that he was transferred when the line closed.

151

Bampton Stone Quarries; c.1900.   *R. J. Kingdon collection*

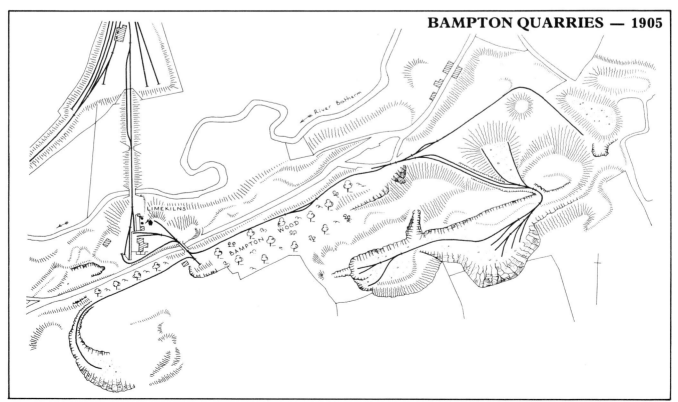

BAMPTON QUARRIES — 1905

LIMEKILNS

River Batherm

BAMPTON WOOD

Presentation at Bampton, 1958. The occasion is the retirement presentation to Walter Pash, signalman at Morebath Junction, by Mr. C. Soper station master at Bampton (Mr. Soper had arrived at Bampton at the end of October 1950, having previously been station master at Camerton on the Cam Valley branch south of Bath). From left to right are; Bert Curtis, Reg Bull, Fred Bird, Fred Edworthy, Albert Cotterell, Arthur Ball, Ron Manley, Charlie Tout, Bill Williams, Don Chorley, Walter Pash, Frank Manley, Mr. Soper and Wilf Jefferies.

R. J. Kingdon collection

The cutting north of the station. Note the elevated position of the 'down' home signal; c.1960.

S. J. Dickson

153

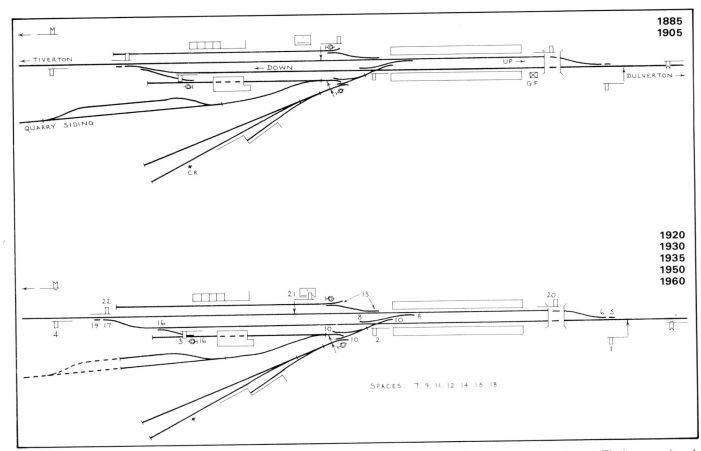

1885
1905

← M

← TIVERTON

← DOWN

UP →

DULVERTON →

G.F.

QUARRY SIDING

CR

1920
1930
1935
1950
1960

← M

22
19 17
4
3
16
21
13
8
10
8
10
2
10
20
6 5
1

SPACES: 7. 9. 11. 12. 14. 15. 18.

No. 1466 with the 17.15 from Dulverton to Exeter waits for 'line clear' following the arrival of No. 1451 with the 16.25 from Exeter. The latter terminated at Bampton (17.23), transferring to the 'down' platform on the clearance of the 17.15, where it waited until 18.10 before returning to Exeter (running non-stop to Tiverton, the only advertised passenger train not to stop at the intermediate halts).

M. Hale

154

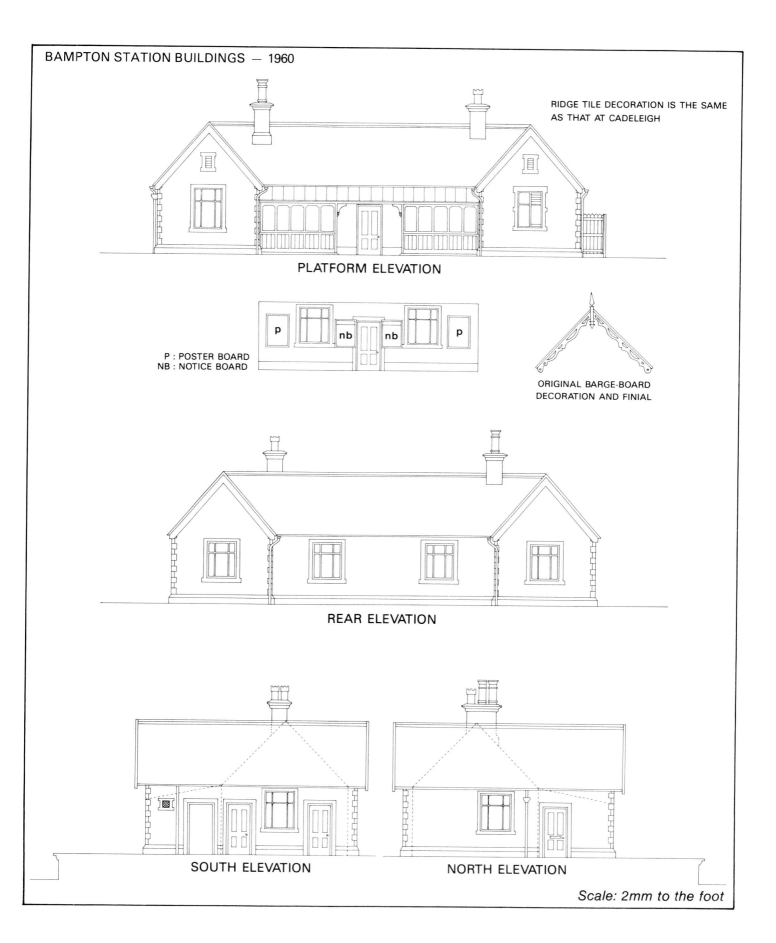

BAMPTON STATION BUILDINGS — 1960

RIDGE TILE DECORATION IS THE SAME
AS THAT AT CADELEIGH

PLATFORM ELEVATION

P : POSTER BOARD
NB : NOTICE BOARD

p   nb   nb   p

ORIGINAL BARGE-BOARD
DECORATION AND FINIAL

REAR ELEVATION

SOUTH ELEVATION   NORTH ELEVATION

Scale: 2mm to the foot

0-6-0PT No. 9629 approaching with the 14.08 from Exeter to Dulverton on 8th July 1959. *Peter W. Gray*

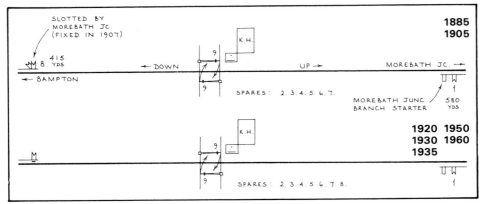

Lower Lodfin Crossing

No. 1421 with the 15.25 from Exeter passing through the ridge-gap utilised by both road and railway. 15th June 1963. *Peter W. Gray*

The view east in 1930. The Devon & Somerset loops were not lengthened until
1937.   *R. J. Kingdon collection*

Morebath Junction

The junction layout in 1953.   *D. Butterfield*

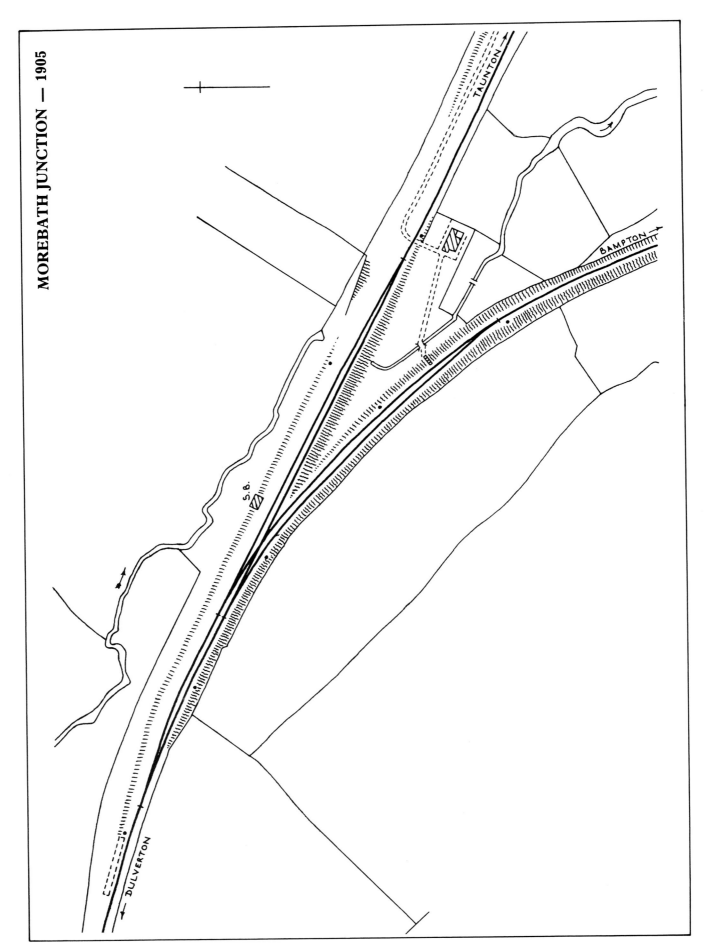

MOREBATH JUNCTION — 1905

'43XX' class mogul No. 7326 taking the D & S line with a train from Barnstaple Junction to Taunton on 2nd October 1962.   *R. A. Lumber*

The view looking west in 1965.   *S. J. Dickson*

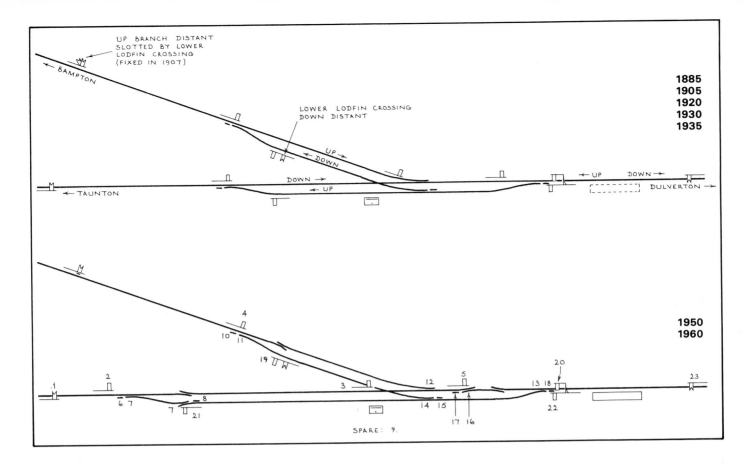

UP BRANCH DISTANT
SLOTTED BY LOWER
LODFIN CROSSING
(FIXED IN 1907)

← BAMPTON

1885
1905
1920
1930
1935

LOWER LODFIN CROSSING
DOWN DISTANT

← UP →

← DOWN

DOWN →

← UP

← TAUNTON

UP → ← DOWN →

DULVERTON →

M

4

10 11

19

1950
1960

2

1

6 7

7

21

3

8

12

5

13 18

20

22

23

14 15

17 16

SPARE: 9.

The halt in 1930; looking east.   *R. J. Kingdon collection*

Morebath Junction Halt

The halt in 1960 looking west. Note the hurricane lamp left inside the glass housing of the old oil lamp.   *Lens of Sutton*

Built to the familiar design, this northernmost halt (22 miles 71 chains) opened on Saturday 1st December 1928. The platform was identical with those at Cove and Burn, the only difference being that the shelter had a canopy projecting over the entrance. This addition may seem like a minor modification, but it was a boon in this open, windswept location, giving a little extra protection from wind and rain. The halt was a quarter of a mile to the south of the village of Morebath, but there was no proper metalled road or even footpath, just a trodden track through fields. In rainy weather schoolchildren and shoppers would trudge through the wet grass in boots, carrying their 'town' shoes with them. Once at the halt, the shoes would be substituted, and the boots placed tidily under the bench in the waiting shelter. The repeat performance happened in the afternoon — and the boots never went missing!

All the Taunton to Barnstaple line trains also stopped at the halt (the only exceptions being the through trains to and from Ilfracombe on summer Saturdays). Most of the trains on this service were two or three coaches long and hauled by a 2-6-0 43XX Class locomotive. Many travellers must have wondered why their train had apparently stopped in the middle of nowhere, for even if their coach had drawn past the halt, it was hardly a conspicuous structure! Thus the halt had the enviable facility of through trains to the major towns of the region — Taunton, Barnstaple, Tiverton and Exeter — but it was a facility that few appreciated because only a few lived near the halt!

The halt in 1963.
R. J. Kingdon collection

Busy time at Dulverton. Auto-fitted prairie No. 5524 waits in the Exe Valley platform loop while Southern 'N' class 2-6-0 No. 31846 pauses for line clear on a Taunton – Barnstaple stopping train. Running into the 'up' platform is '43XX' class 2-6-0 No. 6398 on a Taunton freight. 10th October 1959.

Peter W. Gray

Dulverton

The broad gauge line between Taunton and Barnstaple, built by the Devon & Somerset Railway Company, opened throughout on 1st May 1873, and with it the station of Dulverton. The line had picked its way through quite difficult countryside in terms of grade, and the constraints of topography forced it to turn westwards at Brushford rather than continue the further two miles north to Dulverton itself. The early station, with its two 300 foot long platforms and small yard, was built in a style considerably different from that adopted for Exe Valley stations. In May 1881 the Devon & Somerset was narrowed while the decision had already been taken to make Dulverton the terminus of the Tiverton & North Devon Railway. The opening of the latter in 1884, and of the Exe Valley through-

one containing the main building and station master's house — was rebuilt and lengthened to 445 feet, and located on it was a new and much enlarged signal box (a 54-lever frame: 48 levers in use and 6 spaces in case of further layout changes). The 'down' platform was converted into an 'island' 435 feet long, thus giving Exe Valley trains their own platform. Branch locomotives were able to run round their trains without having to block the main line at the Barnstaple end of the station, while new sidings made the transfer of wagons much easier. A new loading dock and cattle pens were provided, while access to the turntable was changed to the opposite end of the station. The two-ton crane in the goods shed was supplemented by a 5-ton crane in the new yard. In 1937 the loops were extended, and the Exe Valley run-round loop and

General view of the station and yard on 2nd July 1963 from the road overbridge. *R. C. Riley*

out the following year, did not lead to any immediate expansion at the station, although a siding with small turntable (23ft. 9in. in diameter) was added from the signal box end of the 'down' siding. Against this, however, the short siding near the cattle pens and the yard to the 'up' main connection were actually removed.

The need to run round Exe Valley engines; shunt stock into sidings to clear the main line; and transfer freight between the D & S and Exe Valley, began to tax the very limited accommodation at the station, and so a programme of expansion and rebuilding began. The new scheme was commissioned on 6th January 1910. The station buildings and goods shed were left intact, but everything else was redesigned about them. The 'up' platform — the

crane road were altered. The platforms at the Taunton end of the station were lengthened by some 40 feet, and both home signals renewed. With only minor alterations to signalling, this layout remained until 1963.

In addition to its function as both rural railhead and interchange station, Dulverton attracted a measure of what it now called tourist traffic, the southern part of Exmoor with its deep, wooded valleys being so near and an obvious attraction. This was quickly appreciated by the Great Western, as is witnessed by the advert placed in the 'Exeter Flying Post' on Wednesday July 29th 1885. For people who did not wish to walk the two miles to Dulverton, ponies and traps were on hand and, later charabancs.

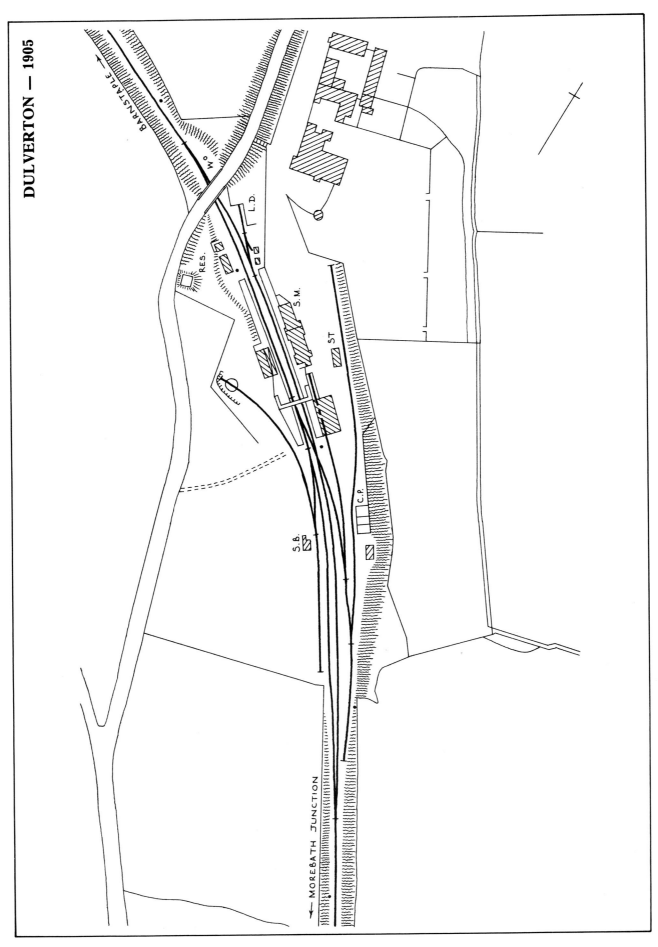

DULVERTON — 1905

BARNSTAPLE

RES.

L.D.

S.M.

ST

S.B.

C.P.

MOREBATH JUNCTION

Looking east, c.1960. *Nelson Collection; courtesy OPC*

Looking west, c.1960. *Nelson Collection; courtesy OPC*

'Island' platform building viewed from the south; c.1960. *S. J. Dickson*

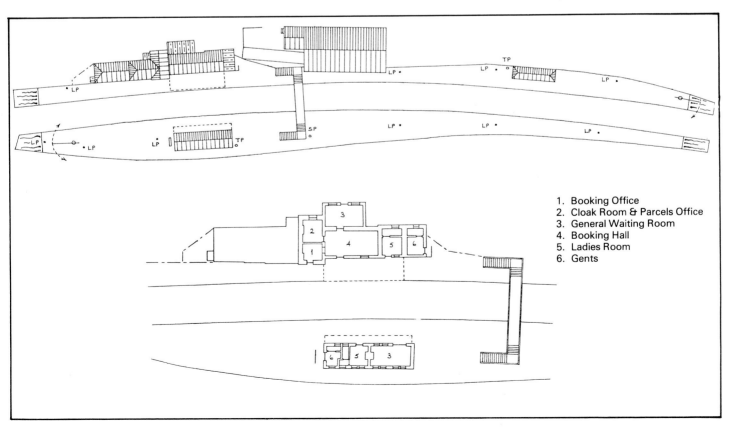

1. Booking Office
2. Cloak Room & Parcels Office
3. General Waiting Room
4. Booking Hall
5. Ladies Room
6. Gents

No. 1421 running into the Exe Valley platform on 22nd June 1963. The auto-coach next to the engine is W22OW *Thrush*, one of only two trailers given names.

M. J. Fox; courtesy Tiverton Museum

Rail-borne horse boxes would arrive for the Exmoor Hunt, the short 2-wagon dock adjacent to the 'up' platform having been designed for this traffic. Some timber from local forests was sent out by rail, much of it going as pit-props or as 'round' timber for railway use. Cattle from Brushford Market were also dispatched by train.

The poor roads — especially in an east-west direction — kept traffic levels constant well into the post-war period, but the loss of the Exe Valley and the inevitable encroachment of road vehicles hit Dulverton hard. Its goods facilities were withdrawn on and from 6th July 1964, by which date some of the sidings had already been removed (in April of that year the coal siding, 'up' spur, horse-box siding, turntable siding and run-round loop had all been lifted). On 5th August 1964 the engineering department moved in again to remove all remaining sidings except the long loading dock road, this being retained for engineers' use. The station was now reduced to one siding and the two main platform lines. The full implementation of the Beeching Plan was to massacre the railway network in the West Country, and although services on the old D & S survived the axeing of the Exe Valley and Tiverton Branch, railwaymen knew that the writing was on the wall. Manpower shortages now became a problem on the line as men left as soon as they could find work away from the railway. A number of stations lost their signal boxes, and with them their crossing loops, as services were retimed and staff shortages grew. Dulverton signal box closed at the end of July 1966, barely nine weeks before the whole line closed down. For a number of years the station site became overgrown and depressingly derelict, but today the main station buildings and goods shed have been incorporated as an annex to a nearby hotel, and have been attractively restored, while the whole yard area has been landscaped.

Exe Valley Trains

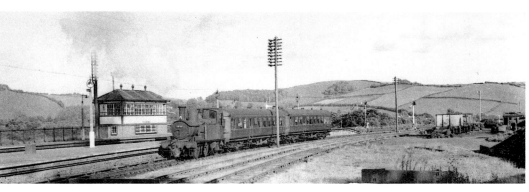

No. 1451 propelling the 19.10 to Exeter out of the back platform road on a fine summer's evening in July 1963.

R. A. Lumber

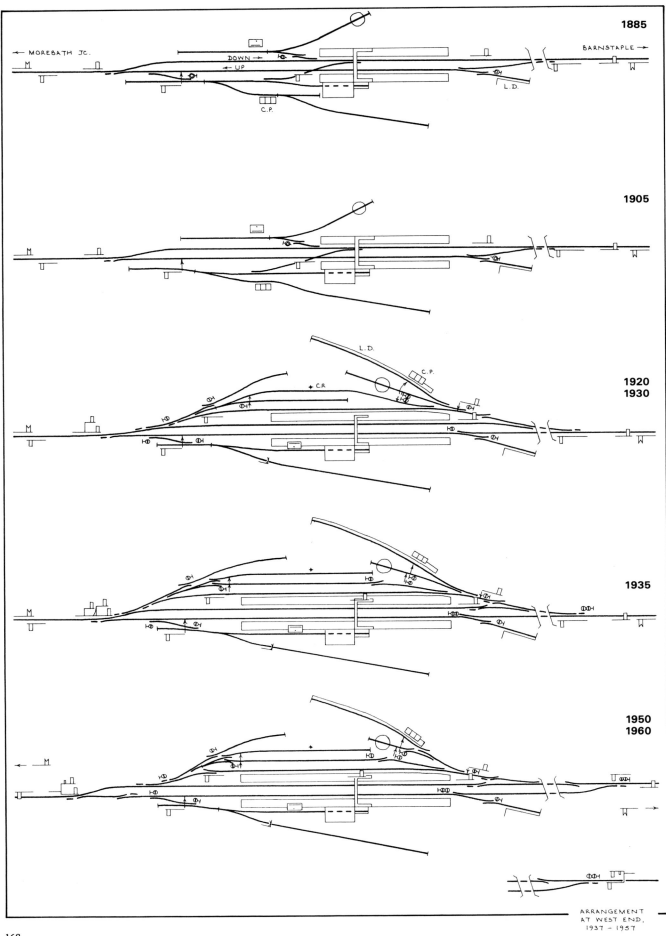

1885

MOREBATH JC.

DOWN

UP

M

C.P.

L.D.

BARNSTAPLE

W

1905

M

W

1920
1930

L.D.

C.P.

C.R.

M

W

1935

M

W

1950
1960

M

W

ARRANGEMENT
AT WEST END,
1937 – 1957

'43XX' class No. 7337 arriving with the 11.05 (S.O.) Ilfracombe to Wolverhampton train on 27th July 1963. *R. A. Lumber*

No. 6343 takes on water at Dulverton whilst working the 08.03 Taunton to Barnstaple train on 28th March 1959. *J. E. Bell*

Devon & Somerset Trains

No. 1420 leaving for the Junction on 31st August 1961. *M. J. Fox; courtesy Tiverton Museum*

Entrance to the halt, from the road bridge. Notice all the classic branch-line halt accoutrements. 4th November 1961. *Peter W. Gray*

Looking towards Tiverton. *Lens of Sutton*

Looking towards Tiverton Junction. *Lens of Sutton*

Halberton Halt

This well-used halt was situated 2 miles 44 chains from Tiverton and 2 miles 10 chains from Tiverton Junction. Opened on Monday 5th December 1927, it was a scheduled stop for all passenger trains on the Tiverton Branch. Being only quarter of a mile or so from the village of Halberton, villagers found it provided a quick and convenient service to Tiverton and, by changing there or at the Junction, to places farther afield.

As was explained in chapter two the Tiverton Branch was built originally in the broad gauge and was intended to be double track. The bridges on the branch in consequence had a particularly wide span for the single 4ft. 8½in. line that used them from 1884. Halberton Halt was built beneath the road overbridge from the village, utilising the 'spare' width for the platform and the bridge itself for increased shelter. The platform was 109ft. long overall and built of wooden facing and edging boards, identical in fact with West Exe Halt which opened three months later. Unlike West Exe, however, a corrugated iron waiting shelter was installed, while oil lamps were provided to light the platform and approach footpath.

Apart from its unusual site, Halberton Halt furnished another idiosyncratic feature, namely the bicycles invariably left on the platform. The halt could be reached easily by road, there were no lanes or fields to cross, and so some villagers and people from the nearby farms used to cycle to the halt to save time. In wet weather, the prime location to leave the bike was underneath the bridge and it was the early-risers who secured this spot!

The halt was administered by Tiverton Junction, and the degree of use was such that, although the Tivvy Bumper did not carry a guard, a porter was provided on each train whose sole duty was to sell tickets to passengers boarding at Halberton and so cut out a queue at the booking office when passengers left the train. The Tiverton Branch kept a passenger service for a further year after the closure of the Exe Valley, and although its closure was inevitable in the climate that prevailed at the British Railways Board at the time, its loss was much mourned at Halberton.

Looking east. No. 1466 and trailer leaving for the Junction in the sunshine of a frosty December morning in 1963.

M. J. Fox; courtesy Tiverton Museum

Tiverton Junction

A Bristol & Exeter station kown as 'Tiverton Road' was opened on 1st May 1844, acting as a rail-head for the Tiverton area and the upper Culm Valley. Built on Brunel's broad gauge, the station possessed two platforms and a small goods yard on the east side of the site.

With the opening of the branch line to Tiverton on 12th June 1848 a bay platform was added on the 'up' side, and the station's name changed to 'Tiverton Junction'. A few short 'branch' sidings and a small engine shed were also added. The 280 foot long branch bay platform was covered for over half its length by an open-ended wooded trainshed, while the 'up' and 'down' platforms had the conventional valanced canopies. Tiverton trains could arrive in, and depart from, the 'up' main platform, a facility which was essential when locomotives had to run round their train or when trains worked through to and from Exeter. The opening of the Culm Valley Branch to Hemyock on 29th May 1876 turned the 'down' platform into an 'island' and also brought about an interesting mixture of gauges: the Culm Valley was narrow gauge (4ft. 8½in.); the Tiverton Branch was broad gauge (7ft. 0¼in.); and the main line was mixed gauge (3 rails, allowing both narrow and broad gauge trains to use the same track).

The narrowing of the Tiverton Branch in June 1884 and the abandonment of broad gauge on the main line in May 1892 facilitated a more economical and flexible mode of operation at the Junction. The mid-1890s saw the provision of two new sidings on the 'down' side and the installation of a turntable (approximate diameter 30ft.) immediately in front of the engine shed. The

Tiverton Branch at this time was the province of the '517' Class of 0-4-2 tanks, whilst the Culm Valley Branch was worked by 2-4-0 tanks which had originally worked on the South Devon Railway in broad gauge days and had been specially converted to suit the tight curves of the Hemyock line. The main station building was on the 'up' platform, being reached by a footbridge linking both the island platform and the station approach on the east side. The water tank adjacent to the Culm Valley platform line was supplied by a well several yards west of, and at a lower level than, the station, a pumping house being installed to raise the water. From the tank, water was piped to the station buildings, goods shed, cattle pens, engine shed and water cranes.

The early years of the twentieth century saw a lengthening of the branch sidings to accommodate the increasing volume of traffic being generated to and from Tiverton. The local butcher, Lloyd Maunder, had built slaughter houses on the land between the engine shed and branch sidings, and a connection had been put in to provide a meat loading bay. The butter factory just to the west of the station, on the Halberton road, was also sending produce out by rail. It is no surprise therefore that when the stations on the Taunton-Exeter line were remodelled in the early 1930s, Tiverton Junction should undergo a marked expansion.

In March 1932 the massive task began of rebuilding the station and transforming the track layout. The whole job was completed by early October — no mean feat. The increased number of sidings reflected the growing amount of freight transferring between main line and branches, as well as the traffic generated at

Looking north; late 1920s. Tiverton Branch trains worked out of the covered bay platform on the far left of the picture. *British Railways/OPC*

A 1921 view, looking south towards Exeter (before quadrupling of the track). *L&GRP; courtesy David & Charles*

the Junction itself — a trait which continued to grow into the 1950s with the Lloyd Maunder meat traffic; butter from the local factory's purpose-built 'butter platform'; milk tankers from the dairy at Hemyock; and oil into Park Sidings.

The functional nature of the new station combined with its main line orientation put it in a different world from the small stone-built rural stations of the Exe Valley, but the two were closely linked in both the passenger and freight spheres. The loss of the Culm Valley, Exe Valley and particularly the Tiverton Branch, put the Junction in a weak economic position now that the age of the internal combustion engine had dawned. Despite the provision of a Western National bus service to connect the Junction with Tiverton, the trains booked to stop were pitifully few and did not satisfy the mainly local nature of Tiverton's sphere of influence. Bit by bit the freight began to die away: the

Tiverton goods ceased running in June 1967; the meat and butter traffic disappeared and all the 'up' side sidings were removed. In November 1973 the lucrative milk traffic from Hemyock was lost to road haulage, and most of the 'down' sidings were lifted. With the passenger service down to about three trains each way a day, the huge signal box which once had over one hundred and twenty levers was little more than a section break presiding over a rather faded and shabby station. In September 1983 the afternoon shift (one man) at the station was deleted, while in May 1984 came the announcement that the station would close on completion of a new 'Parkway' style station to be built near the M5 motorway junction at Sampford Peverell. This will remove the need for the loop lines at the Junction and with the completion of Exeter's multiple-aspect signalling scheme in 1986, will also see the end of the signal box.

Looking south after reconstruction. *British Railways/OPC*

View south. The Tiverton Branch may be seen curving in on the far right of the picture.   *British Railways/OPC*

View north along the Culm Valley platform; c.1960.   *Nelson Collection; courtesy OPC*

Left: No. 1450, having taken on water, will move further back into the branch platform prior to working the 13.42 over to Tiverton. The DMU has just arrived with a stopping service from Exeter to Taunton. 18th August 1964.

I. G. Holt

Right: Southern end of the Junction layout, c.1893, viewed from the Tiverton Branch. The signal box was one of only a few built by the Bristol & Exeter to their own design (the others on the main line and branches were erected by signalling contractors Saxby & Farmer). Opened in 1874, the box remained until the station layout was altered in 1932.

Tiverton Museum

Below left: No. 1469 propelling its trailer over the cluster of points en route for Tiverton in October 1957.

R. E. Toop

Below right: No. 1442 taking on water in the Tiverton Branch platform. The 'Butter' platform is to the right of the train. 4th May 1964.

R. A. Lumber

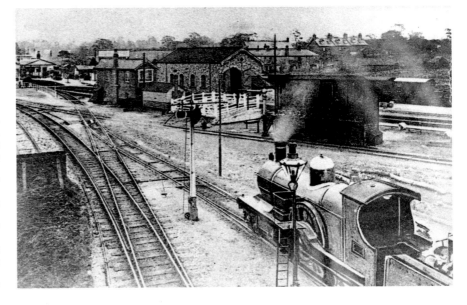

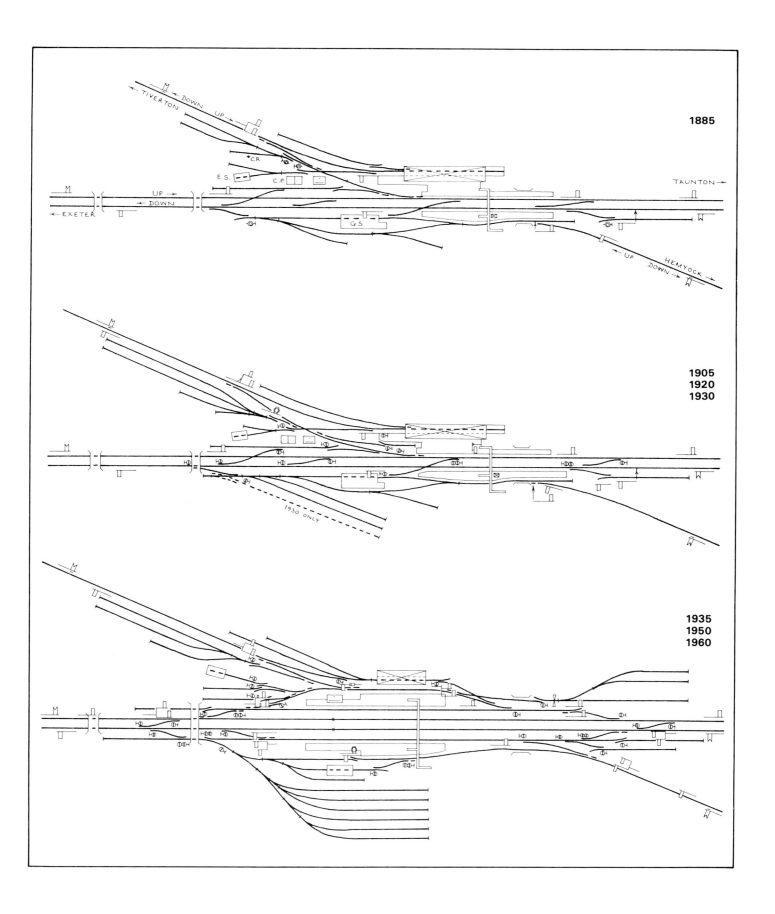

1885

1905
1920
1930

1930 ONLY

1935
1950
1960

Appendix I
Gradient Profile

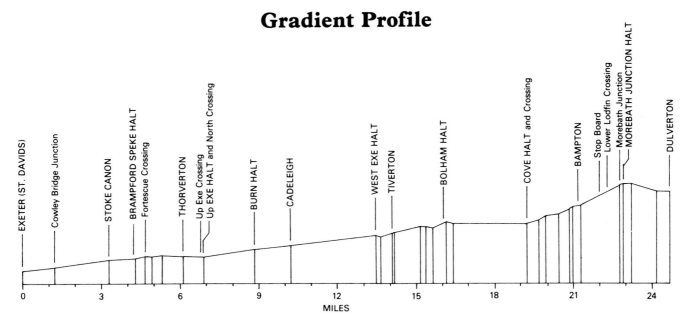

TIVERTON BRANCH		
GRADIENTS STEEPER THAN 1 : 200		
LENGTH OF INCLINE	GRADIENT 1 in	FALLING TOWARDS
28 chains	123	Tiverton
20 chains	86	Tiverton
35 chains	136	Tiverton Jcn.
1m. 02 ch.	86	Tiverton Jcn.
18 chains	91	Tiverton
50 chains	157	Tiverton
14 chains	141	Tiverton
33 chains	103	Tiverton

EXE VALLEY BRANCH			
GRADIENTS STEEPER THAN 1 : 200			
INCLINE BETWEEN	LENGTH OF INCLINE	GRADIENT 1 in	FALLING TOWARDS
Brampford Speke & Thorverton	32 chains	100	Brampford Speke
Brampford Speke & Thorverton	18 chains	100	Thorverton
Brampford Speke & Thorverton	32 chains	132	Brampford Speke
Up Exe and Cadeleigh	73 chains	165	Up Exe
Cadeleigh and Tiverton	38 chains	132	Cadeleigh
Cadeleigh and Tiverton	10 chains	73	Tiverton
Cadeleigh and Tiverton	12 chains	150	Cadeleigh
Tiverton and Bampton	6 chains	103	Tiverton
Tiverton and Bampton	78 chains	119	Tiverton
Tiverton and Bampton	13 chains	163	Bampton
Tiverton and Bampton	17 chains	100	Bampton
Tiverton and Bampton	32 chains	77	Tiverton
Tiverton and Bampton	18 chains	100	Bampton
Tiverton and Bampton	18 chains	66	Tiverton
Tiverton and Bampton	41 chains	176	Tiverton
Tiverton and Bampton	30 chains	79	Tiverton
Tiverton and Bampton	7 chains	66	Tiverton
Bampton & Morebath Junction	57 chains	66	Bampton
Bampton & Morebath Junction	36 chains	66	Bampton
Bampton & Morebath Junction	12 chains	100	Bampton

Appendix II

EXE VALLEY : OPERATING NOTES/RESTRICTIONS

WORKING OF BRANCH

Tank engines only must be used for working the Branch Line between Stoke Canon and Dulverton. A tender engine — engine leading — may, however, be worked over the Branch between Stoke Canon Junction and Dulverton, on a through train.

THORVERTON

No Passenger train is to be shunted into the Siding at the West end of the Station.

TIVERTON

(a) Shunting Operations

A Klaxon Horn is fixed on a telegraph post adjacent to the Down Exe Valley Line Home Signal to control shunting movements between the shunting spur, the Exe Valley Line and Tiverton Yard.

The plunger is fixed on a lamp post at the Yard exit.

The standard code of signals shewn in the Rule Book must be observed, allowing communication between Shunter and Enginemen.

Drivers must not shunt in any direction until the required code is sounded on the Klaxon Horn.

(b) Propelling Empty Coaching Stock Trains between Tiverton and West Exe Halt

An empty Coaching Stock train may be propelled as between Tiverton and West Exe Halt, providing the train does not exceed an engine and four vehicles and the brake compartment is leading, in which the Guard must ride and keep a sharp look-out and be prepared to hand-signal to the Driver.

(c) Exchange of Electric Train Staff

When trains are crossed at Tiverton, and delay would be saved, a Porter must collect the Staff from the Up train and take it to the Signal Box, and then deliver the Staff to the Down train, after being requested by the Signalman to do so.

BAMPTON

(a) Securing Vehicles detached from Passenger Trains

No vehicle must be detached and allowed to remain on the Main Line.

Vehicles detached from Up trains must be placed in the Siding before departure of the train, and vehicles detached from Down trains must either be placed into the Sidings by the train engine, or pushed into the Sidings by hand before the train leaves the Station.

(b) Cove Quarry — Blasting Instructions

Blasting may be permitted in small charges at agreed times, subject to the train service and during daylight and in clear weather only.

Whenever the Quarry Company requires to blast, their Foreman will apply to the Crossing Keeper at Cove. The Crossing Keeper must obtain the necessary permission from the Signalman at Bampton.

Immediately blasting is finished the Quarry Company's Foreman must give an assurance to the Cove Crossing Keeper that the line is clear. The Crossing Keeper must so advise the Bampton Signalman.

(c) Cove Siding — Ground Frame

The points giving access to the Siding are controlled from the lever frame in the Level Crossing Signal Cabin, worked as a Ground Frame. The levers are unlocked by the Key on the Train Staff, and are to be attended by the Guard. The signals and gate bolts are not so released or locked, and are the responsibility of the Crossing Keeper.

(d) Stop Board — 0m. 61ch.

Down Freight Trains must stop at the Board fixed at 0m. 61ch., between Lower Lodfin Crossing and Bampton, for the Guard to pin down Wagon Brakes. The train must also stop near the Bampton Down Starting Signal for the brakes to be released.

TIVERTON JUNCTION

An appointed man may, when necessary, be permitted to fetch the Train Token from, or take it to the Tiverton Branch Train, after being requested by the Signalman to do so.

Appendix III

ENGINE RESTRICTIONS

EXE VALLEY BRANCH

Route Colour	Engines Authorised	Local Prohibitions
Yellow	All Uncoloured and Yellow types	Permitted tender engines may work over the Branch on through trains , if required. BAMPTON — Scott's Siding. No engine to pass Stopboard. THORVERTON — Mill Siding. No engine to pass gate.
	Southern Region 'West Country' Class (except rebuilt engines of this class)	Applicable in cases of emergency only. Speed NOT to exceed 20 m.p.h. All Permanent Speed Restrictions less than 20m.p.h. to be rigidly observed. 'West Country' Class Engines must NOT be coupled to any other engine. TIVERTON — Bay Lines. BAMPTON — Crossover to Goods Yard.

TIVERTON BRANCH

Dotted Red	All types except 60XX	Red types — Speed restricted to 20m.p.h. TIVERTON — 'Red' engines prohibited on all sidings except that alongside Unwin's Yard and connection to Main Line and Double Compound. Goodland's Lower Siding: All engines prohibited except 0-6-0T, 16XX, 54XX, 57XX and 0-6-0, 2251 Classes at SLOW SPEED only. Goodland's Top Siding: All 'Red' and 'Blue' engines except 2-6-2T, 51XX.

Appendix IV

SIGNAL FUNCTIONS/LOCATIONS: 1960

DESCRIPTION OF SIGNAL	LEVER NO.	DISTANCE FROM BOX (Yd.)	DESCRIPTION OF SIGNAL	LEVER NO.	DISTANCE FROM BOX (Yd.)
THORVERTON					
UP DISTANT (FIXED)	—	856	DOWN ADVANCED STARTER	17	302
UP HOME	2	170	DOWN STARTER	18	57
UP STARTER	3	74	DOWN HOME	19	196
UP ADVANCED STARTER	4	293	DOWN DISTANT (FIXED)	—	827
CADELEIGH					
DOWN DISTANT (FIXED)	—	1672	UP MAIN TO GOODS LOOP	16	153
DOWN HOME	2	157	UP ADVANCED STARTER	17	290
DOWN STARTER	3	77	UP STARTER	18	70
			UP HOME	19	153
			UP DISTANT (FIXED)	—	780
TIVERTON					
UP DISTANT (FIXED)	—	930	DOWN INNER HOME TO BAY	35	134
UP HOME	1	264	DOWN START (SHUNT)	36	190
UP MAIN STARTER	2	78	DOWN STARTER	37	190
BAY STARTER	3	26	DOWN INNER HOME TO DOWN PLATFORM	38	134
DOWN TO UP MAIN	4	80			
UP MAIN ADVANCED START	5	310	BRANCH HOME	39	265
UP MAIN SHUNT	6	310	DOWN MAIN HOME	40	290
UP MAIN TO BRANCH START	7	78	DOWN MAIN DISTANT (FIXED)	—	1145
DOWN MAIN TO BRANCH	8	80	BRANCH DISTANT (FIXED)	—	1810
BRANCH ADVANCED STARTER	9	330			
BAMPTON					
DOWN DISTANT (FIXED)	—	1096	UP STARTER	20	191
DOWN HOME	1	278	UP INNER HOME	21	6
DOWN STARTER	2	80	UP OUTER HOME	22	198
DOWN INTERMEDIATE START	3	68	UP DISTANT (FIXED)	—	736
DOWN ADVANCED STARTER	4	208			
MOREBATH JUNCTION					
DOWN MAIN DISTANT	1	1290	BRANCH STARTER	19	75
DOWN MAIN OUTER HOME	2	445	UP MAIN TO BRANCH	20	205
DOWN MAIN INNER HOME	3	20	UP MAIN STARTER	21	339
BRANCH DISTANT (FIXED)	—	1070	UP MAIN HOME	22	205
BRANCH HOME	4	163	UP DISTANT	23	1216
DOWN STARTER	5	77			

Appendix V

SPEED RESTRICTIONS

NAME OF PLACE	DIRECTION OF TRAIN		Miles per Hour
	From	To	
Exeter Middle Box	All trains entering or leaving Bay Line..........	....	5
Cowley Bridge Junction	All W.R. Trains through Junction...............	....	50
Stoke Canon	Up Main..................................	Up Platform Line.................................	20
Stoke Canon	Up Main..................................	Branch Platform Line...........................	20
Stoke Canon	Branch Platform Line...........................	Down Main over connections at West End....	15
Stoke Canon	Up Platform Line.................................	Branch..	15

EXE VALLEY BRANCH — The speed of all Up and Down Trains between Stoke Canon Junction and Morebath Junction must not exceed 35 m.p.h. and must be further restricted to a lower speed as shown below:

Thorverton	Trains entering or leaving Station Loop........	....	15
Cadeleigh	Trains entering or leaving Station Loop........	....	15
Tiverton	Tiverton Branch.................................	Exe Valley Branch..............................	10
Tiverton	Exe Valley Branch...............................	Tiverton Branch................................	10
Tiverton	Single Line......................................	Double Line.....................................	10
Tiverton & Bolham Halt	7m. 10ch..	7m. 50ch..	20
Bampton	Trains entering or leaving Station Loop........	....	15
Bampton & Morebath Junction	1m.p...	1m. 20ch..	20
Morebath Junction	Trains entering or leaving Loops..............	....	15
Morebath Junction	All Down Trains between Station and 182m. 50ch....................................	....	40
Morebath Junction and Dulverton	All Down Trains between 182m. 50ch. and Dulverton Station...........................	....	50
	All Up Trains between Dulverton and Morebath Junction.............................	....	50

TIVERTON BRANCH — The speed of all Up and Down Trains must not exceed 45 m.p.h. and must be further restricted to a lower speed as shown below:

Tiverton Junction	All trains between Tiverton Jc. & 179m. 30ch...	....	35
Tiverton	All trains over Junction with Exe Valley Line	....	10
Red Engines not to exceed speed of 20 m.p.h.			

Appendix VI

Appendix VII

WORKING TIMETABLES : EXPLANATION OF REFERENCES

SO	Saturdays Only		a	Arrives 1½ minutes earlier
SX	Saturdays Excepted		b	Arrives 3 minutes earlier
TO	Tuesdays Only		c	Arrives 7 minutes earlier
TX	Tuesdays Excepted			
ThO	Thursdays Only			Where no separate time is shown for
ThSO	Thursdays and Saturdays Only			arrival and departure, the time indicated is
CR	Calls when required			the Departure time.
Q	Runs when required			
N	Stop not advertised in public timetable			
			X	Indicates points at which trains are
E.B.V. †	Engine and Brake Van			booked to cross each other on a single line.
E.C.S. †	Empty coaching stock train		*	Wait for 'Line Clear'
			•	Shunt
L.E. ‖	Light Engine		→	For continuation of train timings, see subsequent column
M.P.	Mileage post		←	Train timings continued from a previous
M	Miles			column
C	Chains (1 chain = 22 yards)		‡	Advertised time in public timetable.
R	Riverside Yard			
				Times shown in small type indicate at what time a train should pass a Station or Signal Box.

TIVERTON BRANCH

Single Line, Broad Gauge; Tiverton Junction to Tiverton.

Length: 4m 54ch.   Journey time: 12 minutes.

DEPARTURES From Tiverton				
WEEKDAYS	1850	1861	1869	1877
AM	6.48	8.40	8.44	7.50
	8.00	9.47	10.12	9.00 E
	9.48	11.45	11.25	9.55
	11.49			11.10
PM	12.40	12.55	12.00	12.20
	1.40	2.20	2.22	2.10
	2.50	3.46	3.37	3.37
	4.45	5.00	5.26	5.45
	5.57	7.45	6.05	7.10
	7.20	8.30	8.14	8.20
			9.40	9.40
			10.25	
SUNDAYS AM	6.48	8.40	8.40	8.39
	9.48	9.50	10.30	10.14
PM	2.50	3.46	3.46	3.44
	9.10	9.10	5.54	5.45

ARRIVALS	E : Through Train to or from Exeter			
WEEKDAYS	1850	1861	1869	1877
AM	7.28	9.12	9.35	8.37 E
	8.42	10.45	10.42	9.35
	10.37		11.55	10.55
				11.45
PM	12.30	12.25	1.00	12.50
	1.22	1.30	2.52	1.29
	2.25	2.55	4.07	2.44
	3.34	4.18	5.57	4.30
	5.30	5.55	6.34	5.23
	6.37	8.25	9.05	6.35
	8.05	9.03	10.10	7.43
			10.55	9.20
				10.10
SUNDAYS AM	7.28	9.12	9.12	9.09
	10.28	10.30	11.00	10.44
PM	3.34	4.18	4.18	4.18
	9.55	9.55	6.24	6.20

TRAIN SERVICES, AUGUST 1884 TO APRIL 1885 INCLUSIVE

TIVERTON BRANCH

STATION	DOWN TRAINS						WEEKDAYS										
	GOODS	GOODS	PASS.	PASS.	PASS.	PASS.		PASS.	PASS.	PASS.	PASS.	PASS.	PASS.	PASS.		PASS.	PASS.
TIVERTON JUNCTION..dep	TX 6.30	TO 7.10	EC 8.25	9.20	10.16	E 11.33	....	12.13	EC 1.17	3.33	4.18	EC 5.23	E 6.16	7.28	....	9.23	10.03
TIVERTON............arr	6.50	7.30	8.37	9.32	10.28	11.45	..	12.25	1.29	3.45	4.30	5.35	6.28	7.40	..	9.25	10.15

STATION	UP TRAINS						WEEKDAYS										
	MIXED	PASS.	PASS.	PASS.	PASS.		PASS.	PASS.	PASS.		PASS.	PASS.	PASS.	PASS.	PASS.	L.E.
TIVERTON............dep	....	7.50	EC 9.00	9.45	11.10	11.52	....	E 12.45	3.16	3.55	....	E 5.55	7.05	8.25	9.00	9.40	10‖25
TIVERTON JUNCTION..arr	..	8.04	9.12	9.57	11.22	12.04	..	12.57	3.28	4.07	..	6.07	7.17	8.37	9.12	9.52	10‖35

DOWN TRAINS	SUNDAYS					
	L.E.	PASS.	PASS.	L.E.	PASS.	PASS.
TIVERTON JUNCTION..dep	8‖10	8.58	10.34	3‖00	4.08	5.55
TIVERTON............arr	8‖22	9.09	10.46	3‖13	4.20	6.07

UP TRAINS	SUNDAYS					
	PASS.	PASS.	L.E.	PASS.	PASS.	L.E.
TIVERTON............dep	8.39	10.14	11‖00	3.48	5.33	6‖30
TIVERTON JUNCTION..arr	8.51	10.26	11‖13	4.00	5.45	6‖42

E : THROUGH TRAIN TO OR FROM EXETER
EC : CONVEYS THROUGH COACH TO/FROM EXETER T.F.O.
TX : TUESDAYS EXCEPTED
TO : TUESDAYS ONLY
TFO : TUESDAYS AND FRIDAYS ONLY

TIVERTON & NORTH DEVON LINE

UP TRAINS		WEEKDAYS				
MILEAGE M C	STATION	MIXED	PASS.		PASS.	PASS.
- -	TIVERTON............dep	8.00	11.35	....	3.53	7.10
5 11	Cove Siding...............	CR	-	..	-	-
7 05	Bampton............arr	8.20	11.49	....	4.07	7.24
	............dep	8.25	11.55	..	4.09	7.26
8 54	Morebath Junction.......	8.35	12.02	....	4.16	7.33
10 45	DULVERTON............arr	8.40	12.08	..	4.21	7.38

DOWN TRAINS		WEEKDAYS				
M.P. MILEAGE M C	STATION	PASS.		PASS.	MIXED	PASS.
- -	DULVERTON............dep	8.55	....	12.30	4.45	8.00
- -	Morebath Junction........	9.01	..	12.36	4.51	8.06
1 49	Bampton............arr	9.06	....	12.41	4.56	8.11
	............dep	9.11	..	12.43	5.10	8.13
3 43	Cove Siding............	-	....	-	CR	-
8 54	TIVERTON............arr	9.25	..	12.57	5.30	8.27

SINGLE LINE worked by Train Staff & Ticket   JULY — DECEMBER, 1885

MILEAGE M	C	STATION	UP TRAINS WEEKDAYS MIXED	PASS.	PASS.		PASS.	PASS.	PASS.
0	0	EXETER .... dep	6.50	9.45	10.55	....	1.05	3.05	6.25
3	40	Stoke Canon Junction	6.59	9.51	11.03	..	1.13	3.13	6.33
4	19	Brampford Speke ...... arr	7.03	9.54	11.06	....	1.16	3.17	6.35
		.... dep	7.04	9.55	11.07	..	1.17	3.18	6.36
6	11	Thorverton ...... arr	7.10	10X00	11X12	....	1X22	3.24	6.41
		.... dep	7.18	10.01	11.13	..	1.23	3.25	6.42
6	73	Up Exe & Silverton .... arr	7.22	10.04	11.16	....	1.26	3.28	6.45
		.... dep	7.23	10.05	11.17	..	1.27	3.29	6.46
10	18	Cadeleigh & Bickleigh .. arr	7.33	10.12	11.24	....	1.34	3.36	6.53
		.... dep	7.39	10.14	11.26	..	1.36	3.38	6.54
14	9	TIVERTON .... arr	7.51	10.23	11.35	....	1.45	3.48	7.03
		.... dep	7.59	..	11.37	..	1.47	3X51	7.07
19	20	Cove Siding	CR	....	—	....	—	—	—
21	14	Bampton ...... arr	8.16	..	11.51	..	2.01	4.05	7.21
		.... dep	8.21	....	11.53	....	2.03	4.07	7.23
22	63	Morebath Junction	8.30	..	12.00	..	2.10	4.15	7.30
24	54	DULVERTON .... arr	8X35	....	12X05	....	2.15	4X20	7.35

CROSSING ARRANGEMENTS

1. The 6.50am Train from Exeter will cross the 7.35am Train from Barnstaple at Dulverton.
2. The 9.45am Train from Exeter will cross the 9.05am Train from Dulverton at Thorverton.
3. The 10.55am Train from Exeter will cross the 10.50am Train from Tiverton at Thorverton; and the 11.25am Train from Barnstaple at Dulverton.
4. The 1.05pm Train from Exeter will cross the 12.30pm Train from Dulverton at Thorverton.
5. The 3.05pm Train from Exeter will cross the 2.40pm Train from Dulverton at Tiverton; and the 3.40pm Train from Barnstaple at Dulverton.

TIVERTON BRANCH

SINGLE LINE worked by Train Staff & Ticket   JULY — DECEMBER, 1885

MILEAGE M	C	STATION	UP TRAINS WEEKDAYS MIXED	PASS.	PASS.	E.C.S.	PASS.		PASS.	PASS.	PASS.	PASS.	PASS.	PASS.	L.E.
0	0	TIVERTON .... dep	7.50	9.05	9.46	TO 11†10	11.52	....	2.35	3.16	3.55	5.55	7.05	8.45	....	10‖25
4	54	TIVERTON JUNCTION ... arr	8.04	9.17	9.58	11†22	12.03	..	2.47	3.28	4.07	6.07	7.17	8.57	..	10‖35

MILE-POST MILEAGE M	C	STATION	DOWN TRAINS WEEKDAYS PASS.	PASS.		PASS.	PASS.	MIXED	PASS.
—	—	DULVERTON .... dep	9X05	....	..	12X30	2X40	4.45	8X00
—	—	Morebath Junction	9.11	..	....	12.36	2.46	4.52	8.06
1	49	Bampton ...... arr	9.16	....	....	12.41	2.51	4.58	8.11
		.... dep	9.18	..	....	12.43	2.53	5.03	8.13
3	43	Cove Siding	—	....	..	—	—	CR	—
8	54	TIVERTON .... arr	9.32	..	....	12.57	3.07	5.20	8.27
		.... dep	9.35	10.50	..	12.59	3X55	5.25	8.30
12	45	Cadeleigh & Bickleigh .. arr	9.45	11.00	....	1.09	4.05	5.36	8.40
		.... dep	9.46	11.01	..	1.10	4.06	5.41	8.41
15	70	Up Exe & Silverton ..... arr	9.54	11.09	....	1.18	4.14	5.50	8.49
		.... dep	9.55	11.10	..	1.19	4.15	5.51	8.50
16	52	Thorverton ...... arr	9.58	11.13	....	1.22	4.18	5.54	8.53
		.... dep	10X00	11X14	..	1X24	4.19	5.59	8.54
18	44	Brampford Speke ...... arr	10.05	11.19	....	1.29	4.24	6.05	9.00
		.... dep	10.07	11.21	..	1.31	4.26	6.07	9.02
19	23	Stoke Canon Junction	10.11	11.25	....	1.35	4.29	6.11	9.05
—	—	EXETER .... arr	10.18	11.33	..	1.42	4.36	6.20	9.12

1. The 9.05am Train from Dulverton will cross the 7.55am Train from Taunton at Dulverton; and the 9.45am Train from Exeter at Thorverton.
2. The 10.50am Train from Tiverton will cross the 10.55am Train from Exeter at Thorverton.
3. The 12.30pm Train from Dulverton will cross the 11.20am Train from Taunton at Dulverton; and the 1.05pm Train from Exeter at Thorverton.
4. The 2.40pm Train from Dulverton will cross the 1.30pm Train from Taunton at Dulverton; and the 3.05pm Train from Exeter at Tiverton.
5. The 8.00pm Train from Dulverton will cross the 6.55pm Train from Taunton at Dulverton.

STATION	DOWN TRAINS WEEKDAYS GOODS	GOODS	PASS.	PASS.	PASS.	PASS.		PASS.	PASS.	PASS.	PASS.	PASS.	PASS.	PASS.
TIVERTON JUNCTION ... dep	TX 6.30	TO 7.10	8.25	9.27	10.16	TO 11.33	....	12.13	2.58	3.33	4.18	6.16	7.28	10.03
TIVERTON .... arr	6.50	7.30	8.37	9.39	10.28	11.45	..	12.25	3.10	3.45	4.30	6.28	7.40	10.15

STATION	UP TRAINS SUNDAYS PASS.	PASS.	L.E.	PASS.	PASS.	L.E.
TIVERTON .... dep	8.39	10.14	11‖00	3.48	5.33	6‖30
TIVERTON JUNCTION ... arr	8.51	10.26	11‖13	4.00	5.45	6‖42

STATION	DOWN TRAINS SUNDAYS L.E.	PASS.	PASS.	L.E.	PASS.	PASS.
TIVERTON JUNCTION .. dep	8‖10	8.58	10.34	3‖00	4.08	5.55
TIVERTON .... arr	8‖22	9.09	10.46	3‖13	4.20	6.07

1905   OCTOBER — DECEMBER

STATION	PASS.	PASS. TC	PASS.	GOODS	PASS.	GOODS	PASS.	PASS.
EXETER............dep	7.16	9.11	10.46	11.30	12.56	....	3.17	7.02
Stoke Canon........arr	7.22	9.17	10.52	....	1.02	..	3.23	7.08
............dep	7.23	9.18	10.53	..	1.03	....	3.24	7.09
Stoke Canon Junction..a	....	..	....	11X38	....	..		
............dep	7.24	9.19	10.54	11X40	1.04	..	3.25	7.10
Brampford Speke....arr	7.26	9.21	10.56	....	1.06	..	3.27	7.12
............dep	7.27	9.22	10.57	..	1.07	..	3.28	7.13
Thorverton........arr	7.32	9.27	11.02	11.50	1X12	..	3X33	7.18
............dep	7.33	9.28	11.03	12.10	1X14	..	3X36	7.19
Up Exe............arr	7.36	9.31	11.06	....	1.17	..	3.39	7.22
............dep	7.37	9.32	11.07	..	1.18	..	3.40	7.23
Cadeleigh & Bickleigh...a	7.44	9X38	11X13	12.25	1.24	..	3.46	7.29
............dep	7.46	9X41	11X15	12.38	1.25	..	3.47	7.30
TIVERTON............arr	7.54	9.49	11.23	12X50	1.33	..	3.55	7X39
............dep	7.57	9.55	11.25	..	1.35	2.10	3.57	7X41
Cove Siding............	....	..	..	..	CR	....	..	
Bampton............arr	8.09	10.08	11.38	....	1.48	2X30	4.10	7.54
............dep	8.11	10.10	11.40	..	1.49	2.55	4.12	7.58
Morebath Junction......	8.16	10.15	11.45	....	1.54	3.05	4.17	8.03
DULVERTON............arr	8.21	10.20	11.50	..	1.59	3.10	4.22	8.08

STATION	PASS.	PASS.		PASS.	PASS. TH	PASS.	GOODS	PASS.
DULVERTON............dep	9.01	10.40	....	12.10	2.33	5.01	6.00	8.50
Morebath Junction......	9.06	10.45	..	12.15	2.38	5.06	6.07	8.55
Bampton............arr	9.11	10.49	....	12.19	2X43	5.10	6.15	9.00
............dep	9.13	10.51	..	12.21	2X46	5.12	6.35	9.01
Cove Siding............	....	..	....	..	....	..	CR	
TIVERTON............arr	9.25	11.03	..	12.33	2.58	5.24	6.55	9.13
............dep	9.30	11.06	....	12X53	3.15	5.27	7X40	9.15
Cadeleigh & Bickleigh...a	9X38	11X14	..	1.01	3.23	5.35	7.50	9.23
............dep	9X39	11X15	....	1.02	3.24	5.36	8.00	9.24
Up Exe............arr	9.47	11.23	..	1.09	3.31	5.43	..	9.32
............dep	9.48	11.24	....	1.10	3.32	5.44	..	9.33
Thorverton........arr	9.51	11.27	..	1X13	3X35	5.47	8.15	9.36
............dep	9.52	11.28	..	1X16	3X38	5.48	8.35	9.37
Brampford Speke....arr	9.57	11.33	..	1.21	3.43	5.53	..	9.42
............dep	9.58	11.34	..	1.22	3.44	5.54	..	9.43
Stoke Canon Junction..a	..	....	..	..	....	..		
............dep	10.00	11.36	....	1.24	3.46	5.56	8.45	9.45
Stoke Canon........arr	10.01	11.37	....	1.25	3.47	5.57	..	9.46
............dep	10.02	11.40	....	1.27	3.48	5.58	....	9.47
EXETER............arr	10.08	11.48	..	1.35	3.56	6.05	8.55	9.55

TC : Through train from Christow ⎫ Teign Valley Line
TH : Through train to Heathfield ⎭

TIVERTON BRANCH

1905   OCTOBER — DECEMBER

DOWN TRAINS WEEKDAYS

MILEAGE M C	STATION	GOODS	PASS.	GOODS	PASS.	PASS.	PASS.	PASS.		PASS. T.O.	GOODS	PASS.	PASS.		MIXED	PASS.
0 0	TIVERTON JUNCTION....dep	6.10	7.30	8.02	8.20	9.05	10.03	11.50	....	12.25	1.30	3.13	3.55	..	4.50	5.58
4 54	TIVERTON................arr	6.25	7.40	8.17	8.30	9.15	10.15	12.00	..	12.35	1.45	3.23	4.05	....	5.02	6.08

SUNDAYS

		PASS.	PASS.	PASS.	PASS.		GOODS	L.E.	PASS.	PASS.		PASS.	PASS.	PASS.	
	TIVERTON JUNCTION....dep	6.38	7.35	8.23	10.10	....	8.00	8||20	9.10	10.45	....	2.10	3.05	6.15	....
	TIVERTON................arr	6.48	7.45	8.33	10.20	..	8.15	8||30	9.20	10.55	..	2.20	3.15	6.25	..

UP TRAINS WEEKDAYS

MILEAGE M C	STATION	MIXED	PASS.		PASS.	GOODS	PASS.	PASS.		PASS. T.O.	GOODS T.X.	GOODS T.O.	PASS.	PASS.	PASS.	GOODS
0 0	TIVERTON................dep	7.00	7.48	....	8.38	9.17	9.32	11.20	..	12.08	12.40	12.55	2.30	3.32	4.20	5.25
4 54	TIVERTON JUNCTION....arr	7.12	7.58	..	8.48	9.30	9.42	11.30	....	12.18	12.55	1.10	2.40	3.42	4.30	5.40

SUNDAYS

		PASS.	PASS.	PASS.	PASS.	L.E.		PASS.	GOODS	PASS.	PASS.		PASS.	PASS.	PASS.	
	TIVERTON................dep	6.18	6.55	7.55	9.50	10||30	..	8.45	9.25	9.55	11.05	....	2.35	5.45	6.35	....
	TIVERTON JUNCTION....arr	6.28	7.05	8.05	10.00	10||40	....	8.55	9.40	10.05	11.15	..	2.45	5.55	6.45	..

EXE VALLEY LINE
WORKED BY THE ELECTRIC TRAIN STAFF 1920   JANUARY — APRIL

MILEAGE M	C	STATION	UP TRAINS WEEKDAYS PASS.	PASS.		GOODS		PASS.	PASS.	
0	0	EXETER (ST. DAVID'S).....dep	....	7.40	10.40	..	11.40	..	3.40	5.50	....
3	30	Stoke Canon.........arr	..	7.46	10.46	....	..	....	3.46	5.56	..
		............dep	....	7.48	10.48	..	....	..	3.48	5.58	....
3	40	Stoke Canon Junction......	..	7.49	10.49	....	11.50	....	3.49	5.59	..
4	19	Brampford Speke.............	....	..	10.52	..	....		3.52	6.02	
6	11	Thorverton.........arr	..	7.54	10.57		12.00		3.57	6X07	..
		............dep	....	7.55	10.58	..	12.25	..	3.58	6X08	....
6	73	Up Exe.................	..	7.58	11.01	....	..	....	4.01	6.11	..
10	18	Cadeleigh.........arr	....	8.04	11.07	..	12X40	..	4.07	6.17	..
		............dep		8.07	11.10	....	1.25	....	4.10	6.20	
14	9	TIVERTON...........arr	..	8.15	11.18	..	1.38	..	4.18	6X28	....
		............dep	..	8.18	11.22		2.20	....	4.20	6X30	..
19	20	Cove Siding..........	...	..	....	..	CR	..	....	..	....
21	14	Bampton.........arr	..	8.30	11.35		2.40	...	4.32	6.42	..
		............dep		8.32	11.38		3.10	....	4.35	6.45	....
22	63	Morebath Junction..........	..	8.37	11.43	....	3.20	....	4.40	6.50	
24	54	DULVERTON...........arr	....	8.42	11.48	..	3.25	..	4.45	6.55	....

TIVERTON BRANCH
WORKED BY TRAIN STAFF AND TICKET 1920   JANUARY — APRIL

MILEAGE M	C	STATION	UP TRAINS WEEKDAYS MIXED	PASS.	PASS.	GOODS	PASS.	PASS.		GOODS	PASS.	PASS.		MIXED	PASS.	L.E.	
0	0	TIVERTON.........dep	7.05	8.00	9.15	9.30	10.35	11.30	....	1.00	2.45	3.40	....	5.20	6.55	8X25	....
4	54	TIVERTON JUNCTION......arr	7.17	8.10	9.25	9.45	10.45	11.40	..	1.15	2.55	3.50	..	5.32	7.05	8X35	..

MILE POST MILEAGE M	C	STATION	DOWN TRAINS WEEKDAYS PASS.		PASS.	GOODS	PASS.	GOODS	PASS.	
—	—	DULVERTON.........dep	....	9.05	..	12.15	4.50	5.10	....	7.25	....
—	—	Morebath Junction............	..	9.10	..	12.20	4.57	5.15	..	7.30	..
1	49	Bampton.........arr	..	9.14	..	12.24	5.10→	5.19	....	7.34	..
		............dep	..	9.17	..	12.26	..	5.21	5.40←	7.36	..
3	43	Cove Siding..........		..	..	....		CR	..		
8	54	TIVERTON.........arr	..	9.29	..	12.38	..	5.33	5.58	7.48	..
		............dep	..	9.32	..	12.40	....	5.40	6X35	7.51	..
12	45	Cadeleigh.........arr	..	9.40	..	12X48	..	5.48	6.45	7.59	..
		............dep	..	9.41	..	12X49	..	5.51	6.55	8.00	..
15	70	Up Exe.............	..	9.49	..	12.57	..	5.59	..	8.08	..
16	52	Thorverton.........arr	..	9.51	..	12.59	..	6X03	7.10	8.11	..
		............dep	..	9.52	..	1.00	..	6X10	7.30	8.12	..
18	44	Brampford Speke.............	..	9.57	..	1.05	....	6.16	....	..	
19	23	Stoke Canon Junction......	..	9.59	..	1.07	..	6.20	7.40	8.18	
—	—	Stoke Canon.........arr	..	10.00	..	1.08	....	6.21	..	8.19	
		............dep	..	10.03	..	1.12	..	6.25	..	8.23	
—	—	EXETER (ST. DAVID'S).....arr	..	10.10	..	1.20	..	6.33	7.50	8.30	....

NO SUNDAY SERVICE

MILEAGE M	C	STATION	DOWN TRAINS WEEKDAYS GOODS		PASS.	GOODS	PASS.	PASS.	PASS.	PASS.		GOODS	PASS.	PASS.		MIXED	PASS.
0	0	TIVERTON JUNCTION......dep	5.30	....	7.30	8.20	8.50	9.55	11.05	11.55	..	1.45	3.20	4.05	..	6.00	8.05
4	54	TIVERTON.........arr	5.45	..	7.40	8.35	9.00	10.05	11.15	12.05	....	2.00	3.30	4.15	....	6.12	8.15

EXETER TO DULVERTON   DULVERTON TO EXETER

1930

SINGLE LINE worked by Electric Train Staff

UP TRAINS — WEEKDAYS

1930 JULY — SEPTEMBER

M	C	Station	AUTO	AUTO	AUTO	AUTO	GOODS	AUTO	GOODS	AUTO	AUTO	AUTO	AUTO		AUTO	AUTO	AUTO
0	0	EXETER (ST. DAVID'S)......dep	6.20	7.05	8.20	10.05	10R15	11.30	..	12.50	2.20	3.50	4.38	....	6.10	7.40	9.33
3	30	Stoke Canon......arr	6.26	7.11	8.26	10.11	....	11.36	..	12.56	2.26	3.56	4.44	..	6.16	7.46	9.39
		......dep	6.26½	7.12	8.28	10.12	..	11.37	..	12.57	2.27	3.57	4.45	..	6.16½	7.47	9.40
3	40	Stoke Canon Junction......	6.27½	7.13	8X29	10.13	10.23	11.38	..	12.58	2.28	3.58	4.46	..	6X17½	7.48	9.41
4	19	Brampford Speke Halt......arr	6.29½	7.15	8.31	10.15	..	11.40	..	1.00	2.30	4.00	4.48	..	6.19½	7.50	9.43
		......dep	6.30	7.15½	8.31½	10.16	..	11.41	..	1.00½	2.31	4.01	4.48½	..	6.20	7.50½	9.44
6	11	Thorverton......arr	6.35	7.20½	8.36½	10.21	10X31	11.46	..	1.05½	2.36	4.06	4X53½	..	6.25	7.55½	9X49
		......dep	6.35½	7.21½	8.37	10.22	10X55	11.48	..	1.06½	2.39	4.07	4X57	..	6.25½	7.56½	9X53
6	73	Up Exe Halt......arr	6.37½	7.23½	8.39	10.24	..	11.50	..	1.08½	2.41	4.09	4.59	..	6.27½	7.58½	9.55
		......dep	6.38	7.24	8.39½	10.25	..	11.51	..	1.09	2.42	4.10	5.00	..	6.28	7.59	9.56
8	68½	Burn Halt......arr	6.41½	7.27½	8.43	10.28	..	11.54	..	1.12½	2.46	4.13½	5.03½	..	6.31½	8.02½	9.59½
		......dep	6.42	7.28	8.43½	10.29	..	11.54½	..	1.13	2.47	4.14	5.04	..	6.32	8.03	10.00
10	18	Cadeleigh......arr	6.45	7.31	8.46½	10X32	11.07	11.57½	..	1.16	2X50	4.17	5.07	..	6X35	8.06	10.03
		......dep	6.47	7.34	8.48	10X36	11.30	12.00	..	1.18	2X55	4.19	5.09	..	6X37	8.08	10.05
13	40	West Exe Halt......arr	6.54	7.41	8.55	10.43	..	12.07	..	1.25	3.02	4.26	5.16	..	6.44	8.15	10.12
		......dep	6.55	7.42	8.56	10.44	..	12.08	..	1.26	3.03	4.27	5.17	..	6.45	8.16	10.13
14	9	TIVERTON......arr	6.57	7X44	8X58	10.46	11.42	12X10	..	1.28	3.05	4X29	5.19	..	6.47	8X18	10.15
		......dep	7.00	7.50	9X02	10.50	→	12X23	12.30	1.35	3.07	4X32	....	..	6.50	8X20	10.30
16	5	Bolham Halt......arr	(To Tiverton Jc.)	7.54½	9.06½	10.54½		(To Tiverton Jc.)	..	1.39½	3.11½	4.36½	....		6.54½	8.24½	(To Tiverton Jc.)
		......dep		7.55	9.07	10.55			..	1.40	3.12	4.37			6.55	8.25	
19	18	Cove Halt......arr		8.01	9.13	11.01			CR	1.46	3.18	4.43			7.01	8.31	
		......dep		8.01½	9.13½	11.01½			CR	1.46½	3.18½	4.43½			7.01½	8.31½	
21	14	Bampton......arr		8.05½	9.17½	11.05½			12.49	1.51½	3.22½	4X47½			7.05½	8.35½	
		......dep		8.07	9.19	11.08			1.15	1.53	3.24	4X50			7.07	8.37	
22	63	Morebath Junction......	..	8.11	9.23	11c20			1.25	1.57	3.28	4.54			7.11	8.41	..
22	71	Morebath Junction Halt...arr	....	8.12	9.24	11.21				1.58	3.29	4.55			7.12	8.42	....
		......dep	..	8.13	9.25	11.22				1.59	3.30	4.56			7.13	8.43	..
24	54	DULVERTON......arr	....	8.18	9.30	11.27			1.30	2.04	3.35	5.01	....	..	7.18	8.48	....

DOWN TRAINS — WEEKDAYS

M	C	Station	AUTO	AUTO	AUTO	AUTO		AUTO	AUTO	AUTO	GOODS	AUTO	GOODS	AUTO	AUTO		AUTO
-	-	DULVERTON......dep	....	8.25	9.50	11.50	....	..	2.15	3.50	4.15	5.20	....	..	7.35	..	9.02
-	-	Morebath Junction Halt...arr	..	8.30	9.55	11.55	..	....	2.20	3.55	..	5.25	..	....	7.40	..	9.07
		......dep	....	8.31	9.55½	11.55½	..	....	2.20½	3.56	....	5.26	..	..	7.41	..	9.08
0	0	Morebath Junction......	..	8.32	9.56½	11.56½	..	....	2.21½	3.57	4.21	5.27	..	..	7.42	..	9.09
1	49	Bampton......arr	(From Tiverton Jc.)	8.35	9.59½	11.59½		....	2.24½	4.00	4.30	5.30			7.45	(From Tiverton Jc.)	9.12
		......dep		8.37	10.01	12.01			2.26	4.02	5X00	5.31			7.47		9.13
3	45	Cove Halt......arr		8.41	10.05	12.05			2.30	4.06		5.35			7.51		9.17
		......dep		8.41½	10.05½	12.05½			2.30½	4.07		5.35½			7.51½		9.18
6	58	Bolham Halt......arr		8.48½	10.12	12.12			2.37	4.14		5.42			7.58		9.24½
		......dep		8.49	10.12½	12.12½			2.37½	4.15		5.42½			7.58½		9.25
8	54	TIVERTON......arr	7X44	8X53	10.16½	12X16½	....	..	2.41½	4.20	5o19	5.46½	....	7.12	8.02½	..	9.29
		......dep	8.00	9X00	10.24	12.19		1.45	2.44	4X33	→	5.48	6.15	7.15	8X21	....	9.31
9	23	West Exe Halt......arr	8.01	9.01	10.25	12.20		1.46	2.45	4.34		5.49		7.16	8.22		9.32
		......dep	8.01½	9.02	10.26	12.21		1.47	2.46	4.35		5.50		7.17	8.23		9.33
12	45	Cadeleigh......arr	8.08½	9.09	10X33	12.28		1.54	2X53	4.42		5.57	6X27	7.24	8.30		9.40
		......dep	8.09½	9.10	10X35	12.29		1.55	2X54	4.43		5.58	6X45	7.25	8.31		9.41
13	74½	Burn Halt......arr	8.12½	9.13	10.38	12.31½		1.58	2.56½	4.46		6.00½		7.27½	8.33½		9.43½
		......dep	8.13	9.13½	10.38½	12.32		1.59	2.57	4.47		6.01		7.28	8.34		9.44
15	70	Up Exe Halt......arr	8.17	9.17½	10.42½	12.36		2.03	3.01	4.51		6.05		7.32	8.38		9.48
		......dep	8.17½	9.18	10.43	12.36½		2.04	3.01½	4.52		6.05½		7.33	8.38½		9.49
16	52	Thorverton......arr	8.19½	9.20	10X45	12.38½		2.06	3.03½	4X55		6.07½	6.57	7.35	8.40½		9X51
		......dep	8.20	9.21	10X46	12.39½		2.07	3.05	4X57		6.08½	7.22	7.36	8.42		9X52
18	44	Brampford Speke Halt...arr	8.24	9.25	10.50	12.43½		2.11	3.09	5.01		6.12½		7.40	8.46		9.56
		......dep	8.24½	9.26	10.50½	12.44		2.12	3.10	5.02		6.13		7.41	8.47		9.57
19	23	Stoke Canon Junction......	8X26½	9.28	10.52½	12.46		2.14	3b15	5.04		6c22	7.30	7.43	8.49		9.59
-	-	Stoke Canon......arr	..	8.27½	9.29	10.53½	12.47		2.15	3.16	5.05		6.23		7.44	8.50		10.00
		......dep	..	8.28	9.30	10.54	12.49		2.16	3.17	5.06		6.24		7.45	8.51		10.01
-	-	EXETER (ST. DAVID'S)......arr	..	8.34	9.36	11.00	12.55		2.22	3.23	5.12		6.30	7R38	7.51	8.57	....	10.07

TIVERTON BRANCH

JULY — SEPTEMBER, 1930

DOWN — WEEKDAYS

M.P. MILEAGE M	C			GOODS	GOODS		EX					T.O.					GOODS					E.B.V.	
179	10	TIVERTON JN..d	....	6.30	7.15	..	7.32	8.30	9.52	11.30	....	..	12.09	..	12.43	1.18	..	2.05	....	3.51	5.05	..	6†40	..
181	20	Halberton Halt....	....	..	..	..	7.38	8.36	9.58	11.36	..	...	12.15	....	12.49	1.24	..	....	3.57	5.11	....	..	..
183	64	TIVERTON....arr	....	6.44	7.29	..	7.44	8.42	10.04	11.42	....	12.21	..	12.55	1.30	....	2.20	....	4.03	5.17	..	6†55	..

SUNDAYS

		EX				Th SO							E.B.V. PM					
	TIVERTON JN..d	7.00	7.38	....	9.05	11.55	....	..	....	..	....	..	5†15	..	..	..	..	..
	Halberton Halt....	7.06	7.44	..	9.11	12.01	..	..	....	..	....	..		..	....	..	..	..
	TIVERTON....arr	7.12	7.50	....	9.17	12.07	....						5†25	..				

EX   Through train to or from Exeter, via Exe Valley

NB.   All Passenger Trains are AUTO.

UP — WEEKDAYS

MILEAGE M	C		EX				GOODS SX				T.O.		EX			E.B.V.				GOODS	
—	—	TIVERTON....dep	7.00	7.55	....	9.18	....	10.10	..	11.05	..	11.50	....	..	12.23	1.00	1†40	....	3.20	4.15	5.50	..
2	44	Halberton Halt....	7.07	8.02	..	9.25	..	....	..	11.12	..	11.57	..	..	12.30	1.07	..	....	3.27	4.22	....	..
4	54	TIVERTON JN...a	7.12	8.07	....	9.30	....	10.25	....	11.17	....	12.02	....	..	12.35	1.12	1†50	....	3.32	4.27	6.05	..

SUNDAYS

				GOODS		EX	L.E. Th O	E.C.S. SO			MEAT PM				
	TIVERTON....dep	6.08	7.15	8.30	9.45	....	10.30	....	12‖15	12†15	..	....	5.45	....	..	....	..
	Halberton Halt....	6.15	7.22	8.37	..	....	10.37	..	....	..	....	..	..	....	..	....	..
	TIVERTON JN...a	6.20	7.27	8.42	10.00	....	10.42	....	12‖25	12†25	..	....	5.57	..	....	..

SUNDAYS ONLY

	AUTO		AUTO	AUTO
EXETER (ST. DAVID'S)........dep	9.50	....	1.10	8.15
Stoke Canon................arr	9.56	..	1.16	8.21
...................dep	9.57	..	1.17	8.22
Stoke Canon Junction........	9.58	..	1.18	8.23
Brampford Speke Halt....arr	10.00	....	1.20	8.25
.........................dep	10.01	..	1.21	8.26
Thorverton................arr	10.06	..	1.26	8.31
.........................dep	10.07	..	1.28	8.33
Up Exe Halt..............arr	10.09	....	1.30	8.35
.........................dep	10.10	..	1.31	8.36
Burn Halt.................arr	10.13½	....	1.34½	8.39½
.........................dep	10.14	..	1.35	8.40
Cadeleigh.................arr	10.17	....	1.38	8.43
.........................dep	10.19	..	1.40	8.45
West Exe Halt............arr	10.26	....	1.47	8.52
.........................dep	10.27	..	1.48	8.53
TIVERTON.................arr	10.29	....	1.50	8.55

	AUTO		AUTO	AUTO
TIVERTON.................dep	10.40	....	2.00	9.05
West Exe Halt............arr	10.41	..	2.01	9.06
.........................dep	10.41½	....	2.02	9.07
Cadeleigh.................arr	10.48½	..	2.09	9.14
.........................dep	10.49½	..	2.10	9.15
Burn Halt.................arr	10.52½	..	2.13	9.18
.........................dep	10.53	....	2.13½	9.18½
Up Exe Halt..............arr	10.57	..	2.17½	9.22½
.........................dep	10.57½	....	2.18	9.23
Thorverton................arr	10.59½	..	2.20	9.25
.........................dep	11.00½	..	2.21	9.26
Brampford Speke Halt....arr	11.04½	..	2.25	9.30
.........................dep	11.05	....	2.26	9.31
Stoke Canon Junction........	11.07	..	2.28	9.33
Stoke Canon................arr	11.08	..	2.29	9.34
.........................dep	11.09	..	2.30	9.36
EXETER (ST. DAVID'S)........arr	11.16	....	2.36	9.42

NO SERVICE TIVERTON TO DULVERTON

1935 JULY — SEPTEMBER

EXETER TO DULVERTON

SINGLE LINE worked by Electric Train Staff — WEEKDAYS — SUNDAYS

M	C	Station					Goods				SO	SX	SO								Sun	Sun	Sun
0	0	EXETER (ST. DAVIDS) ... dep	6.20	7.05	8.20	10.05	10R15	11.35	..	12.30	1.50	2.15	2.37	....	3.40	4.38	6.10	7.50	9.35	....	9.55	1.10	8.15
3	30	Stoke Canon ... arr	6.26	7.11	8.26	10.11	....	11.41	....	12.36	1.56	2.21	2.43	..	3.46	4.44	6X16	7.56	9.41	..	10.01	1.16	8.21
		... dep	6.26½	7.12	8.28	10.11½	10.23	11.42	..	12.36½	1.56½	2.22	2.44	....	3.47	4.45	6X17	7.56½	9.42	....	10.02	1.17	8.22
4	19	Brampford Speke Halt ...	6.30	7.15½	8.31½	10.15	....	11.45½	....	12.40	2.00	2.26	2.48	..	3.51	4.48½	6.20½	8.00	9.46	..	10.06	1.21	8.26
6	11	Thorverton ... arr	6.35	7.20½	8.36½	10.20	10.31	11.50½	..	12X45	2.05	2.31	2X53	....	3.56	4X53½	6.25½	8.05	9X51	....	10.11	1.26	8.31
		... dep	6.35½	7.21½	8.37	10.20½	10X55	11.51½	....	12X46	2.06	2.32	2X58	..	3.57	4X57	6.26	8.05½	9X56½	..	10.12	1.28	8.33
6	73	Up Exe Halt ...	6.38	7.24	8.39½	10.23	..	11.54	..	12.48½	2.08½	2.35	3.01	....	4.00	5.00	6.28½	8.08	9.59	....	10.15	1.31	8.36
8	68½	Burn Halt ...	6.42	7.28	8.43½	10.27	....	11.58	....	12.52	2.12½	2.39	3.05½	..	4.04	5.04	6.32½	8.12	10.03	..	10.19	1.35	8.40
10	18	Cadeleigh ... arr	6.45	7.31	8.46½	10X30	11.07	12.01	..	12.55	2.15½	2X43	3.08½	....	4.07	5.07	6X35½	8X15	10.06	....	10.22	1.38	8.43
		... dep	6.47	7.34	8.48	10X32	11.30	12.03	....	12.57	2.17½	2X47	3.12	..	4.09	5.09	6X37	8X17	10.08	..	10.24	1.40	8.45
13	40	West Exe Halt ... arr	6.54	7.41	8.55	10.39	..	12.10	..	1.04	2.24½	2.54	3.19	....	4.16	5.16	6.44	8.24	10.15	....	10.31	1.47	8.52
		... dep	6.55	7.42	8.56	10.40	....	12.11	....	1.05	2.25	2.55	3.20	..	4.17	5.17	6.45	8.25	10.16	..	10.32	1.48	8.53
14	9	TIVERTON ... arr	6.57	7X44	8X58	10.42	11.42	12X13	..	1.07	2X27	2.57	3.22	....	4X19	5.19	6.47	8.27	10.18	....	10.34	1.50	8.55
		... dep	7.00	7X49	9X02	10.45	→	12X22	← 12.30	1.13	2X30	3.00	....	..	4X22	..	6.50	8.29	10.30	..	....	..	....
16	5	Bolham Halt ...	TJ	7.54	9.07	10.50	..	TJ	..	1.18	2.35	3.05	..	....	4.27	....	6.55	8.34	TJ	....	..	....	..
19	18	Cove Halt ...	....	8.00½	9.13½	10.56½	....	..	CR	1.24½	2.41½	3.11½	....	..	4.33½	..	7.01½	8.40½	....	..	....	..	....
21	14	Bampton ... arr	..	8.04½	9.17½	11.00½	..	....	12.49	1.28½	2.45½	3X15½	..	....	4.37½	....	7.05½	8.44½	..	....	..	....	..
		... dep	....	8.06	9.19	11.02	....	..	1.05	1.31	2.47	3X18	....	..	4.40	..	7.07	8.46	....	..	....	..	....
22	63	Morebath Junction ...	..	8.09	9.22	11.05	..	....	1.15	1*41	2.50	3.21	..	....	4.43	....	7.10	8.49	..	....	..	....	..
22	71	Morebath Junction Halt ...	...	8.12	9.25	11.08	....	..	....	1.43	2.53	3.24	....	..	4.46	..	7.13	8.52	....	..	....	..	....
24	54	DULVERTON ... arr	..	8.17	9.30	11.13	..	....	1.20	1.48	2.58	3.29	..	....	4.51	....	7.18	8.57	..	....	..	....	..

TJ Through train to Tiverton Junction

DULVERTON TO EXETER

M.P. Mileage M	C	Station								Goods										Sun	Sun	Sun	Sun
–	–	DULVERTON ... dep	....	8.24	9.50	11.55	....	..	2.00	3.03	3.40	..	5.20	..	....	7.35	9.06	..	....	..	....	..	....
–	–	Morebath Junction Halt ...	..	8.29	9.55½	11.59½	..	....	2.05½	....	3.46	....	5.26	....	..	7.41	9.12	....	..	....	..	....	..
0	0	Morebath Junction ...	....	8.30	9.56½	12.00½	....	..	2.06½	3.10	3.47	..	5.27	..	....	7.42	9.13	..	....	..	....	..	....
1	49	Bampton ... arr	..	8.33	9.59½	12.03½	..	....	2.09½	3X16	3.50	....	5.30	....	..	7.45	9.16	....	..	....	..	....	..
		... dep	....	8.35	10.01	12.05	....	..	2.12	3.26	3.51	..	5.31	..	....	7.47	9.17	..	....	..	....	..	....
3	45	Cove Halt ...	..	8.40	10.05½	12.09½	..	....	2.16½	....	3.56	....	5.35½	....	..	7.51½	9.21½	....	..	....	..	....	..
6	58	Bolham Halt ...	TJ	8.48	10.12½	12.16½	....	..	2.23½	..	4.03½	..	5.42½	..	TJ	7.58½	9.28½	..	....	..	....	..	....
8	54	TIVERTON ... arr	7X44	8X52	10.16½	12X20½	..	....	2X27½	3.44	4.07½	....	5.46½	....	7.06	8.02½	9.32½	....	..	....	..	....	..
		... dep	7X50	9X00	10.20	12X24	....	1.25	2X34	→ ..	4X33	..	5.48	← 6.15	7.08	8.05	9.35	..	....	10.45	....	2.00	9.05
9	23	West Exe Halt ... arr	7.51	9.01	10.21	12.25	..	1.26	2.35	....	4.34	....	5.49	....	7.09	8.06	9.36	....	..	10.46	..	2.01	9.06
		... dep	7.51½	9.02	10.22	12.26	....	1.27	2.36	..	4.35	..	5.49½	..	7.09½	8.07	9.37	..	....	10.46½	....	2.02	9.07
12	45	Cadeleigh ... arr	7.58½	9.09	10X29	12.33	..	1.34	2X43½	....	4.42	....	5.56½	6.27	7.16½	8X14	9.44	....	..	10.53½	..	2.09	9.14
		... dep	7.59½	9.10	10X33	12.34	....	1.34½	2X46	..	4.43	..	5.57½	6X45	7.17	8X18	9.45	..	....	10.54½	....	2.10	9.15
13	74½	Burn Halt ...	8.03	9.13½	10.36½	12.37	..	1.38	2.49	....	4.47	....	6.01	....	7.20	8.21½	9.48½	....	..	10.58	..	2.13½	9.18½
15	70	Up Exe Halt ...	8.07½	9.18	10.41	12.41½	....	1.42½	2.53½	..	4.52	..	6.05½	..	7.24½	8.26	9.53	..	....	11.02½	....	2.18	9.23
16	52	Thorverton ... arr	8.09½	9.20	10X43	12X43½	..	1.44½	2X55½	....	4X54	....	6.07½	6.57	7.26½	8.28	9X55	....	..	11.04½	..	2.20	9.25
		... dep	8.10	9.21	10X44	12X47	....	1.45	2X57	..	4X56	..	6.08	7.17	7.27½	8.29	9X56	..	....	11.05½	....	2.21	9.26
18	44	Brampford Speke Halt ...	8.14½	9.26	10.48½	12.51½	..	1.49½	3.02	....	5.01	....	6.12½	....	7.32	8.34	10.01	....	..	11.10	..	2.26	9.31
19	33	Stoke Canon ... arr	8.17½	9.29	10.51½	12.54½	....	1.52½	3.05	..	5.04	..	6X15½	..	7.35	8.37	10.04	..	....	11.13	....	2.29	9.34
		... dep	8.18	9.30	10.52	12.56	..	1.53	3.06	....	5.06	....	6X17	7.25	7.36	8.38	10.05	....	..	11.14	..	2.34	9.36
–	–	EXETER (ST. DAVIDS) ... arr	8.24	9.36	10.58	1.02	....	1.59	3.12	..	5.12	..	6.23	7R33	7.42	8.44	10.11	..	....	11.20	....	2.40	9.42

TJ Through train from Tiverton Junction

DOWN   WEEKDAYS

M.P. MILEAGE M	C		GOODS J	E.B.V. Q	GOODS		AUTO	AUTO	AUTO		GOODS	AUTO		AUTO TO	AUTO	AUTO		GOODS SX	AUTO SO	AUTO			
179	10	TIVERTON JN..d	6.30	7†15	7.15	..	7.32	8.23	9.35	..	10.40	11.30	....	..	12.05	12.40	1.25	..	2.15	2.20	3.35	..	....	..
181	20	Halberton Halt	..	..	..	..	7.38	8.29	9.41	....	..	11.36	..	....	12.11	12.46	1.31	..	..	2.26	3.41	..	..	..
183	64	TIVERTON....arr	6.44	7†25	7.29	..	7.44	8.35	9.47	..	10.55	11.42	....	..	12.17	12.52	1.37	..	2.30	2.32	3.47	..	....	..

	AUTO	AUTO	L.E.		MOTOR	AUTO	AUTO	AUTO ThO	PASS. SO				E.B.V. PM	SUNDAYS
TIVERTON JN..d	4.30	5.05	6||35	..	6.54	7.35	9.02	11.25	11.55				4†45	..	....	..
Halberton Halt	4.36	5.11	....	..	7.00	7.41	9.08	11.31	12.01				..	..
TIVERTON....arr	4.42	5.17	6|50	..	7.06	7.47	9.14	11.37	12.07				4†55	..	....	..

J From Exeter   E To Exeter
Q EBV will only run when there is no freight booked   T To Taunton

UP   WEEKDAYS

MILEAGE M	C		AUTO	AUTO	AUTO		E.B.V. T	GOODS T		AUTO	AUTO TO		AUTO	AUTO	E.B.V. SX	AUTO SO		AUTO	AUTO SO	AUTO	AUTO	
—	—	TIVERTON....dep	7.00	7.50	9.05	..	10†05	10.20	....	11.10	11.47	..	....	12.22	1.00	1†45	2.00	..	3.13	3.50	4.10	4.45	..
2	44	Halberton Halt	7.07	7.57	9.12	....	..	....	..	11.17	11.54	..	....	12.29	1.07	....	2.07	....	3.20	3.57	4.17	4.52	
4	54	TIVERTON JN...a	7.12	8.02	9.17	..	10†15	10.35	....	11.22	11.59	..	....	12.34	1.12	2†00	2.12	....	3.25	4.02	4.22	4.57	..

	GOODS	MOTOR	AUTO	AUTO	L.E.	AUTO E	L.E. ThO			E.C.S. AM		MEAT PM	SUNS.
TIVERTON....dep	..	5.50	6.20	7.10	8.35	9||45	10.30	11||50		12†15	....	5.05	....
Halberton Halt	..	....	6.27	7.17	8.42	....	10.37	....		....	..	....	..
TIVERTON JN...a	..	6.05	6.32	7.22	8.47	10|00	10.42	12||00		12†25	..	5.15	....

1950   JUNE — SEPTEMBER   SINGLE LINE worked by Electric Token   **1950**

DOWN   WEEKDAYS

M.P. MILEAGE M	C		GOODS	GOODS A			TO B				GOODS				
179	10	TIVERTON JN..d	6.30	6.50	..	7.30	8.15	9.40	..	10.35	11.35	....	..	12.56	1.40	..	2.25	..	3.30	4.25	5.32	..
181	20	Halberton Halt	..	....	..	7.36	8.21	9.46	....	10.41	11.41	..	....	1.02	1.46	..	....	..	3.36	4.31	5.38	..
183	64	TIVERTON.....arr	6.45	7.05	..	7.42	8.27	9.52	..	10.47	11.47	....	..	1.08	1.52	..	2.40	....	3.42	4.37	5.44	....

			L.E. SX					
TIVERTON JN..d	....	..	6||05	..	7.05	9.05	....	10.00	....	..
Halberton Halt	..	....	..	....	7.11	9.11	..	10.06	..	..
TIVERTON.....arr	....	..	6||18	..	7.17	9.17	..	10.12	..	..

A From Exeter (dep. 3.45a.m.)
B Connects with 5.30a.m. Paddington
C To Taunton
D From Exeter (dep. 9.00a.m.) via Exe Valley
E From Dulverton (dep. 10.10p.m.)
F To Exeter, via Main Line
G From Exeter (7.55p.m.) via Exe Valley;
    returns ECS to Exeter via Main Line.

UP   WEEKDAYS

MILEAGE M	C					TO E.C.S.	TX GOODS C	TO GOODS C		SO GOODS D			SX E.B.V.	SO L.E.		
—	—	TIVERTON....dep	7.13	7.45	9.00	....	10†00	....	10.40	10.50	..	11.05	11.50	....	..	12.30	1.20	..	2†00	2||00	..	....	..
2	44	Halberton Halt	7.20	7.52	9.07	..	....	....	..	..	..	11.12	..	....	12.37	1.27	....	....	..	..
4	54	TIVERTON JN...a	7.25	7.57	9.12	....	10†12	....	10.55	11.05	..	11.17	12.05	....	..	12.42	1.32	..	2†10	2||10	..	....	..

				SX GOODS				SX L.E.	E	ThO E.C.S.	SO L.E.	SUNDAYS	E.C.S. PM
TIVERTON....dep	....	3.00	4.05	4.45	....	5.15	....	6.20	8.46	9.30	10||20	10.20	10.40	....	11†05	11||05	..	....	..	8†40 G
Halberton Halt	..	3.07	4.12	4.52	..	....	..	6.27	8.53	9.37	..	10.27	10.47	F	F		..
TIVERTON JN...a	..	3.12	4.17	4.57	....	5.30	....	6.32	8.58	9.42	10||30	10.32	10.52	....	11†15	11||15	..	....	..	8†50

1950 continued

EXETER TO DULVERTON

1950 JUNE – SEPTEMBER — WEEKDAYS / SUNDAYS

SINGLE LINE worked by Electric Train staff or Token

Mileage M	Mileage C	Station				Goods	SO	SX	SX	SO	SO	SX	SO	SX	SO				ThSO	Sundays	Sundays	Sundays	Sundays
0	0	EXETER (ST. DAVIDS)... dep	6.00	6.30	7.55	9R00	9.53	10.08	....	..	....	1.46	1.47	3.55	4.00	5.55	6.45	8.51	10.15	8.40	10.15	4.20	7.55
3	30	Stoke Canon .... arr	6.06	6.36	8.01	....	9.59	10.14	..	....	..	1.52	1.53	4.02	4.07	6.01	6.51	8X57	10.21	....	..	....	..
		.... dep	6.07	6.37	8.02	9X08	10.02	10.16	....	..	....	1.52½	1.54	4.04	4.09	6.02	6.52	8X58	10.22	8.46	10.21	4.26	8.01
4	19	Brampford Speke Halt....	..	6.40½	8.06	....	10.07	10.20	..	....	..	1.56	1.57½	4.08	4.13	6.05½	6.55½	9.01½	10.26	8.50½	10.25½	4.31	8.06
6	11	Thorverton .... arr	6.14	6.45½	8X11	9.22	10.13	10.25	....	..	....	2.01	2.02½	4.14	4.18	6X10½	7.00½	9.06½	10.31	8.55½	10.30½	4.36	8.11
		.... dep	6.15	6.46½	8X16	9.40	10.16	10.25½	..	....	..	2.01½	2.03	4X20		6X11	7.01	9.07	10.32	8.56½	10.31	4.37	8.12
6	73	Up Exe Halt	....	6.49	8.18½	..	10.20	10.28	....	..	....	2.04	2.05½	4.22½		6.13½	7.03½	9.09½	10.35	8.59	10.33½	4.40	8.15
8	68½	Burn Halt	..	6.53	8.22½	....	10.26	10.32	..	....	..	2.08	2.09½	4.26½		6.17½	7.07½	9.13½	10.40	9.03	10.37½	4.44	8.20
10	18	Cadeleigh .... arr	6.23	6.56	8.25½	9.52	10.30	10.35	....	..	....	2.11	2.12½	4.30		6.20	7X10	9.16	10.44	9.06½	10.40½	4.47½	8.23½
		.... dep	6.24	6.58	8.27½	10.05	10X37		..	....	..	2.11½	2.13	4.30½		6.20½	7X10½	9.16½	10.45	9.07	10.41	4.48	8.24
13	40	West Exe Halt....... arr	....	7.05	8.34½	..	10.44		....	..	....	2.18½	2.20	4.37½		6.26½	7.17½	9.23½	10.52	9.14	10.48	4.55	8.31
		.... dep	..	7.06	8.35	....	10.45		..	....	12.10	2.19	2.21	4.38		6.28	7.18	9.24	10.53	9.15	10.49	4.56	8.33
14	9	TIVERTON .... arr	6.32	7.08	8X37	10.15	10.47		....	..	12.12	2.21	2.23	4.40		6.30	7.20	9.26	10.55	9.17	10.51	4.58	8.35
		.... dep	6.36	7.11	8X41	→	10.49		← 11.06	← 11.50	12.14	2.24	2.26	4.43		6.33	7.23	9.29	11†05	....	..	....	8†40
16	5	Bolham Halt	....	7.17	8.46	..	10.54		..	TJ	12.19	2.29	2.31½	4.48		6.38	7.28	9.34	TJ	..	....	..	TJ
19	18	Cove Halt	6.47	7.24	8.52½	....	11.00½		CR	..	12.25½	2.35½	2.38	4.54½		6.44½	7.34½	9.40½	..	....	..	....	..
21	14	Bampton .... arr	6.51	7X28	8.56½	..	11.04½		11.26	....	12.29½	2.39½	2.42	4.58½		6.48½	7X38½	9.44½	....	..	....	..	....
		.... dep	6.52	7X32	8.57½	....	11.05½		12.00	..	12.30	2.40	2.42½	4.59½		6.49	7X39	9.45½	..	....	..	....	..
22	63	Morebath Junction	6.55	7.35	9.00½	..	11.08½		12.09	....	12X36	2.43	2.45½	5.02½		6.52	7.42	9.48½	....	..	....	..	....
22	71	Morebath Junction Halt..	6.57½	7.37½	9.03	....	11.11		....	..	12.38	2.45½	2.48	5.05		6.54½	7.44½	9.51	..	....	..	....	..
24	54	DULVERTON .... arr	7.02	7.42	9.07	..	11.15		12.14	....	12.42	2.49½	2.52	5.09		6.58	7.48	9.55	....	..	....	..	....

TJ To Tiverton Junction, thence returning to Exeter via Main Line.

NB. All Passenger Trains are AUTO.

DULVERTON TO EXETER

M.P. Mileage M	M.P. Mileage C	Station			SX	SO	SO E.C.S.			SX Goods	SX	SO			SX								
–	–	DULVERTON .... dep	7.15	8.05	9.55		11†26	....	12.47	1.15	3.10	3.32	5.20	....	..	7.20	8.00	10.10	..	....	..	....	..
–	–	Morebath Junction Halt....	7.21	8.11	9.59½		....	..	12.51½	..	3.14½	3.36½	5.24½	..	....	7.26	8.04½	10.15	....	..	....	..	....
0	0	Morebath Junction	7.22	8.12	10.00½		11.31	....	12.52½	1.22	3.15½	3.37½	5.25½	....	..	7.27	8.05½	10.16	..	....	..	....	..
1	49	Bampton .... arr	7X25	8.15	10.03½		....	..	12.55½	1.26	3.18½	3.40½	5.28½	..	....	7X32	8.08½	10.19	....	..	....	..	....
		.... dep	7X30	8.16	10.05		11X34	....	12.56½	1.46	3.19½	3.41½	5.29½	....	..	7X40	8.09	10.20	..	....	..	....	..
3	45	Cove Halt	7.34½	8.21	10.09½		....	..	1.01	CR	3.24	3.46	5.34	..	....	7.44½	8.13½	10.25	....	..	....	..	....
6	58	Bolham Halt	7.41½	8.29	10.16½		..	....	1.08	....	3.31	3.53	5.41	....	..	7.51½	8.20½	10.32	..	....	..	....	..
8	54	TIVERTON .... arr	7.46	8X34	10.21		11†47	..	1.12½	2.05	3.36½	3.57½	5.45½	..	....	7.56	8.25	10.37	....	..	....	..	....
		.... dep	7.51	8X40	10.25		11†50	....	1.15	→	4.00	4.00	5.50	....	← 6.35	7.58	8.28	10.40	..	9.30	11.05	....	5.10
9	23	West Exe Halt........ arr	7.52	8.41	10.26		11†51	..	1.16	..	4.01	4.01	5.51	..	....	7.59	8.29	TJ	....	9.31	11.06	..	5.11
		.... dep	7.57	8.42	10.27		..	....	1.16½	....	4.01½	4.01½	5.52	....	..	7.59½	8.30	....	..	9.33	11.08	....	5.13
12	45	Cadeleigh .... arr	8.04	8.49	10X34		....	..	1.23½	..	4.08½	4.08½	5.59	..	6.47	8.06½	8.37	..	....	9.40	11.15	..	5.20
		.... dep	8.04½	8.49½	10.37½	10.38	..	....	1.24	....	4.09	4.09	5.59½	....	7X11	8.07	8.37½	....	..	9.41	11.16	....	5.21
13	74½	Burn Halt	8.07½	8.52½	10.40½	10.42	....	..	1.27	..	4.12	4.12	6.02½	..	....	8.10	8.40½	..	....	9.44½	11.19½	..	5.25
15	70	Up Exe Halt	8.12	8.57	10.45	10.48	..	....	1.32	....	4.16½	4.16½	6.07	....	..	8.14½	8.45	....	..	9.49	11.24	....	5.30
16	52	Thorverton .... arr	8X14	8.59	10.47	10.53	....	..	1.34	..	4X18½	4X18½	6X09	..	7.21	8.16½	8.47	..	....	9.51	11.26	..	5.32
		.... dep	8X17	8.59½	10.48	10.56	..	....	1.35	....	4X19	4X23	6X12	....	7.45	8.17	8.47½	....	..	9.51½	11.26½	....	5.33
18	44	Brampford Speke Halt.....	8.22	9.04	10.52½	11.02	....	..	1.40	..	4.23½	4.28	6.16½	..	....	8.21½	8.52	..	....	9.56	11.31	..	5.38
19	33	Stoke Canon .... arr	8.25	9X07	10.55½	11.06	..	....	1.43	....	4.26½	4.32	6.19½	....	..	8.24½	8X55	....	..	....	..	....	..
		.... dep	8.28	9X09	10.57	11*14	....	..	1.46	..	4.27	4.36	6.20	..	7.54	8.25	8X58	..	....	9.59	11.34	..	5.41
		EXETER (ST. DAVIDS)... arr	8.34	9.15	11.03	11.21	..	....	1.52	....	4.33	4.42	6.26	....	8R02	8.31	9.04	....	..	10.05	11.40	....	5.48

SX SO

TJ To Tiverton Junction

1960 JUNE — SEPTEMBER

EXETER TO DULVERTON

WEEKDAYS

SINGLE LINE worked by Electric Train Staff or Token

MILEAGE M	C				SO	SX ‡-7.53	SO	SX GOODS	Q GOODS	SO	SX		SO ‡-1.43	SX	SX	SO ‡-3.45	SX	SX		SX F		SX ‡-9.10	SO
0	0	EXETER (ST. DAVIDS)... dep	6.00	6.30	7.53	7‡55	9.30	10R55	....	..	11.44	..	1‡44	2.08	3.25	3‡47	4.35	..	5.48	7.15	7.40	9‡12	9.40
3	30	Stoke Canon .... arr	6N06	....	7.59	8.01	9.36	....	..	....	11.51	....	1.50	....	..	....	4X41	....	5.54	7.21	..	....	..
		.... dep	6N07	6.36	8.00	8.02	9.37	11.05	....	..	11.52	..	1.51	2X14	3.33	3.53	4X44	..	5.55	7.22	7.46	9.18	9.46
4	19	Brampford Speke Halt....	..	6.40	8.04	8.06	9.41	....	..	....	11.56	....	1.55	2a19	3.37	3.56½	4.48	....	5.59	7.26	7.50	9.22	9.50
6	11	Thorverton .... arr	6.14	6.45	8X09	8X11	9.46	11.14	....	..	12.01	..	2X00	2.24	3.42	4.01½	4.52	..	6.04	7X31	7X55	9.27	9.55
		.... dep	6.15	6.46	8X17	8X17	9.47	11.24	..	....	12.03	....	2X01	2.25	3.44	4.02	4.53	....	6.05	7X32	8X00	9.28	9.56
6	73	Up Exe Halt	....	6.49	8.20		....	..	....	..	....	..	2.04	..	3K47	4.04½	4.56	..	6.08	7.35	....	..	....
8	68½	Burn Halt	6N21	6.53½	8.24½		..	....	..	....	..	....	2.08½	....	..	4.08½	..	....	..	....	..	....	..
10	18	Cadeleigh .... arr	6.24	6.56½	8.27½		9.55	11.36	....	..	12.11	..	2.11½	2.33	3.53	4X11	5.02	..	6X14	7X43	8.08	9.36	10.04
		.... dep	6.25	6.57½	8.29		9.56	11.51	..	....	12.12	....	2.13	2.34	3.54	4X12	5.03	....	6X16	7X51	8.09	9.37	10.05
13	40	West Exe Halt ...... arr	....	7.04½	8.36		10.03	..	....	..	12.19	..	2.20	2.41	4.01	4.19	5.09	..	6.23	7.58½	8.16	9.44	10.12
		.... dep	..	7.06	8.37		10.04	....	..	12.10	12.20	....	2.21	2.42	4.03	4.20	5.10	TJ	6.24	7.59	8.17	9.45	10.13
14	9	TIVERTON .... arr	6.33	7.08	8X39		10.06	12.04	....	12.12	12.22	..	2.23	2.44	4X05	4.22	5.12	5.18	6.26	8.01	8X19	9.47	10.15
		.... dep	6.35	7.12	8X44		10X15	....	..	12.15	12.29	....	2.26	2.49	4X15	4.25	..	5.25	6.30	....	8X22	10†05	10.19
16	5	Bolham Halt	6.40½	7.17½	8.49½		10.20½	..	....	12.20½	12.34½	..	2.31½	2.54½	4.20½	4.30	....	5.30½	6.35½	..	8.27	TE ..	10.24½
19	18	Cove Halt	6.47½	7.24½	8.56½		10.27½	....	..	12.27½	12.41½	....	2.38½	3.01½	4.27½	4.36½	..	5.36½	6.42½	....	8.33½	....	10.31½
21	14	Bampton .... arr	6.51½	7X28½	9.00½		10.31½	..	....	12.31½	12.45½	..	2.42½	3.05½	4.31½	4.40½	....	5X40½	6.46½	..	8.37½	..	10.35½
		.... dep	6.52½	7X30	9.01½		10.33	....	12.12	12.33	12.46½	....	2.44	3.07	4.32½	4.41	..	....	6.48	....	8.39	....	10.37
22	63	Morebath Junction	6.55	7.33	9.04½		10.36	..	12.20	12.36	12.50	..	2.47	3.10	4.35	4.44	....	..	6.51	..	8.42	..	10.40
22	71	Morebath Junction Halt..	..	7.36	9.07½		10.39	....	..	12.39	12.52	....	2.50	3.12	4.39	4.46½	..	....	6.54	....	8.45	....	10.43
24	54	DULVERTON .... arr	7.00	7.40	9.11		10.43	..	12.26	12.43	12.56	..	2.54	3.17	4.43	4.50	....	..	6.58	..	8.49	..	10.47

TJ From Tiverton Junction
TE Returns ECS to Exeter via Tiverton Jc.
F Runs July & August only

DULVERTON TO EXETER

M.P. MILEAGE M	C				SX	SO	SO	Q GOODS		SO	SX	SO	SX	SX			SX	SX GOODS		SX F	SX	SO	SO E.C.S.
-	-	DULVERTON .... dep	7.15	8.10	9.28	9.45	11.30	11.50	....	1.05	1.10	3.25	3.42	..	....	5.30	....	..	7.10	..	9.15	9.25	11†00
-	-	Morebath Junction Halt....	7.20	8.15	9.33	9.50	11.35	....	..	1.10	1.15	3.30	3.47	....	..	5.35	..	....	7.15	....	9.19½	9.29½	..
0	0	Morebath Junction	7.21	8.16	9.34	9.51	11.36	11.56	....	1.11	1.16	3.31	3.48	..	....	5.36	....	..	7.16	..	9.20	9.30	11.05
1	49	Bampton .... arr	7X24½	8.19	9.37	9.54	11.39	12.04	..	1.14	1.19	3.34	3.51	....	..	5X39	..	....	7.19	....	9.23	9.33	..
		.... dep	7X30	8.20	9.38	9.55	11.40	..	....	1.15	1.20	3.35	3.52	..	....	5X42	6.00	..	7.20	..	9.23½	9.33½	11.08
3	45	Cove Halt	7.35	8.25	9.43	10.00	11.45	....	..	1.20	1.25	3.40	3.57	....	..	5.45	..	....	7.25	....	9.28	9.38	..
6	58	Bolham Halt	7.42½	8.32½	9.50½	10.07½	11.52½	..	....	1.27½	1.32½	3.47½	4.04½	..	....	5.52½	...	..	7.32½	..	9.35	9.45	....
8	54	TIVERTON .... arr	7.47	8X37	9.55	10X12	11.57	....	..	1.32	1.37	3.52	4X09	....	..	5.57	6.15	....	7.37	....	9.39½	9.49½	11†22
		.... dep	7.51	8X41	10.01	10X17	12†07	..	....	1.37	1.43	4.01	4X12	5.22	....	6.00	6.28	6.35	7.40	8X22	10‖20	10.20	11†30
9	23	West Exe Halt .... arr	7.52	8.42	10.02	10.18	12†08	....	..	1.38	1.44	4.02	4.13	5.23	..	6.02	TJ	....	7.41	8.23	TJ	TJ	TE
		.... dep	7.53	8.43	10.03	10.19	....	..	....	1.39	1.45	4.03	4.14	5.24	....	6.03	....	..	7.42	8.24	....	..	....
12	45	Cadeleigh .... arr	8.00	8.50	10.10	10.26	..	....	..	1.46	1.52	4X10	4.21	5.31	..	6X10	..	6.47	7X49	8.31	..	....	..
		.... dep	8.01	8.51	10.12	10.27	....	..	....	1.47	1.53	4X13	4.22	5.32	....	6X17	....	6.58	7X50	8.32	....	..	....
13	74½	Burn Halt	8.04½	....	..	....	..	....	..	1.51	1.57	4.17	4.26	....	..	....	..	....	..	....	..	....	..
15	70	Up Exe Halt	8.09½	..	....	..	....	..	....	1.56	2.02	4.22	4.31	..	....	..	....	..	....	..	....	..	....
16	52	Thorverton .... arr	8X12	8.59	10.20	10.35	..	....	..	1X58	2.04	4.24	4.33	5.40	..	6.25	..	7.08	7X58	8.40	..	....	..
		.... dep	8X17	9.00	10.21	10.36	....	..	....	2X02	2.05	4.25	4.34	5.41	....	6.26	....	7X32	7X59	8.41	....	..	....
18	44	Brampford Speke Halt.....	8.22	9.05	10.26	10.41	..	....	..	2.07	2.10	4.30	4.39	5.46	..	6.31	..	....	8.04	8.46	..	....	..
19	33	Stoke Canon .... arr	8.25	9.08	10.29	10.44	....	..	....	2.11	2.13	4.33	4X43	..	....	6.34	....	..	8.07	8.49	....	..	....
		.... dep	8.26	9.09	10.30	10.49	..	....	..	2.15	2.14	4.34	4X45	5.49	..	6.35	..	7.41	8.08	8.50	..	....	..
		EXETER (ST. DAVIDS)... arr	8.32	9.15	10‡36	10.55	....	..	....	2.21	2.20	4.40	4‡52	5.55	....	6‡41	....	7R50	8.14	8.56	....	..	12†12
					‡-10.39								‡-4.54			‡-6.46							

TJ To Tiverton Junction
TE Returns ECS to Exeter via Tiverton Jc.
F Runs July & August only

1960 continued   SUNDAYS July & August, 1960

UP

MILEAGE M	C							
0	0	EXETER (ST. DAVIDS)...dep	8.30	10.15	..	4.03	6.15	7.54
3	30	Stoke Canon...arr	..	..	...	..	..	..
		...dep	8.36	10.21	..	4.09	6.21	8.00
4	19	Brampford Speke Halt....	8.40½	10.25½	..	4.14	6.26	8.06
6	11	Thorverton...arr	8.45½	10.30½	..	4.19	6.31	8.11
		...dep	8.46½	10.31	..	4.20	6.32	8.12
6	73	Up Exe Halt...	..	..	..	..	..	..
8	68½	Burn Halt...	..	..	..	..	..	..
10	18	Cadeleigh...arr	8.54	10.38	..	4.28	6.40	8.21
		...dep	8.55	10.39	..	4.29	6.41	8.22
13	40	West Exe Halt...arr	9.02	10.46	..	4.36	6.48	8.29
		...dep	9.03	10.47	..	4.37	6.49	8.31
14	9	TIVERTON...arr	9.05	10.50	..	4.40	6.52	8.34
		...dep						8.50
16	5	Bolham Halt...						TE
19	18	Cove Halt...						
21	14	Bampton...arr						
		...dep						
22	63	Morebath Junction...						
22	71	Morebath Junction Halt..						
24	54	DULVERTON...arr						

DOWN

M.P. MILEAGE M	C		Through Train to Newton Abbot						Via Tiverton Junction
–	–	DULVERTON...dep							
–	–	Morebath Junction Halt...							
0	0	Morebath Junction...							
1	49	Bampton...arr							
		...dep							
3	45	Cove Halt...							
6	58	Bolham Halt...							
8	54	TIVERTON...arr							
		...dep		9.20	11.05	..	4.55	7.00	8.50
9	23	West Exe Halt...arr		9.22	11.07	..	4.57	7.02	..
		...dep		9.23	11.08	..	4.58	7.03	..
12	45	Cadeleigh...arr		9.30	11.15	..	5.05	7.10	
		...dep		9.31	11.16	..	5.06	7.11	
13	74½	Burn Halt...		..	..	..	..		
15	70	Up Exe Halt...		..	..	..	..		
16	52	Thorverton...arr		9.39	11.24	..	5.14	7.19	
		...dep		9.40	11.25	..	5.15	7.20	
18	44	Brampford Speke Halt...		9.45	11.29	..	5.20	7.25	
19	33	Stoke Canon...arr		..	..	..	..		
		...dep		9.48	11.32	..	5.23	7.28	
		EXETER (ST. DAVIDS)...arr		9.54	11.39	..	5.29	7.34	9.40

TIVERTON BRANCH
Worked by Electric Token

1960 JUNE — SEPTEMBER

DOWN   WEEKDAYS

M.P. MILEAGE M	C		Goods	Goods E		SO	SX		SO	SX	SO	SX		TX Goods Q	To					
179	10	TIVERTON JN..d	..	6.30	6.50	..	8.10	8.15	..	8.45	9.02	9.30	9.40	..	10.25	10.35	..	11.25	..	..	12.50	1.40	..	..
181	20	Halberton Halt....	..	..	..	..	8.16	8.21	..	8.51	9.08	9.36	9.46	..	..	10.41	..	11.31	..	..	12.56	1.46	..	..
183	64	TIVERTON...arr	..	6.45	7.05	..	8.22	8.27	..	8.57	9.14	9.42	9.52	..	10.40	10.47	..	11.37	..	..	1.02	1.52	..	..

	SX		Goods		SO	SX	SX B	SO		SX L.E.		SX F		SO	SX	
TIVERTON JN..d	2.22	..	3.20	..	4.18	4.22	5.06	5.30	..	6║05	..	7.00	7.33	..	8.40	8.45	..	9.25	..	..
Halberton Halt..	2.28	..	..	..	4.24	4.28	5.12	5.36	..	..	..	7.06	7.39	..	8.46	8.51	..	9.31	..	..
TIVERTON...arr	2.34	..	3.35	..	4.30	4.34	5.18	5.42	..	6║18	..	7.12	7.45	..	8.52	8.57	..	9.37	..	..

E To or From Exeter   D From Dulverton
B To or From Bampton   F Runs July & August only

UP   WEEKDAYS

MILEAGE M	C		SO	SX	SO	SX	TX L.E. Q	To E.C.S.		Goods		SX Goods	SO	SX L.E.
–	–	TIVERTON...dep	..	7.41	8.30	8.45	9.00	9.16	..	10║00	10†00	..	10.55	..	11.40	..	..	12.25	1.20	..	2.00	2.35	2║40	..
2	44	Halberton Halt....	..	7.48	8.37	8.52	9.07	9.23	..	..	..	..	11.02	..	..	..	12.32	1.27	..	2.07	..	..
4	54	TIVERTON JN...a	..	7.53	8.42	8.57	9.12	9.28	..	10║12	10†12	..	11.07	..	11.55	..	..	12.37	1.32	..	2.12	2.50	2║50	..

	SO	SX	SX Goods	B	SX E.C.S.	SX	SO	SX E.C.S.	SO	SX L.E.	SO E.C.S.	SUNDAYS PM
TIVERTON...dep	4.00	4.35	4.45	..	5.20	..	6.28	..	7†20	8.12	9.00	..	9.50	10.00	10†05	..	10.20	10║20	11†30	..	8.50	..
Halberton Halt..	4.07	4.42	4.52	..	..	..	6.35	..	8.19	9.07	..	9.57	10.07	..	10.27	..	..	8.57	..
TIVERTON JN...a	4.12	4.47	4.57	..	5.35	..	6.40	..	7†30	8.24	9.12	..	10.02	10.12	10†15	..	10.32	10║30	11†40	..	9.02	..

f   e   d d d   e